*Across the Narrow Seas*

ECCLESIASTICI CAP. XLIII.

*In sermone eius siluit ventus, et cogitatione sua placauit abyssum.*

PSALMO CVI.

*Et clamauerunt ad Dominum cum tribularentur : et de necessitatibus eorum eduxit eos .*

*Et statuit procellam eius in auram: et siluerunt fluctus eius.*

*Et lætati sunt quia siluerunt: et deduxit eos in portum voluntatis eorum.*

Ee 3

# *Across the Narrow Seas*

Studies in the history and bibliography
    of Britain and the Low Countries

Presented to Anna E C Simoni

*Edited by Susan Roach*

The British Library . 1991

© 1991 The contributors

First published 1991 by
The British Library
Great Russell Street
London WC1B 3DG


*British Library Cataloguing in Publication Data*
Across the narrow seas: studies in the history and
  bibliography of Britain and the Low Countries.
  I. Simoni, Anna E. C. II. Roach, Susan
  327.492041

ISBN 0 7123 0260 3


*Frontispiece:* title-page of *IEROSOLYMITANA
PEREGRINATIO . . . NICOLAI CHRISTOPHORI
RADZIVILI DVCIS OLICAE ET NIESVISII
PALATINI VILNENSIS . . ,* published in
Antwerp by the Plantin Press, 1614.
( BL G.1782).


Designed by Alan Bartram
Typeset in 10 on 12pt Lasercomp Janson
by August Filmsetting, Haydock, St Helens
Printed in England by St Edmundsbury Press
Bury St Edmunds

# Contents

# Foreword

Anna Simoni's contacts with the Low Countries go back more than 50 years; her involvement in Dutch studies came almost 20 years later and started – like so many important personal moves in life – by accident. Anna joined the British Museum library in 1950 as an Assistant Keeper second class. Having come to grips with Panizzi's cataloguing rules, she compiled (with Dennis E. Rhodes) two volumes of additions to Halkett and Laing's *Dictionary of Anonymous and Pseudonymous English Literature* (1956, 1962) and took her early steps on the road of a lifetime's devotion to Dutch literary and bibliographical studies by reading the proofs of the *Short-Title Catalogue of Books printed in the Netherlands and Belgium ... 1470 to 1600, now in the British Musuem* (1965). As she had some knowledge of Dutch and of Holland – acquired during a brief visit to Scheveningen in 1938 – she was made responsible for the library's Dutch collections, their acquisitions and cataloguing. It would not be unfair to say that she was thrown in at the deep end, but she swam, and mastered her new element with a thoroughness and an enthusiasm that have remained her chief characteristics over the following decades. Both were based on her insatiable curiosity, her need to know and her determination to find out. This determination led her to explore obscure and seemingly unlikely sources; it also led her to find, make and keep a host of devoted helpers and friends, in the Netherlands, in Flanders and in Britain. Her inquisitiveness, her ever-widening knowledge, and – above all – her boundless generosity attracted other scholars in her field, whether already established or young and untried, who relied on her help and who shared their own knowledge with her. She never failed to encourage scholarly talent in those around her and her enthusiasm was an inspiration to many of her colleagues in the British Library and elswhere.

Though she had studied in Turin, Genoa and Glasgow, where she obtained a degree in classics, she was largely self-taught in Dutch bibliography. This makes her achievements the more remarkable. In the British Library she has left three monuments behind: the collection of Dutch clandestine material with her catalogue *Publish and be free* (1975), her massive *Catalogue of Books from the Low Countries 1601-1621 in the British Library* (1990) and, perhaps most important of all for generations of scholars to come, the British Library's holdings of Dutch material which she built up from a relatively modest collection to arguably the best outside the Netherlands. She made many friends in the process, several of whom have contributed to this Festschrift: an act of respect, appreciation and love to Anna on her 75th birthday.

MIRJAM M. FOOT
Director, Collections & Preservation
British Library

Bert van Selm

# *Bewitched by books: Anna Simoni*

*Every large library with a great history seems to inexperienced visitors like a maze in which, without expert help, they can waste a lot of time. How fortunate I was that when I first visited the British Library on 6 September 1976 Anna Simoni was there to be my guide to one of the largest and most fascinating collections of older Dutch imprints outside the Low Countries. Neither before nor since in any other library have I received such a warm and friendly welcome as on that day in the imposing building in Great Russell Street. Not only did she give me a concise survey of the possibilities for finding systematically the collection of 17th-century imprints from the Dutch Republic, she also immediately invited me to a tasty lunch. Both these acts are highly typical of Anna as a helpful curator and an engaging personality. Both before and after me she has welcomed and advised young scholars from the Low Countries. Through her good offices the old and rare Dutch works in London no longer remain unread in the stacks. On the contrary, because of her these sources have been used increasingly in cultural and historical research in the Low Countries and abroad.*

*Anna Simoni's publications also perform a bridging role: to open up and publicise the collections of Neerlandica in the British Library. Who knew before 1975 that the BL possessed such an extensive collection of clandestine books that appeared in the Netherlands during the occupation of 1940-45? Those who know her life-history will understand why Anna felt attracted to these often modest little books. Even if the literary, intellectual or aesthetic worth of these works is not very great, their emotional value can scarcely be overestimated. It was these books that gave comfort to people in difficult circumstances; they gave a feeling of freedom and fellowship in a time of crude violence and barbaric oppression, they bolstered hope for a better future. If ever a prize is given for the catalogue with the best title, then* Publish and be free *must be a candidate. This work contains much more than just formal bibliographical descriptions; the plentiful information about authors, designers, printers and publishers does full justice to the importance that illegally and clandestinely printed books had and have, namely as shining examples of spiritual freedom stretching into the distant future.*

*Few people will feel called upon in middle age to begin a new, large-scale project: to describe and make accessible 17th-century books from the Low Countries. The courage and energy with which Anna embarked upon her self-appointed task commands admiration. These books in particular pose countless questions which take a long time to answer. In any event a comprehensive knowledge of Dutch bibliography, literature and art-history is a primary requisite. Numerous works appeared anonymously or pseudonymously. Anna's aim was to arrange them, as far as possible, under the name of the real author. In many articles in the specialist journals, but above all in her magnum opus, the* Catalogue of Books from the Low Countries 1601-1621 *in the British Library, she reported on her findings, for example the discovery of the original work on which the Dutch translation is based.*

*Many modern managers of research libraries just cannot understand why the description of older books takes so much time and trouble. Often they have no idea at all of the problems which confront the scholar. For it isn't sufficient to establish who is the author and who the translator; we also need to find out where, when and by whom a work was printed and published. For the 17th century certainly there is very little bibliographical apparatus available to unmask the numerous fictitious addresses or to ascribe the many anonymous works to a particular workplace. Anna has rightly seen it as one of the curator's tasks to solve bibliographical puzzles as far as possible. In so doing she has acted as a true ambassadress of the Dutch book. Because of the relatively small linguistic area of Dutch, awareness abroad of Dutch book-history has been very limited. With her publications, reviews and countless translations from Dutch into English, Anna has made an unparalleled contribution to a greater knowledge of the bibliographical research that is carried out in the Low Countries.*

*Anna always knows how to formulate the right questions in a clear way and she calls on her many Belgian and Dutch friends when she can't find the answer herself. Few others have as much insight into the skill and care with which older books were made, and she is fully alive to the great culturo-historical value of the sources which surround her daily. This deeply-rooted awareness is apparent not only in her many publications, but above all in conversation with colleagues and visitors at the British Library.*

*With this volume Anna Simoni's friends in Britain and the Low Countries have the opportunity to thank her for the great work which she has done in the service of the Dutch book. But I hope even more that this volume speaks her language: a language of warm humanity and friendship.*

(Translated by Susan Roach)

# Editor's Introduction

*Across the Narrow Seas* (a phrase borrowed from Lotte Hellinga's essay) could be the title of an account of Anna Simoni's own journeys back and forth between the Low Countries and Britain. Since the time she passed through the Netherlands on her way to the safety of Britain just before the outbreak of the Second World War she has crossed the North Sea and the Channel on numerous occasions, to visit libraries, to call on booksellers and, always, to maintain the personal and professional friendships to which she has committed herself so enthusiastically.

I first approached friends and colleagues of Anna in 1988 with my ideas for a volume of essays to celebrate her 75th birthday in 1991. The contributors were asked to suggest essays dealing with relations between Britain and the Low Countries in the earlier centuries which have so fascinated Anna. I had in mind a broad range of approaches: literary, bibliographical, cultural, political and art-historical. The resulting volume has elements of all these approaches and also covers a wide time-span, from the dawn of printing to the end of the Napoleonic Wars.

The title has taken on two shades of meaning, on the one hand indicating a fixed position on one side of the water, and on the other denoting movement to and fro. The first meaning is reflected in the essays on Low Countries topics of special interest to Anna: freedom of the press in Leiden; Flemish engravings accompanying Neo-Latin poems; the printer Henrick van Hastens, and the binding of a volume published by Theodorus Crajenschot. The second meaning comes out in a number of different ways. The English travel to the Low Countries, either in person or in the form of their (translated) writings; Dutchmen come to London and visit the British Museum, celebrate the coronation of James I or, in the most famous example, take the crown from James II! One essay traces the origin and subsequent travels of a Dutch word. Books roam freely and come to rest in libraries in Ireland, Germany and London. Printers, artists and mapmakers influence each other without apparently finding the intervening waters a barrier to communication.

The geographical area of the Low Countries dealt with here is essentially that of the modern Netherlands and Belgium but includes French towns like Douai and Saint-Omer which have in the past belonged to Flanders. It would have been a very tricky exercise to standardise throughout these essays the use of the various adjectives, Belgian, Dutch, Flemish, Netherlandic, in view of the complex history and changing status of the territories in question. I think that meanings will be clear in what each contributor has chosen for his or her essay.

In the Europe of the 1990s and the next century the destinies of Britain and the Low Countries are set to become more and more intimately connected, but what I hope this volume shows is that we have been linked by ties of friendship and mutual influence for many centuries.

It has been a great privilege and pleasure to work with the contributors to this volume. I am grateful to them all for their co-operation and support. I would like especially to mention four people who have been conspirators in this clandestine project from the very beginning: abroad, the late Bert van Selm whom we all sadly miss; in the British

Library, Dennis Rhodes and David Way, and in the home camp, Anna's husband, Bill Harvey, who has undertaken photography under false pretences and had to commit all sorts of minor perjury to keep the project a secret.

SUSAN ROACH
9 July 1991

## Acknowledgements

We are grateful to the following for their kind permission to reproduce illustrations: Arme Klarenabdij, Ghent (page 6); Bodleian Library, Oxford (page 10); The British Library Board (frontispiece, pages 33, 39, 41, 48, 49, 59, 62, 168); Green Studio, Dublin (page 190); Mr W. Harvey (page viii); Mr F. Knuf (pages 208, 209); H. E. Huntington Library, San Marino (pages xvi, 152); Lambeth Palace Library, London (page 95); Library of Congress, Washington, DC (page 44); the Honourable Society of the Middle Temple, London (by kind permission of the Masters of the Bench) (page 46); Öffentliche Kunstsammlung, Kupferstichkabinett Basel (pages 84, 85); Rijksmuseum, Amsterdam (page 6); Royal Library, Brussels (pages 68, 70, 72); Royal Library, The Hague (Pages 18, 19, 153); Stedelijk Museum 'De Lakenhal', Leiden (page 178); University Library, Ghent (pages 108, 109); University Library, Jena (page 8); University Library, Utrecht (page 162).

# List of Contributors

A. F. ALLISON, formerly Assistant Keeper at the British Museum; editor, with D. M. Rogers, of *The Contemporary Printed Literature of the English Counter-Reformation between 1558 and 1640* (1989-    ).

T. A. BIRRELL, Emeritus Professor of English and American literature at Nijmegen University and author of *English Monarchs and their Books.*

THEO BÖGELS teaches English Literature at the Free University of Amsterdam. His *Govert Basson: Printer, Publisher and Bookseller in Leiden 1612-1630* will appear shortly.

ERNST BRACHES teaches Bibliography at the University of Amsterdam.

ELLY COCKX-INDESTEGE is on the staff of the Rare Books Department, Royal Libarary, Brussels; she is the author of articles on the history of the book, bibliography and rare book cataloguing.

CHRISTIAN COPPENS is curator of Manuscripts and Rare Books at Louvain University Library and publishes on book- and library-history in periodicals such as *The Book Collector, Gutenberg Jahrbuch* and *Quaerendo.*

MIRJAM M. FOOT, Director of Collections & Preservation, British Library, formerly Head of West European Collections; author of *Pictorial Bookbindings* (1986) and numerous articles on the history of bookbinding.

ARIE-JAN GELDERBLOM teaches Dutch Renaissance literature at Utrecht University. His recent publications include articles on the country-house poem and on the authors Coornhert, Huygens, Vondel, Luyken, and Wolff & Deken.

J. A. GRUYS is Curator of Early Printed Books in the Royal Library, The Hague, and Project Leader of the STCN; he has written a number of books and articles in the field where the history of the booktrade, of libraries and of scholarship comes together.

CIS VAN HEERTUM is a curator in the Dutch Section at the British Library.

LOTTE HELLINGA-QUERIDO is Deputy Director, British Library, Humanities and Social Sciences. She is a specialist in fifteenth-century printed books and has published widely on the subject.

PAUL HOFTIJZER is a lecturer at the Sir Thomas Browne Institute of the University of Leiden. He has written on early-modern Anglo-Dutch relations and the history of Dutch printing and bookselling.

GERVASE HOOD is a professional archivist, and works as an editor for the Public Record Office, London.

JONATHAN I. ISRAEL is Professor of Dutch History at University College London. His most recent work is *Empires and entrepôts: the Dutch, the Spanish monarchy and the Jews, 1585-1713 (1990)*.

FRITS KNUF is an antiquarian bookseller based in Buren, The Netherlands.

DAVID PAISEY is a curator in the German Section at the British Library; he has written extensively on the history of the book in Germany.

DENNIS E. RHODES, formerly Deputy Keeper in the Department of Printed Books, British Library; author of various studies on incunabula and Italian and Spanish bibliography.

SUSAN ROACH is a curator in the Dutch and German Sections at the British Library.

MARCUS DE SCHEPPER is head of the Bureau Bibliografie Neerlandistiek at the Royal Library, Brussels.

†BERT VAN SELM taught at the Institute of Dutch Language and Literature, University of Leiden, and he was also Professor of the History of the Book Trade, University of Amsterdam.

HELEN WALLIS, formerly the Map Librarian of the British Library; author of books and articles on map librarianship and the history of cartography, exploration and discovery.

# Abbreviations

| | |
|---|---|
| *BCNI* | *Bibliotheca catholica neerlandica impressa* 1500-1727 (The Hague, 1954) |
| BL | British Library, London |
| *BLC* | *The British Library General Catalogue of Printed Books to 1975.* 360 vols. (London [etc], 1979-87) |
| CUL | Cambridge University Library |
| *DNB* | *Dictionary of National Biography* (London, 1885-) |
| GAL | Gemeente Archief Leiden |
| *GK* | BL General Catalogue *see BLC* |
| *GW* | *Gesamtkatalog der Wiegendrucke* (Leipzig, 1925-  ) |
| MP | Member of Parliament |
| MS(s): | Manuscript(s) |
| *NNBW* | *Nieuw Nederlandsch biografisch woordenboek* (Leiden, 1911-37) |
| *OED* | *Oxford English Dictionary* |
| *STC²* | A. W. Pollard and G. R. Redgrave, *A short-title Catalogue of Books printed in England, Scotland, & Ireland and of English Books printed abroad, 1475-1640.* Second edition, completed by Katharine F. Pantzer. 2 vols. (London, 1976-86) |
| *STCN* | *Short-Title Catalogue Netherlands* (in progress, based at the Royal Library, The Hague) |
| TCD | Trinity College, Dublin |
| *TLS* | *Times Literary Supplement* |
| Wing | Donald Wing, *Short-Title Catalogue of Books printed in England, Scotland, Ireland, Wales and British America and of English Books printed in other countries 1641-1700.* Second edition. 3 vols. (New York, 1972-88) |

Fig.1    William Caxton presents his English translation of Raoul le Fèvre, *Recueil des Histoires de Troie* to Margaret of York, Duchess of Burgundy. (H. E. Huntington Library, San Marino, California.)

Lotte Hellinga-Querido

# *Reading an engraving: William Caxton's dedication to Margaret of York, Duchess of Burgundy*

The beginning of printing in English did not take place in England itself but in another linguistic area, just across the Narrow Seas, in Flanders. Here the main language was the particular branch of Dutch known as Flemish, while the high culture in the cities of Flanders and Brabant, and of the Burgundian court that often chose to reside in them, was almost exclusively in French. In this essentially bilingual environment the first book printed in the English language came into being. The fact that this important event in the history of English culture did not take place on English soil was a direct result of the Anglo-Burgundian alliance which was confirmed in 1468 by the marriage of the Duke of Burgundy, Charles the Bold, with Margaret of York, sister of Edward IV.

Not surprisingly, the first book printed in English, William Caxton's translation of Raoul le Fèvre's *Recueil des Histoires de Troies,*[1] has always been regarded from a strictly English point of view, as has the unique copper engraving that is found in one copy of the book. I shall here attempt to change that point of view, and to consider the engraving in a context of other books commissioned by Margaret of York, bearing in mind that they were all executed in Flanders and Brabant.

The engraving, which is preserved in only one copy of the *Recuyell* (now in the H. E. Huntington Library), shows William Caxton presenting his translation of the *Recueil des Histoires de Troie*[1] to his patron Margaret of York. It has been reproduced many times since its significance was first brought to light by Montague Peartree in 1905.[2] It has even become one of the images (together with his device and perhaps the illustrations for *The Mirror of the World*) by which England's first printer is best remembered. There is not a little irony in the fact that the figure seen here as central to the scene, Margaret of York, Duchess of Burgundy and sister of the King of England, Edward IV, enjoys not a fraction of the fame now bestowed on the man depicted as her humble servant, William Caxton.

The engraving represents a lively scene, in an almost theatrical setting, and suggests therefore a sharply defined moment in time, in a development of the form of dedication miniatures connected with the court of Burgundy which became increasingly anecdotal by playing on the more usual formal setting. Instead of the enthroned prince surrounded by his courtiers, the author or scribe kneeling in front of him, we may witness a scene in which the Duke visits the scribe in his *atelier*, or even, in a particularly engaging miniature, Charles the Bold hiding behind a pillar as he is spying on the scribe (David Aubert) or on the artist, the miniaturist Loyset Liedet.[3]

The Caxton engraving is on several counts an astonishing document: it continues the tradition established by the miniaturists, and we shall see that it is even closely connected with it. But the traditional message is expressed in a new medium, one that had not been used at that time in combination with movable type, a combination that was to remain very unusual for several decades.[4] We have here one of those rare moments when the transition into a new medium (from manuscript to print) is made deliberately explicit, and has found an exceptional form to celebrate it. Less deliberate, and more a matter of hindsight, is that the momentous event of the first appearance of the English language in print is the focus of the scene. The engraving in the H. E. Huntington Library is part of a copy that had once belonged to Elizabeth Woodville, Edward IV's queen and therefore sister-in-law of Margaret of York.[5] We are now reasonably certain that the *Recuyell* was completed in 1473, but although the engraving is likely to be integral to the copy in which it survives[6] it is conceivable that it was printed at a later date on the page that had been left blank in the letterpress printing of the book. We shall see that the presentation scene is closest to a miniature which is found in a manuscript with the date 1476 (the Jena *Boethius*, see below). It is also remarkable that in this same year a series of copper engravings was produced in Bruges. They were made for an edition of a French translation of Boccaccio's *De casibus virorum illustrium* printed in Bruges by Colard Mansion; in this luxuriously laid out book spaces were left open which in several copies are occupied by a spectacular series of up to nine copper engravings.[7] There is not much to suggest a link in design between Caxton and Mansion's engravings, but their technique would not exclude the possibility that they were executed by the same engraver. If the Caxton engraving was made at about the same time, in 1476, well after the printing of the *Recuyell*, we might think, just for once, that we have here a true reportage of the ceremonial dedication, instead of the usual fiction which anticipated the event that was not to take place until the book had been completed. It has even been argued on the basis of this engraving that Caxton must have offered a manuscript version to his patroness, later to be followed by the more vulgar form of print for his friends.[8] We shall see that the engraving continuously confronts us with the question of what has to be taken literally, and what has a symbolic meaning. Even if we go along with the simple fact that Caxton is seen here presenting a real book, we must not lose sight of the fact that the essential object of his dedication is his translation, and that the book stands as a symbol for this work, whatever its material form. Meanwhile there is realism in the physical portrayal of Margaret of York, as is evident from the resemblance to her known portraits, and we are therefore justified in thinking that this is also a real portrait of Caxton, the only one known. On closer inspection, however, we shall see that the scene contains also a certain amount of fantasy, or rather, that it has to be taken 'literally' in an unexpected sense. This becomes clear when we place the engraving in the context of the other known instances when Margaret of York encouraged the production of books, namely the manuscripts commissioned by her.

In the short years of her marriage to Duke Charles the Bold, between the glittering wedding that took place in 1468 in Bruges which also celebrated the Anglo-Burgundian alliance, and Charles's death before Nancy, early in 1477, Margaret of

York commissioned some 14 manuscripts which still survive. It is also known that she owned manuscripts or presented manuscripts to others which were not necessarily commissioned by her. There is one instance in which a purchase of a very large Breviary is documented, sold from the estate of a canon of the church of St Mary in Courtrai in the year 1476.[9] The most spectacular part of the books connected with Margaret of York are undoubtedly the manuscripts made to her order, spectacular because without exception they are lavishly illuminated. Many of them have a particularly personal character because the portrait of the patroness is a prominent feature in the illumination.

Margaret of York's patronage of William Caxton should be seen in connection with her patronage of scribes and illuminators, and we shall see that when we arrange these commissions as to date and place, Caxton's *Recuyell* with the assumed dating of 1473 can fall, interestingly, just before the beginning of a sequence of manuscripts commissioned in Ghent from the scribe David Aubert. Margaret of York's manuscripts have attracted a great deal of attention in the last 45 years, particularly from art historians. Beginning with Otto Pächt's study of the Master of Mary of Burgundy which appeared first in 1944 (and in monograph form in 1948),[10] interest continued with G. I. Lieftinck's conjectural identification of the miniaturist as one of the artists of the circle of Hugo van der Goes resident at Rooclooster near Brussels,[11] and L.- M.-J. Delaissé's extensive catalogue and brief but perceptive further observations.[12] Pächt, and following him J. J. G. Alexander,[13] tentatively suggested Alexander Bening, but the identity of the miniaturist is by no means certain. The results of these discussions were summarised in listings of all manuscripts connected with Margaret of York by G. Dogaer (1973)[14] and by Muriel T. Hughes.[15] Margaret of York as patron and collector was most recently discussed by Thomas Kren.[16] There is therefore no need here to repeat a listing, and a mere summary, arranged according to place and time of production (in so far as known) may suffice. This list is limited to those manuscripts which are known or must be assumed to have been commissioned by Margaret; those which she acquired by other means are excluded.

## Brussels

Four manuscripts, all undated. They may have preceded the following group, produced in Ghent, but there is no ground for excluding the possibility that they were made simultaneously with the Ghent group.

1. *Benois seront les miserécordieux* (Translated by Nicolas Finet)
With miniature portraits of Margaret of York, once seen kneeling with the St Gudule and Grand Sablon churches of Brussels in the background, and, in a most unusual compartmented miniature, seen seven times administering the works of Mercy. These miniatures are generally ascribed to the Brussels *atelier* of Dreux Jean.[17]

2. Nicolas Finet, *Dyaloge de la Duchesse de Bourgogne et Jesu Christ*
With a portrait miniature showing Margaret kneeling at the feet of the Risen Christ. Although close in execution to the previous manuscript, (to which it is also linked by Nicolas Finet, respectively translator and author who was Margaret's almoner), this

miniature is generally ascribed to the master of Girard de Rousillon. It is remarkable that in these two related manuscripts Margaret is seen dressed in very similar fashion, in a brocaded gown, close fitting with an ample train, and with a black hennin with white wimple.[18]

3. *Une bonne information pour tous ceulz et celles quy ont la grace de acquerir les pardons et indulgences quy sont a Romme (Mirabilia Rome)*
Written by the same scribe as the two previous manuscripts. The style of the seven miniatures depicting scenes related to the churches in Rome resembles that of Dreux Jean, although the possibility has been left open to ascribe them to the Master of the Vasque de Lucène who painted Brussels MS 10778.[19]

4. The fourth manuscript thought to be produced in Brussels cannot be ranged with the previous three as to text, scribes or miniaturists. It is Pierre de Vaux, *Vie de Sainte Colette*, and was probably commissioned by the Duchess or by the ducal pair with the express purpose of presentation to the convent of the Clarisses at Ghent. It bears a dedication inscription in the hand of Margaret, but one of its miniatures shows Charles and Margaret both kneeling in prayer behind the saint. This must be the reason why it is thought that the ducal couple commissioned this manuscript jointly. We shall see that there are more miniatures in which Charles is depicted as part of the scene, although there is no ground for the assumption that he had any part in the commissioning. His presence may well have another significance, emphasising that it is he who determines the *persona* of Margaret.[20]

## Ghent

### (A) SCRIBE: DAVID AUBERT

1. Guy de Thurno, *La vision de l'âme*
With date 1 February 1474.
This is the earliest date for a commission, 'par le commandement et ordonnance de treshaulte et tresexcellente princhesse madam marguerite de yorch. Par la grace de dieu Duchesse de bourgoing. de lothryk, de brabant'... (etc, etc). It ends (34 verso): 'A este escript en la ville de gand par david, son escripuain Lan de grace Mil. CCCC Soixante et quatorze le premier du mois de feurier' (contractions expanded).[21]

2. Closely connected to the previous manuscript is *Les visions du Chevalier Tundale*
With date March 1474.
In one (or possibly two) of its 20 miniatures Charles the Bold and Margaret of York are shown as the guests of the protagonist, Tundalus. The patroness is mentioned in terms as in the previous manuscripts. The miniatures of these two manuscripts were tentatively ascribed by Delaissé to Simon de Marmion, and more positively so by Thomas Kren and Roger Wieck.[22]

3. Frère Laurent, *Somme le Roi*
With date 1475.[23]

4. *Traités moraux et religieux*
With date March 1475.
With miniature (ascribed to the Master of Mary of Burgundy) showing Margaret in

prayer, accompanied by two kneeling ladies and a male figure standing in the background.[24]

5. Boethius, *De Consolatione philosophiae* (in French)
With date 1476.
With dedication miniature (ascribed to the Master of Mary of Burgundy) showing the scribe offering the manuscript to Margaret. The scene is set in front of a building, and Margaret is accompanied by five ladies. (See fig.4.)[25]

Although undated we may range with this group:
6. *Bible moralisée*
In the hand of David Aubert, commissioned by Margaret or by the ducal pair, and with miniatures stylistically related to the previous manuscripts.[26]

(B) SCRIBE UNKNOWN:

7. *Traités de morale, Imitatio Christi*
Ghent, but not by David Aubert. With a miniature portrait showing Margaret alone in prayer at an altar.[27]

## Place of production unknown

1. *L'Apocalypse de St. Jean*, possibly produced in Ghent but not by David Aubert. The miniatures are ascribed to the Master of Mary of Burgundy.[28]

2. Book of Hours, known as the Spencer-Churchill Hours. Possibly adapted for Margaret of York.[29]

3. Sarum Breviary, possibly adapted for Margaret of York by the addition of illuminated leaves.[30]

4. Charles Soillot, *Le Débat de Félicité*
Copied from a manuscript produced for Charles the Bold who had commissioned the text.[31]

There is no doubt whatever about the patron of these manuscripts. Amid the lavish decorations of the margins we find Margaret's coat of arms, banderolles with her motto 'Bien en aviegne' ('may good come of it'), and the initials C and M for Charles and Marguerite. In addition there are the miniature portraits. They number eight in all, or 14 if we count the compartments in the *Benois seront les miserécordieux* separately, and in the present short list they are found in Brussels 1, 2 and 4, Ghent 2, 4, 5, and 7. They are very similar in the portrayal of this elegant figure, although some allowance for a stylised representation has to be made. We have noted already that the Brussels miniatures show consistency in dress and head-ornaments. Margaret's sartorial representation in the Ghent group is equally consistent: a close fitting dress of undecorated material, a V-necked bodice with a wide belt, a train bordered with ermine, a hennin with a wimple. The attendant ladies are dressed in very similar styles. When we divide the portrait miniatures according to these criteria (headwear, dress) there is only one exception: in the *Vie de Sainte Colette* Margaret is seen wearing an elaborate

Fig.2    Margaret of York and Charles the Bold in Prayer.
Miniature in Pierre de Vaux, *Vie de Sainte Colette.*
(Ghent, Arme Klarenabdij, MS 8.)

Fig.3    Charles the Bold and Margaret of York in a hunting scene.
Tapestry, Brussels, Lille or Tournay, 1468.
(Amsterdam, Rijksmuseum, RBK 1955-97.)

cap with transparent veils (see fig.2), a headdress which she also appears to be wearing on a tapestry now in the Rijksmuseum in Amsterdam, where she is seen with her spouse, who is here sporting a natty embroidered hunting hat (see fig.3).[32] It is possible that we have seen that hat somewhere else?

Our curiosity about the ducal wardrobe is the immediate result of the liveliness and immediacy with which these scenes are presented. Although they are the work of several miniaturists, they are united in portraying their subject as immersed in activity, or in relation to other figures, in a way that resembles the modern notion of reportage, although we need not entertain for long the idea of a duchess, besieged by her miniaturists, even requesting them to remove themselves. In two miniatures (Brussels 4 and Ghent 2) we are left in no doubt that she is portrayed in the company of her spouse Duke Charles, who in many of the other manuscripts is explicitly represented by the initial C as part of the monogram CM in the borders or in the miniature itself.

With this background of miniatures of very similar nature it is time to take a closer look at the engraving in the *Recuyell* copy. In costume and in style of presentation it is close indeed to the David Aubert-series, and this is presumably one of the reasons why Otto Pächt recognised here the design of the 'Mary of Burgundy' master, an identification that has remained unopposed. The scene is particularly close to the Jena *Boethius* of 1476 (fig.4) in that we may recognise the same five ladies here, but the engraving offers a much busier scene. As in the miniatures the engraving leaves us in no doubt at whose court we are present: a baldequin over a bed is decorated with the initials CM joined by a love-knot and below them is Margaret's motto 'bien en aviegne'. In front of the bed, but much in the background of the scene, two courtiers are whispering together, in contrast to the five ladies whose attention is demurely directed to the central scene, their downcast eyes deferential in the extreme. The rich jewellery of the two ladies in front may suggest that they were not just ladies in waiting, but belonged in a different way to Margaret's entourage. One of them was possibly her step-daughter Mary of Burgundy, to whom she was close, and in whose company she was painted on other occasions. One of these ladies tenderly strokes a very small dog, a puppy really. It is at this point that we are confronted with obvious symbolism, for the dog is the well-known emblem for faith: 'your loyal friend' is what this gesture says (a term used in several of Margaret's autograph inscriptions), and perhaps the image even conveys that loyalty, when fostered, will grow. The other animal in the picture, the monkey posturing between the two central figures, is much less discreet. He is the little jester, aping the donor's gesture, but also giving it a deeper dimension: by contrasting it with the monkey's empty and soul-less little hands Caxton's gesture gains in spiritual depth. His act of dedication is anything but empty. The presence of these pets shows, probably unintentionally, yet another aspect of the ducal household, its lack of children. The marriage of Charles and Margaret had remained childless, and the lack of a male heir was a cloud over this union which otherwise appears to have been popular. Of course royal children, even babies or toddlers, would have been shown in their ceremonial best, but the presence of these pets in places so natural for young children, a lady's arms and the floor, seems to show up this emptiness.

Fig.4    Margaret of York and the ladies of her court, Boethius, *De consolatione Philosophiae*, in French. (Jena, Universitätsbibliothek, MS El.F.85.)

There are more players filling up the stage with smaller parts to play than the protagonists. Well in the background are two servants, standing by the dresser with beautiful jugs, the junior one pouring water from an ewer into a dish held by the other. Pouring? Surely we should remember that whoever the master of Mary of Burgundy was, he is unlikely to have been an Englishman, and 'schenken' is the verb that is intended to come to mind. 'Schenken' must be an intentional pun in the context of this dedication scene, for 'schenken' means 'to give', 'to give solemnly', 'to endow', as well as 'to pour'.

This is an obvious element to alert us to the necessity to think in Dutch, if not specifically in Flemish, however English the context in which the engraving is presented to the observer. It leads us to an explanation of the figure who is seen as entering the tableau through a door on the left. Again we can be struck by the theatrical effect: a new character entering will change the dramatic situation. He may be the hero of the play who will not enter until minor roles have established the setting, or he may be a messenger who brings tidings of events which take place beyond the confines of the staged scene. In the theatre a door quite plainly represents a link with the outer world. This is also its function in pictorial terms. André Chastel very rapidly sketched the development of this function, 'la fenêtre ouverte sur le monde', ranging from the Flemish painters early in the 15th century to the Dutch masters of the interior in the 17th century, all to support an analysis of the figure framed in a doorway painted in Velázquez's *Las Meniñas*.[33] This figure, elegantly poised on his way out, bridging two worlds, overlooks a scene which, in the idiom of its own time, has many points in common with the engraving of Margaret of York: the courtly entourage, striking a balance between hierarchical formality and lively domesticity, the presence of an artist as a central figure in the composition along with the little princess, and with it the problem of the position of the artist at court. We may even take a cue from the discreetly implied presence of the highest in the hierarchy, the king and the queen whose faces are merely reflected in a mirror. The question whether this means that they are reflected from the painting on the easel, or from their actual presence in the *atelier*, appears to be a deliberate teaser bequeathed by the artist to posterity which has not neglected to discuss it at great length.[34] The painting and the engraving are in many ways objects without basis for comparison: 200 years divide them, the pictorial medium is different, the scale of the painting yields a fullness of expression that is alien to the 15th century. Yet a comparison is less contrived when we come to realise that this court, and the little *infanta* in the centre, are direct descendants of the court depicted in the Caxton engraving. At the very least it can remind us of the pictorial idiom for symbolically implying a presence in an evidently naturalistic scene.

The figures in *Las Meniñas* are all identified by contemporary documentation, including the *aposentador* in the doorway. We are not quite so lucky with the gentleman entering Caxton's dedication scene. Rather daringly he is depicted as half a man, one long leg, one arm, half a torso, but an almost complete face, a glimpse of full shoulder-length hair, and most complete of all – a dashing hat with a rim and a feather. Have we not seen this hat before? He is entering through a half-opened door, in rather awkward perspective, and in his left hand, which seems to push the door

Fig.5    Margaret of York in Prayer. *Traités moraux et religieux*,
written at Ghent by David Aubert, 1475.
(Oxford, Bodleian Library, MS Douce 365, f.115 r, detail.)

open, he holds a stick. In general symbolism a stick is an attribute of power, but specifically in this combination we may associate it again with a Dutch expression: 'de stok achter de deur' (the stick behind the door) meaning the power to enforce an agreement, or, as the *Woordenboek der Nederlandse Taal* explains, to threaten with a measure which can be made operative at any time.[35] The person entering need not be necessarily threatening, but he is expressly presented as a figure to whom real power is available. Also the foot, almost wedged below the door, has the connotation 'een voet in de deur' with the same meaning as the English 'a foot in the door': this is a person who is intent on entering, by force if necessary. There is therefore a rather threatening meaning in the attributes to the figure, but the element of threat can be mitigated by the playfulness of its expression. We may also associate this man with the rather friendlier appearances he may be making in several miniatures. For the powerful person entering on the scene can hardly be anyone else but Charles the Bold, who may even be identified by that fashionable hat.[36] He was the 'real power' behind any influence Margaret exerted by her patronage. We may recall another appearance of his on the side-lines, in the Liedet miniature of the History of Charles Martel spying on the artist from behind a pillar. With Margaret of York he is shown in prayer in the Sainte Colette manuscript, (bare-headed, of course), and (wearing a hat), as principal guest of Tundalus, taking part in the opening scene of the story. The tapestry in the Rijksmuseum, Amsterdam, shows him in her company, wearing a rimmed, feathered hat. There is yet another miniature with a male figure observing Margaret, but lingering in the background. It is the miniature in the Bodleian *Traités moraux et religieux* (Ghent 4, see fig.5). Margaret accompanied by two kneeling ladies is praying at an altar in a large church apparently following the service from an open Book of Hours, while off centre-stage, in front of a pillar, a tall male figure seems to listen with an inward look of rapt attention. His expression charmingly betrays his absorption in the scene. As in the engraving the figure is not fully depicted: part of his left arm is cut off by the border, and so is his sword, all adding to the impression that he is holding himself back. But for those in the know it would not be difficult to establish his identity, for he wears a heavy gold chain, he has a full head of hair, and from his right hand dangles ... a hat.

The movements of the ducal pair during the years of their marriage are well documented,[37] and it is therefore known that they were seldom together in one place. The scenes depicted by the miniaturists are therefore in all likelihood fictional in so far as they indicate really shared moments of time. Yet, when Delaissé briefly discussed the manuscripts commissioned by Margaret of York he sensitively saw in her active patronage a sign of an interest shared between the spouses.[38] This may equally be expressed by the miniaturists when they imply Charles's presence in the scenes which pay homage to their patron. It is difficult to consider Margaret's bibliophily as anything but genuine, especially in the light of the simple autograph dedications written in some of her manuscripts which have the ring of truth. With her active interest and patronage the English princess followed the tradition established by her Burgundian father-in-law Philip the Good. By her spouse Charles's presence in the background as a spectator, or entering the scene, as an essential part of her identity, the miniaturists and the engraver delicately and playfully praised the English princess for continuing a tradition that was recognised (then as now) as a celebration of the great achievements of the House of Burgundy.

## Notes

1. Raoul le Fèvre, *Le recueil des histoires de Troie*. Translated by William Caxton with the title *Recuyell of the Histories of Troye* [Bruges, William Caxton, *c*.1473]. M. F. A. G. Campbell, *Annales de la typographie néerlandaise au quinzième siècle*, Suppl.I (The Hague, 1878), 1093ᵃ. E. Gordon Duff, *Fifteenth Century English Books* (London, 1917), 242. *Catalogue of Books Printed in the XVth Century now in the British Museum*, pt.IX (London, 1962), p.129. F. R. Goff, *Incunabula in American Libraries: a Third Census of Fifteenth-Century Books Recorded in American Collections* (New York, 1964), L117. *STC²* (1976-86), 15375. This copy: S. de Ricci, *A Census of Caxtons* (Oxford 1909), 3.11.

2. S. Montague Peartree, 'A portrait of William Caxton', *The Burlington Magazine for Connoisseurs*, 7 (1905), pp.383-87. A .W. Pollard, 'Recent Caxtoniana', *The Library*, 2nd series, vol.6 (1905), pp.337-45. Reproduced by Peartree and A. W. Pollard; by Seymour de Ricci as frontispiece to his *Census* cited in note 1 above; in G. D. Painter, *William Caxton: a Quincentenary Biography of England's First Printer* (London, 1976), pl.1; *William Caxton: An Exhibition to commemorate the Quincentenary of the Introduction of Printing into England* (London, The British Library, 1976), pl.13; Lotte Hellinga, *Caxton in Focus* (London, 1982), fig.6, and in a study which also discusses Caxton and Margaret of York: 'Caxton and the Bibliophiles', in [Association internationale de bibliophilie], P. Culot and E. Rouir (eds.), *Onzième Congrès International de Bibliophilie, Bruxelles, 21-27 sept. 1979.* (Brussels, 1981) pp.11-38 (pl.7).

3. Both miniatures are found in the manuscript *Histoire de Charles Martel*, Brussels, Royal Library MS 6-9, written by David Aubert in 1463-65, and illuminated (*c*.1472?) by Loyset Liedet. Illustrated in: *Charles le Téméraire 1433-77: Exposition organisée à l'occasion du cinquième centenaire de sa mort*, Brussels, Royal Library, 1977, Plate III and figs.6, 7. See also: L.-M.-J. Delaissé, *La miniature flamande: Le mécénat de Philippe le Bon*. Brussels, Royal Library, 1959, nos.144-46.

Many scenes representing the dedication by scribe or author to one of the dukes of Burgundy are illustrated in this catalogue.

4. E. von Rath, 'Die Kupferstichillustration im Wiegendruckzeitalter', in: Johannes Hofmann (ed.), *Die Bibliothek und ihre Kleinodien: Festschrift zum 250 jährigen Jubiläum der Leipziger Stadtbibliothek* (Leipzig, 1927), pp.58-68. I am most grateful to my colleague Dr Anneliese Schmidt, Berlin, for providing me with a copy of this publication. Other early books with engraved illustrations are Colard Mansion's *Boccace* of 1476, see below note 7. In Florence the printer Nicolaus Laurentii produced two books with engravings, Antonio Bettini da Siena, *Monte Santo di Dio* printed in 1477 (GW 2204)with three engravings, and the famous Dante *Commedia* with the date 30 August 1481 which contains up to 19 engravings formerly ascribed to Botticelli (GW 7966). In 1479 Johannes Numeister illustrated Johannes de Turrecremata, *Meditationes seu contemplationes devotissimae*, probably printed at Mainz, with 34 metal cuts, using a different technique in metal. These four books are all discussed and illustrated in the exhibition catalogue *Fünf Jahrhunderte Buchillustration: Meisterwerke der Buchgraphik aus der Bibliothek Otto Schäfer*, Nuremberg, Germanisches Nationalmuseum, 1987, nos.11,13,14,17. If the Caxton engraving was produced *c*.1476 it would have preceded these illustrations, but at present this cannot be established with any degree of certainty.

5. S. de Ricci (see note 1) summarised the history of ownership of the copy: Elizabeth, Queen of Edward IV (inserted inscription), later to Major Swinton, by exchange to Laing, sold to the Duke of Roxburghe, hence to the Duke of Devonshire; the book was acquired from Chatsworth by the H. E. Huntington Library.

6. Peartree and Pollard stated that the leaf containing the engraving was pasted in, and Pollard pointed out evidence to show that it was added at an early date. Dr Paul Needham established that the leaf with the engraving,

although now tipped in, appears to be integral to the copy and kindly communicated this finding to me.

7. Giovanni Boccaccio, *De casibus virorum illustrium*, in the earlier French translation of Laurent Premierfait (Bruges, Colard Mansion, 1476), GW 4432. Copies with engravings are recorded at the Boston Museum of Fine Arts (formerly in the collection of the Marquess of Lothian at Newbattle Abbey (nine engravings) and eight at Amiens, Bibliothèque municipale, a state also represented by the copy in the Bibliothek Otto Schäfer, Schweinfurt, but wanting one leaf with engraving. Other copies with engravings are found in Göttingen UB, Providence (RI), Annmary Brown Memorial Library, and the H. E. Huntington Library. In these copies the engravings are printed separately and pasted in. They are discussed and fully reproduced by H. Michel, *L'Imprimeur Colard Mansion et le 'Boccace' de la Bibliothèque d'Amiens* (Paris, 1925). See also H. P. Rossiter, 'Colard Mansion's Boccaccio of 1476', in: Oswald Goetz (ed.), *Essays in honor of Georg Swarzenski* (Chicago, 1951), pp.103-10; F. Anzelewsky, 'Die drei Boccaccio-Stiche von 1476 und ihre Meister', in: *Festschrift Friedrich Winkler* (Berlin, 1959), pp.114-25.

8. George D. Painter suggested that Caxton showed his translation to the Duchess soon after its completion. He considered it possible that the engraving was based on an illumination in the manuscript copy of the *Recuyell* (now lost) which Caxton must have presented to Duchess Margaret. The engraving could represent either of these occasions. See G. D. Painter, *William Caxton: a Quincentenary Biography of England's First Printer* (London, 1976), pp.51,63-4,193. On the liberty taken with the state of completion of books in the conventions of such representations see the remarks of Eberhard König, 'The History of Art and the History of the Book at the Time of the Transition from Manuscript to Print', in: Lotte Hellinga and John Goldfinch (eds.), *Bibliography and the Study of 15th-Century Civilisation* (London, 1987), p.155.

9. The transaction is recorded in the settlement of the estate of Magister Eamundus Munerius, canon of the church of St Mary at Courtrai in Flanders, who died on 10 March 1471. Among the receipts is recorded 'Item a magistro Iohanne Finet, elemosinario domine ducisse, pro magno breviario in duobus voluminibus ad usum Romane ecclesie, Lxxij ıb.par.' (contractions expanded). The list of expenses shows that a barrel was bought to pack one part of the breviary, together with a multi-volume Bible, for sending to Bruges, the Bible to be sold in the market place. One volume had already been dispatched by special messenger. The list of the books in this estate was published by A. Derolez, *Corpus Catalogorum Belgii: De middeleeuwse bibliotheekscatalogi der Zuidelijke Nederlanden*. I. Provincie West-Vlaanderen (Brussels, 1966), no.81, p.127.

10. O. Pächt, 'The Master of Mary of Burgundy', *The Burlington Magazine*, 85 (1944), pp.295ff. O. Pächt, *The Master of Mary of Burgundy* (London, 1948).

11. G. I. Lieftinck, 'De Meester van Maria van Bourgondië en Rooclooster bij Brussel', *Nieuws-Bulletin van de Koninklijke Nederlandse Oudheidkundige Bond*, 17 (1964), pp.257-94. G. I. Lieftinck, 'Boekverluchters uit de omgeving van Maria van Bourgondië, c.1475-c.1495', *Verhandelingen van de Koninklijke Vlaamse Akademie van Wetenschappen, kl.d.Letteren*, jg.31, nr.66, (1969).

12. L.-M.-J. Delaissé, *La miniature flamande: Le mécénat de Philippe le Bon. Exposition* (Brussels, 1959). L.-M.-J. Delaissé, 'Marguerite d'York et ses livres', in: M.-R. Thielemans, *Marguerite d'York et son temps*. Exposition organisée par la Banque de Bruxelles, 28 sept.-7 oct. 1967.

13. J. J. G. Alexander, *Le maître de Marie de Bourgogne: Un livre d'heures d'Engelbert de Nassau, the Bodleian Library, Oxford* (Paris, 1970). (The English version was not available to me.)

14. G. Dogaer, 'Margarete van York, bibliofiele', *Studia Mechliniensia en Handelingen van de Koninklijke Kring voor Oudheidkunde, Letteren en Kunst van Mechelen*, 79 (1975), pp.99-111.

15. Muriel J. Hughes, 'The Library of Margaret of York, Duchess of Burgundy', *The Private Library* (1984), pp.53-78.

16. The chapter 'The Library of Margaret of York and the Burgundian Court' by Thomas

Kren in: Thomas Kren and Roger S. Wieck, *The Visions of Tondal from the Library of Margaret of York* (Malibu, The Paul J. Getty Museum, 1990). At the time of going to press it was unfortunately impossible for me to benefit from the information exchanged at the colloquium on Margaret of York's manuscripts held in June 1990 at the Getty Museum. Another recent publication, Christine Weightman, *Margaret of York, Duchess of Burgundy, 1446-1503* (Gloucester and New York, 1989) is valuable for understanding the background of a woman in her position but does not add significantly to knowledge of her as a patron and collector.

17. Brussels, Royal Library, MS 9296. *La miniature flamande* 177. Hughes 12.

18. BL Add. MS 7970. Hughes 13. Illustrated: *William Caxton: Quincentenary Exhibition.* The British Library, 1976, p.26. Lotte Hellinga, *Caxton in Focus* (London, 1982), pl.VI.

19. New Haven, Yale University Library, Beinecke MS 639. From Sotheby's, London, 22 June 1982, lot 59. I am most grateful to my colleague Janet Backhouse for help in identifying the catalogue. Examination of the (modest) manuscript raises doubts whether it was commissioned for Margaret of York, or simply owned by her.

20. Ghent, Arme Klarenabdij, MS 8. *La miniature flamande* 186. Hughes 21. Facsimile edition: Y. Cazaux, J. Decavele, A. Derolez, C. van Contanje o.f.m., *Vita Sanctae Coletae (1381-1447)* (Tielt, Leiden, 1982).

21. Formerly the late Philip Hofer, deposited at the Houghton Library, Harvard University. In 1987 acquired by the Paul J. Getty Museum, Malibu, California. See Thomas Kren and Roger S. Wieck (note 16 above). *La miniature flamande* 191. Hughes 16.

22. As above note 21. The two manuscripts have been bound together since the nineteenth century. *La miniature flamande* 191. Hughes 17.

23. Brussels, Royal Library, MS 9106. *La miniature flamande* 193. *Charles le Téméraire* (Exhibition 1977) 16, pl.21. Hughes 18.

24. Oxford, Bodleian Library, MS Douce 365. Pächt plates 2,3,44. *La miniature flamande* 192. Hughes 20.

25. Jena, Universitätsbibliothek, MS El.F.85. Pächt 4. *La miniature flamande* 194. Hughes 11.

26. Brussels, Royal Library, MS 9030-37. *La miniature flamande* 197. *Charles le Téméraire* 20. Hughes 4.

27. Brussels, Royal Library, MS 9272-76. *La miniature flamande* 196. *Charles le Téméraire* 17. Hughes 19. Of the five miniatures the one with the portrait of Margaret of York is ascribed to the Master of Mary of Burgundy.

28. New York, Pierpont Morgan Library, MS 484. Pächt 2. *La miniature flamande* 199. Hughes 2. With 78 miniatures.

29. Christie's, London, 26 May 1965, lot 195. Written for Charles the Bold. Inserted at the end of the manuscript is a miniature in different style from the preceding, with the arms of Margaret of York in the border. Hughes 5.

30. Cambridge, St John's College MS H.18. This breviary dating from the early 15th century was adapted for Margaret of York by the insertion of leaves decorated with her coat of arms, monogram and motto. Pächt 6. *La miniature flamande* 198. Hughes 8. It is possible that several fragments in the Cottonian collection now in the British Library originally belonged to this manuscript.

31. BL, MS Arundel 71. Hughes 22.

32. Amsterdam, Rijksmuseum, RBK 1955-97, Brussels, Lille or Tournai, c.1468-70, thought to be produced from a cartoon by Hugo van der Goes (*Charles le Téméraire* (1977), p.66).

33. André Chastel, 'La figure dans l'encadrement de la porte chez Velázquez', in: *Velázquez; son temps, son influence.* Actes du Colloque tenu à la Casa de Velázquez, 7-10 Dec. 1960 (Paris, 1963), pp.141-5. I am most grateful to my colleague Chris Michaelides for tracing this publication.

34. See for a summary of previous literature and a new interpretation of the painting, Jonathan Brown, *Velázquez, Painter and Courtier* (New Haven, London, 1986), pp.256-64. Brown's discussion of the perspective of

the painting and his observation that in the small room where it was originally destined to be hung it must have had a *trompe-l'oeil* effect adds to his interpretation of the deliberate ambiguity of the 'insinuation' of the royal presence.

35. *Woordenboek der Nederlandse Taal* vol.xv, 1201: 'De stok achter de deur: in toepassing op een bedreiging met een maatregel die te allen tijde in werking kan worden gesteld.'

36. For an iconographical survey of Charles the Bold see the 'Introduction à

l'iconographie de Charles le Téméraire' by Micheline Comblen-Sonkes and Anne Rouzet in *Charles le Téméraire* (1977), pp.40-67. Anne Rouzet prepared also the excellent documentation in John Bartier, *Charles le Téméraire* (Brussels, 1970).

37. H. VanderLinden, *Itinéraires de Charles, Duc de Bourgogne, Marguerite d'York et Marie de Bourgogne 1467-1477* (Brussels, 1936).

38. Delaissé, 1967, see note 10 above.

J. A. Gruys

# Post-Incunabula: a Dutch contribution to bibliographical vocabulary

Among the few words given by the Dutch to the English language, surely the most strange and superfluous is 'post-incunabulum'. For why on earth should anyone need a special word to denote 'a book printed between 1500 and 1540'? The answer to this question, and at the same time the sum and conclusion of my argument, is: since in the Royal Library at The Hague this category of books was already placed together in about 1840 by the then librarian J. W. Holtrop, library jargon invented a word to denote this collection. As later librarians such as T. C .L. Wijnmalen (who moved the collection to his own room in 1891, and intended to describe it afresh) and their staff were having frequent contact with the bookseller and publisher Wouter Nijhoff (1866-1947), the concept of 'post-incunabulum' was taken over together with the word by the future author of the *Nederlandsche bibliographie van 1500 tot 1540* when in the 1890s he started collecting material; the word was then spread by him amongst his fellow bibliographers, who, eventually, introduced it to their British connections.

Maria Elisabeth Kronenberg (1881-1970), Wouter Nijhoff's co-author for the first volume of the *Nederlandsche bibliographie* (1923) and sole author of the second and third volumes (1940-1971), was the first scholar to make an inquiry into the history of the word post-incunabulum (Dutch: postincunabel), which was published in 1951 and reprinted in 1961.[1] I shall summarize her article first.

Miss Kronenberg relates that she was struck by J. C. T. Oates's paper on the collection of early printed books of Sir Stephen Gaselee,[2] in which he first cites the latter's use of the word 'post-incunabula', then states that 'any currency which the term may have among English bibliographers is due to Gaselee's influence' (the word 'first achieved the dignity of English print' in 1938 in a paper from his hand), and finally assumes that Gaselee had borrowed the word from Wouter Nijhoff, who had used it in the Introduction to his *Nederlandsche bibliographie* in 1923. She modestly adds that her own use of the word in personal conversation may have contributed to Gaselee's introducing it into English usage.

After establishing that in Germany too the word 'Postinkunabel' passes for a borrowing from Dutch, she decided to find out its origin. She first turned to the *Woordenboek der Nederlandsche taal* s. v. 'incunabel' (vol.6, col.1541; the instalment in question was published in 1909); the derivative 'postincunabel' is called there 'a well-known word among book-lovers', but no further information is given. Under 'postincunabel' the *Woordenboek* (vol.12.2, col.3632, published in 1949) does give some quotations – all

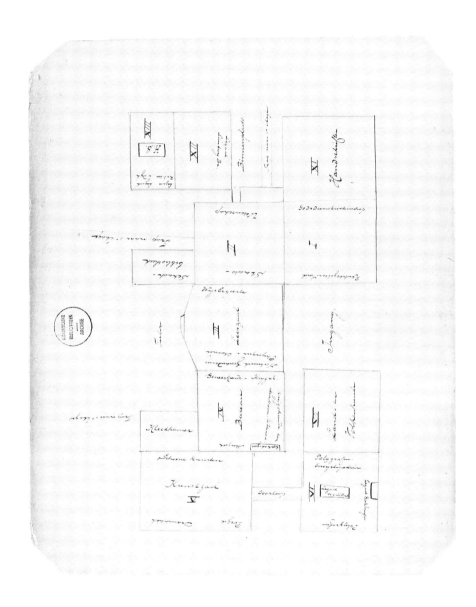

Fig.1    The Royal Library at The Hague in 1891. Ground-floor.

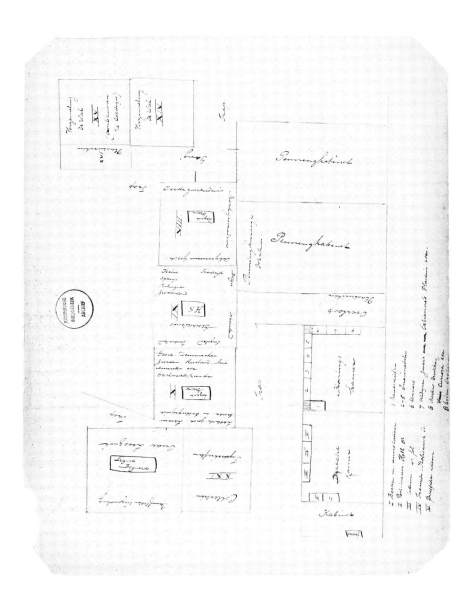

Fig.2   First floor.

borrowed from a paper published in 1923 by Miss Kronenberg herself! Then she examined a long list of articles and personal letters written before 1909, and she found a small series of instances where the word was used; the two earliest (published in January and February 1902, by the Royal Library's sub-librarian W. P. C. Knuttel and by an anonymous writer) were both concerned with Nijhoff's intended bibliography, and both denoted its subject as 'so-called post-incunabula'.[3] Evidently the term was newly introduced then into (at least written) Dutch. Bonaventura Kruitwagen, she adds, declared to her that he was sure that he himself had taken the term from Nijhoff. And so, she concluded, the word was probably coined by Nijhoff in about 1900; at least, earlier instances are lacking, also in papers by Nijhoff where he might have been expected to use the word. In a 1961 Addendum to her article she cites a still earlier example from a letter by Nijhoff himself to the Deventer librarian J. C. van Slee (January 1901).

Thus far Miss Kronenberg. It is clear that more than 30 years' familiarity with the word and concept 'post-incunabulum' had made her blind to the first and principal question: 'Why should there *exist* such a concept?', as well as to the more practical question: 'Why did Nijhoff choose the period 1500-40, and not, for instance, 1500-25 or 1500-50?'. Had she been aware of these questions, the answer to them would have occurred to her readily: Nijhoff simply followed the lead of the Royal Library's collection of post-incunabula, which, as she surely knew, was formed in about 1840 by Holtrop, who placed the books together in the Reading Room.[4] Of course the term as such was used neither by Holtrop nor later in official reports; as a matter of fact, the collection was mentioned none too frequently during the following 50 years.

Before going into details, I must confess that I can explain only tentatively why Holtrop chose to make a special collection of the library's holdings printed between 1500 and 1540; in choosing the year 1540 he did not follow any established librarians' or book collectors' practice.[5] Probably he considered having a thorough control of early 16th-century books necessary when he started compiling his exemplary *Catalogus librorum saeculo XV° impressorum, quotquot in Bibliotheca Regia Hagana asservantur* (published in 1856), and his rearrangement of the library's complete holdings in about 1840 must have made this object comparatively easy to achieve. An argument for ascribing such bibliographical motives to Holtrop is the final arrangement of his collection of 1500-40 editions, which was 'chronological and geographical'.[6] The shelf-marks added in 1891 to part of the mid-19th-century card catalogue of the collection clearly shows its early arrangement: first by country (the Netherlands, France, Italy, Germany), then by format (folio, quarto, octavo), and finally by year of publication.

In 1891 the collection was moved from the (by then former) Reading Room to the Director's Room; the librarian, Wijnmalen, announced his intention to recatalogue it afresh personally[7]. About the same time Nijhoff conceived his plan for a Dutch Bibliography 1500-40, and the first thing he did was to describe the Royal Library's collection of Dutch 'post-incunabula'.[8] And about the same time again, the administrator of the Royal Library, G. J. Bekink, drew a rough plan of the library's arrangement (see illustrations); in it the Director's Room shows five bookcases, containing respectively:

I. *Boeken m. annotatiën* ( = books with ms annotations)
II. *Post-incun. Holl. 8°.* ( = Dutch post-incunabula in 8°)
III. *idem 4° fol.* ( = ditto in 4° and folio)
IV. *Fransch-Italiaansch id.* ( = ditto, French and Italian)
V. *Duitsche idem* ( = ditto, German)

Bekink's ground-plan, and especially its date, needs to be examined carefully, as, apart from other interesting points, it gives the first testimony of the word 'post-incunabula'.

This plan[9] shows the two main floors of the eighteenth-century building used by the library since 1821. The main rooms on the ground-floor are numbered I-VII and XI-XIII, those on the first floor VIII-X, XIV-XV and XXI, or are called 'Oude Leeszaal' (Former Reading Room), 'Penningkabinet' (Coin and Medal Room), 'Directie Kamer' (Director's Room), and 'Koningskamer' (Royalty Room). The 1891 and 1892 Annual Reports of the library[10] make it clear that during those years considerable changes in the arrangement of some rooms and collections were made by Wijnmalen, and the plan shows the resulting situation in most cases. Apart from moving the *post-incunabula* to his own Room ('Directie Kamer'), he also moved to the location shown in the plan the *archief* (next to the 'Directie Kamer'), the *Catalogus* (in Room IV, the 'Bureau'), the *Legaat Groen* (legacy Groen van Prinsterer, in Rooms VIII and X), the *Penningkundige Werken* (numismatic works, in the 'Penningkabinet') and the *Pamfletten Verzameling* (collection of pamphlets, in the 'Oude Leeszaal'). In other cases the plan appears to show the pre-1891 situation: the HS (manuscripts) indicated in Room IX seem to refer to the old show-case for some manuscripts and not yet to the two large new ones that replaced it in 1891; they exhibited 80 manuscripts, 82 incunabula, a Veldener binding, and the Coronation Bible of William and Mary.[11] Other features which were disappearing by 1891/92 but still shown in the plan are the presence in the 'Leeszaal' (Reading Room) and: 'Bureau' (Catalogue Room) of the collections *Wijsbegeerte, Natuurl. geschiedenis* (Philosophy, Natural history), and so on, which had had their place in Rooms III and IV since 1821 but had to be removed when in 1888 the Reading Room and the Catalogue Room were transferred there, to be replaced by a considerable collection of reference works;[12] and the presence of *handschriften* (manuscripts) in the 'Koningskamer', for in 1891 all manuscripts (excepting those in the show-cases) were concentrated in Rooms XI and XIII. The only moment that all the features mentioned thus far existed at the same time was at some time during the year 1891. If the plan dates from that year, only the *Kunstzaal* (Art Room, in Room V) is an anachronism – or rather, anticipates an expected development: though opened to the public only in 1893, it was planned since spring 1890.[13] As all other years would produce more numerous and more serious anachronisms, I think we may safely assume that the plan dates from 1891; and as, consequently, the word 'post-incunabulum' was already current in the Royal Library at that time, there can be little doubt where to look for its cradle.

## Notes

1. M. E. Kronenberg, 'Bijdrage tot de geschiedenis van het woord post-incunabel', *Het boek*, 30, 1949/51, pp.351-56 (reprinted with an Addendum in: M. E. Kronenberg, *Over mensen en boeken* (The Hague, 1961), pp.114-18). F. de Marez Oyens (*Papers of the Bibliographical Society of America*, 81, 1987, p.41, n.13) gives a useful survey of some deviant meanings given to the word 'post- incunable' by various authors.

2. *TLS*, 17 November 1950.

3. To her list should be added: 'de zoogenaamde post-incunabelen, dat wil zeggen, de drukken van 1500-1540' (W. P. C. Knuttel, in *Die Haghe*, 1905, p.266).

4. 'Tevens is er eene tweede verzameling, wel niet zoo zeldzaam, maar toch niet minder belangrijk, bij gelegenheid der revisie van de gansche Bibliotheek vergaderd, bestaande uit werken, gedrukt in de jaren 1500-1540, van welke behoorlijke catalogussen gemaakt zijn, waarvan de titels in de beide catalogussen op hunne behoorlijke plaatsen gevoegd, en de boeken zelve in eene chronologische en geographische orde der uitgave gerangschikt zijn' (Holtrop to the Minister of Home Affairs, 25 March 1842; Royal Library Archive, Letter No.503; the quotation is part of a report on Holtrop's progress in cataloguing since 1835).

5. I do not believe that those 18th- and early 19th-century surveys of early typography that do not confine themselves to the 15th century could have inspired Holtrop to give a separate treatment to the period 1500-40.

6. See n.4. Did he decide on 1540 simply because he did so in 1840?

7. 'Ik moet hierbij nog de mededeeling voegen, dat ik in de Directiekamer, grenzende aan de zaal, waarin de prachtige verzameling van incunabelen wordt bewaard, in eene nieuwe daarvoor opzettelijk vervaardigde en eerst dezer dagen gereed gekomen groote driedubbele kast heb doen overbrengen de niet minder merkwaardige zeldzame collectie van Nederlandsche, Fransche, Duitsche, Engelsche, Italiaansche en Spaansche drukken uit de jaren 1500-1540. Ik stel mij voor zelf daarvan eene nauwkeurige beschrijving te leveren, tegelijk met eene geheele revisie en aanvulling van den door een mijner Ambtsvoorgangers, den heer J. W. Holtrop, in 1856 uitgegeven *Catalogus librorum saeculo XV° impressorum, quotquot in Bibliotheca Regia Hagana asservantur*' (Wijnmalen to the Minister of Home Affairs, 31 December 1891; Royal Library Archive, Letter No.9826).

8. W. Nijhoff in *Het boek*, 1, 1912, p.281: 'Sedert 1894 ben ik bezig aan het samenstellen van eene bibliographie van alle boeken in Noord- en Zuid-Nederland gedrukt tusschen de jaren 1500 en 1540 ... Door mij werden alle groote en de meeste kleine bibliotheken van Nederland systematisch doorzocht. Bij de Koninklijke Bibliotheek was dit al zeer gemakkelijk omdat daar sinds jaren de Nederlandsche drukken van de jaren 1501-1540 bij elkaar staan; ... Toen ik de boeken van de K.B. had beschreven ben ik (in 1902) begonnen deze titels te laten drukken...' (further on he also uses the word 'postincunabels').

9. It turned up some years ago in the manuscript collection, and is now in the Royal Library Archive.

10. *Verslag over den toestand der Koninklijke Bibliotheek in het jaar 1891* and *1892*.

11. A catalogue of the exhibits was published in 1893, both separately and as a part of the Annual Report on 1892 (*Notice d'un choix de manuscrits et d'imprimés exposés dans une des salles da la Bibliothèque Royale*).

12. After this operation was completed in 1893, a 35-page catalogue was published in 1894, both separately and as part of the Annual Report on 1893 (*Lijst van boekwerken, welke ter raadpleging in de Leeszaal geplaatst zijn*).

13. See the Annual Reports on 1890 and 1893.

Dennis E. Rhodes

## *Richard White of Basingstoke: the erudite exile**

When I was first invited to speak at Basingstoke I was at a loss to know what best to talk about, for I felt that my usual kind of lecture on the cataloguing of incunabula would be inappropriate to this audience. But then by a happy coincidence, while studying the British Library's short-title catalogue of Italian books printed between 1465 and 1600 (which for one reason or another I consult every day), my eye lighted quite by chance on the name 'White, Richard, of Basingstoke', who had published one book in Italy in 1568. I had never heard of him before, and I immediately asked myself: what is this native of Basingstoke doing in Italy in the 16th century? Here was my chance to investigate the life and works of a man who was born in this town but who spent most of his life abroad; and I soon saw from the British Library's general catalogue and from the *Dictionary of National Biography* (which has an inadequate article on him by Thompson Cooper published in 1900) that he wrote many books, all in Latin, none of them ever read today.

Richard White was born in 1539, the son of Henry White of Basingstoke and his wife Agnes, daughter of Richard Capelin of Southampton. Henry, whose grandfather had owned almost half the town of Basingstoke, died at the siege of Boulogne in 1544, and Richard also lost his mother while he was still a boy. One of the people who appear to have looked after him was his maternal uncle, John Capelin. In 1553, aged 14, Richard entered Winchester School, where in the previous year Thomas Hide had succeeded as headmaster. Hide, who came from Newbury, was a staunch Roman Catholic, and on the accession of Queen Elizabeth in November 1558 retired to Douai where he died on 9 May 1597, and was buried in the church of St Jacques. He had been a Prebendary of Winchester Cathedral, and wrote several theological treatises, only one of which seems to have been printed, in Louvain, 1579, and again in 1580, secretly in England, but with the false imprint of Louvain.[1] In 1560 Hide was succeeded as schoolmaster of Winchester by Christopher Johnson, who, as we shall shortly see, was to be a good friend of Richard White.

In 1557, aged 18, Richard White, like all good Wykehamists, entered New College, Oxford, and what may appear strange to us but was not unusual for bright young men in those days, he was elected a perpetual Fellow of New College, but did not take the BA degree until 30 May 1559, when he was 20 years old. (I often wonder what happened to these young Fellows of Oxford colleges if they then failed their BA examinations.)

Richard White left New College, and indeed left England, for a different reason: because he was a fervent Catholic, like so many of his contemporaries at Oxford who ended up on the Continent. The stream of English Catholics leaving their own country for France and Belgium from 1558 onwards gathered momentum quickly, and we should remember the case of William Allen, seven years White's senior, head of St Mary Hall, Oxford (later absorbed into Oriel College), who was mainly responsible for the establishment of the English College at Douai. He became a Cardinal in 1587 and died in 1594.

But it was not to Douai that Richard White first went; it was to Louvain, where the University, founded in 1432, was one of the leading intellectual centres of Europe, and a safe home for Catholics. As Dr A. L. Rowse has reminded us: 'Louvain earlier, Douai and the English College at Rome later, were staffed by Oxford Catholics. William Allen wrote to the Jesuit General in 1576 that Oxford was "more responsive to the ancient faith, and from thence we mostly recruit our seminary at Douai…" '[2] But this is anticipating by some 15 years. Richard White arrived in Louvain in 1560, and when the time allowed for his absence had elapsed, New College declared his Fellowship null and void in 1564. He evidently did not inform them that he was not coming back. I quote now from T. F. Kirby's *Annals of Winchester College*: 'Among other Wykehamists who quitted England about the same time [ie about 1560] and for the same reason are Thomas Hardyng, Treasurer of Salisbury Cathedral and Regius Professor of Hebrew; John Rastell, the writer against Bishop Jewell; John Marshall, who was usher under Hyde, and became a Canon of Lille; John Fen, Master of Bury St Edmund's School; Owen Lewse or Lewis, Archdeacon of Cambrai, Vicar-General to Cardinal Borromeo and Bishop of Cassano, 1588-94; Thomas Stapleton, poet and translator, and Richard White, who was more than thirty years Regius Professor at Douai.'[3]

Richard White stayed at Louvain about three years, and gave two orations there, one on 31 January and the other on 28 February 1563. These were entitled *De circulo artium et philosophiae* and *De eloquentia et Cicerone*. According to Allibone and the *DNB* (copied also by Father Godfrey Anstruther OP in his *The Seminary Priests: a dictionary of the secular clergy of England and Wales 1558-1850*, vol.I, 1969), these two orations, together with two epistles from White to his friend Christopher Johnson and from Johnson to White, were published by Johnson in 1564 or 1565. If so, they would constitute White's first publication, when he was barely 25 years old, but they are not in the British Library under his name or that of Johnson. The search for them has at least produced one good result: it has enabled me to correct an error in the catalogue of the British Library, where the two headings 'Johnson, Christopher, of New College, Oxford', and 'Jonsonus, Christophorus', in Latin (Jonsonus here spelt without an 'h') are in fact the same man. Christopher Johnson, Fellow of New College from 1553 to 1560, came from Kyddesley in Derbyshire. From 1560 to 1571 he was Master of Winchester School, practised medicine in St Dunstan's-in-the-West, became a Fellow of the College of Physicians about 1580, and died in July 1597. He had written a life of William of Wykeham, Bishop of Winchester, who had founded New College, Oxford, in 1379 and Winchester College in 1382. Either Johnson was not a Catholic or he did not allow matters of religion to trouble him, but at any rate he did not find it necessary to leave England. To return to Richard White: we find that having matriculated at Louvain on

12 August 1560, he was soon joined by his Winchester masters John Martial (or Marshall) and Thomas Hide, as well as by his three tutors from Oxford, Thomas Stapleton, Nicholas Sanders and John Rastell.[4] When many years later, in 1596, five of Richard White's orations were published at Arras in a book about which I shall have more to say later, they included a prefatory letter addressed by Christopher Johnson to John Capelin, White's uncle, dated from Winchester College on 25 February 1565. In it, Johnson states that White is now in Padua, and had delivered the first two orations in the Law School at Louvain to the admiration of a large audience. The two orations were, after all, published separately, not in 1564 or 1565, but in 1566, by Reginald Wolf in London, a book that is so rare that the only known copies are at Trinity College, Dublin, and (wanting the title page) at the University Library, Cambridge.[5] This is not only Richard White's first book, published when he was 27, but it is the only book he ever published in England; and, as we have already observed, he never published anything in English, only in Latin. In his notes to the first oration, White refers to his great friend Gulielmus Vilsius, and mentions him again later on. At first I had difficulty in identifying this man, who is not in the lists of Oxford alumni; but Father Anstruther has an entry for William Wills, when he writes: 'William Wills taught geometry and astronomy at Oxford to Richard White as the latter tells us in his *Orationes*. Wills matriculated at Louvain in September 1559 and received a licence from Rome dated 18 October 1563 to be ordained. According to Nicholas Sanders he was "Sacrae Theologiae Licentiatus".'

Another, more obscure, Englishman mentioned in the notes to the first oration is John Heming, philosopher, who in 1562, on his departure from Louvain for Trier, wrote a Latin couplet addressed to White. I have not identified Heming further. More famous men quoted by White include Cuthbert Tunstall (1474-1559), Bishop of London and later Bishop of Durham, and Sir Thomas Eliot, or Elyot, author of a well-known book on government first printed in 1531 and many times reprinted. In the second oration he remarks that he used to ask John Danister, who was then at Louvain, to 'communicate to me the observations from Cicero which formerly he had demonstrated to Nicholas Sanders at Oxford'. Once again, I have failed to identify John Danister. Dr Nicholas Sanders, on the other hand, was another don of New College, author of *De visibili monarchia Ecclesiae* and Nuncio to Ireland, where he died about 1580 while trying to raise a rebellion against English rule.

Richard White left Louvain for Italy at some time between February and August 1563, and went straight to the University of Padua. Here he delivered his third oration in August 1563, entitled *Pro divitiis regum*. It was addressed to Anthony Mason, the adopted son of Sir John Mason, statesman and Fellow of All Souls. Young Anthony Mason was being tutored by Robert Pointz and George Catagreus, a lawyer. Robert Pointz, 'student in Diuinitie', is the author of *Testimonies for the real presence of Christes body and blood in the blessed Sacrament of the aultar set foorth at large* (Louvain, 1566). George Catagreus is unknown to me. It is in the notes to his fourth oration, *Pro doctoratu*, delivered at Pavia on 11 November 1566, that White tells us who his Italian lecturers at Padua University were: Marco Mantova Benavides, the celebrated scholar who, amongst many other books, had published one in Latin at Padua in 1555 entitled 'Epitome of illustrious men who either wrote or taught jurisprudence'. Then there were Guido Panciroli, Tiberio Deciano and Joannes Cephalus, of whom the second, Count Tiberio Deciano, native of Udine and former professor of law at Padua, published a huge treatise on criminal law at Frankfurt am Main in 1591. The other two appear not to have published anything. White mentions that he went to greet Donato Rullo, a nobleman from Calabria, who had at one time been in the household of Cardinal Reginald Pole, who had spent some time in Padua and died in 1558.

The fourth oration gives an account of White's own education at Winchester, and names the teachers there and at Oxford to whom he was most indebted. It is from the notes to these orations that we can glean most biographical details about him, although we gain from them absolutely no impressions of the man's own personality: only that he was extremely learned in the law and in British history, and a devoted Catholic throughout his life.

He may have stayed at Padua as long as six years: we do not know when he left Italy. We are told that it was in 1566 he took the degree of Doctor of Civil and Canon Laws at Padua. I cannot confirm this from the Paduan records, for although that University is publishing detailed lists of its students and their degrees, it has not yet published anything for the second half of the 16th century.

In 1568 he published his only book in Italy: a learned Latin disquisition printed by the leading Paduan printer of the day, Lorenzo Pasquati, with the intriguing title *Aelia Laelia Crispis epitaphium antiquum*. It discusses in detail an ancient Roman inscription found in the territory of Bologna, and it was reprinted many years later in a second edition at Dordrecht in 1618. The author's introductory epistle to his friend Christopher Johnson, 'summo moderatori Vicamensis scholae apud Vintoniam', is dated from Padua on 23 November 1567. In it he refers to his two orations which Johnson had already published 'some years ago' (actually it was only the previous year, 1566), and incidentally refers to himself as 'always keeping well away from the printers' office': was this false modesty, or a genuine reluctance to see his own works in print?

Richard White also addresses part of this little book (which is as obscure as any enigma) to the illustrious Count Marco Mantova Benavides, who as we have seen was one of his law teachers at Padua. The enigmatic inscription, found at the villa of Marcantonio della Volta, at the first milestone outside the Mascharella gate of Bologna, tells us that Aelia Laelia Crispis was neither man nor woman, girl nor boy, but all things. This little book, one must admit, is nothing but unintelligible gibberish to us today; perhaps to readers in its own day it had a strange fascination, now quite outmoded.

The *DNB* gives the impression that White never returned to Britain, but he must have come back at least once, probably arriving home in 1568 or 1569, for he says himself in the notes to his fifth oration that on 13 March 1570 he left Britain, arriving at Rouen on 17 April (why over a month to get that far? - is there a mistake in the month?), from where he rode on horseback to Douai which he reached on 29 April 1570. From then on he lived at Douai for the rest of his life. He seems to have published no books between 1568 and 1597, a period of almost 30 years, more or less from his 30th to his 60th year; and during that time we have few precise biographical details about him.

In 1562 Philip II of Spain founded the University of Douai, which flourished until suppressed in 1793. Several English scholars were given chairs, of whom Richard White was one. In 1568 William Allen founded the English College at Douai, which was the most important college on the Continent for training Roman Catholic clergy for the English missions. One of the first people whom White met on arrival at Douai in April 1570 was, as he tells us himself in the notes to his fifth oration, 'Audoenus Ludouicus', Doctor of Laws and Professor, 'well-known to me and a friend, who had studied at the same college in England, and who immediately gave me hospitality'. Owen Lewis, also known as Lewis Owen (1532-94), from Anglesey, scholar of Winchester College in 1547, became a perpetual Fellow of New College, Oxford, in 1554. As the *DNB* says of him: 'being opposed to the innovations in religion, he left the university about 1561 and proceeded to Douai, where he completed his degrees both in law and divinity, and was appointed regius professor of law'. His later years were spent in Italy, and he died at Rome as Bishop of Cassano. It was Lewis who introduced White to Arnold de la Cambe, alias Ganthois (because he was a native of Ghent), who, says White, 'asked me at once to teach his nephews Iacobus and Quintinus Algambei. Shortly afterwards he built a most spacious house for all the law students.' And we know from the diaries of the English College at Douai that on 1 October 1570, this same man, Dom Arnould Ganthois, abbot of Marchiennes, founded Marchiennes College, calling it 'Societas Iuris Peritorum', and placed at its head Dr Richard White. White then admits: 'I was urged to come out into the public, for my silence, as I was aware, was suspect, so I invented 24 *characteres*, or forms of universal law. These were communicated to Richard Hall, the theologian, my friend, and when they were given back to me I was asked to take them to Antwerp and put them in the hands of the great printer Christopher Plantin, but I refused, because I did not consider that so recent a composition was worthy of being published... So the Praesul (or Principal), hearing of my refusal, arranged with Owen Lewis that I should at least give public lectures; and thus, because I could not avoid the general wishes of the people any longer, I began with this oration [*ie* his fifth] on 15 July 1572.'

Thus he was appointed Regius Professor of Law at Douai, and he retained that position for the next 20 or more years. There is also an undated petition to the Pope for a pension to enable him to teach in Flanders or neighbouring countries.

Abbot Arnold de la Cambe, Ganthois, died in his monastery on 1 May 1582, and the British Library possesses a copy of the only book I know of by the theologian Richard Hall, published at Douai in 1585, which gives a long epitaph on the good abbot. This book mentions many other foreign theologians at Douai, among them Englishmen, but not Richard White, who was not yet a priest. White continued to teach law at Douai for many years, and worked on his magnum opus, the *Histories*, which was eventually published in 11 books, the first five at Arras in 1597, the sixth at Douai (but printed at Arras) in 1598, the seventh to the eleventh at Douai between 1600 and 1607. Meanwhile White married twice, and we are told that each wife brought him great wealth. The surname of the first wife was Bonvicta: her own Christian name is not recorded, but her father was Gulielmus and her brothers Amatus and Bernardus, Senators of Douai. The name of the second wife I have not discovered. White had at least two sons, Thomas and Adrian, both of whom edited part of their father's *Histories*, and it seems he may have had a third son, William, since a Gulielmus Vitus is found writing a poem in the ninth book of the *Histories* in 1602. In 1597, when the first five books of his *Histories* were published together, there also appeared at Arras a book of 367 pages by him of commentaries on the ancient Roman laws of the twelve tables, the Institutions and the first part of the Digest. This book too was edited by his son Adrian.

By order of the Pope, White was created (I cannot say in which year, though out of his ordinary turn), 'Magnificus Rector' of Douai University, and about the same time he became a Count Palatine. After the death of his second wife he was, by dispensation of Pope Clement VIII (that is, between 1592 and 1605) ordained priest, and a canonry in the Church of St Peter at Douai was bestowed on him.

According to the *DNB* (quoting from Dodd's *Church History* of 1737-42) 'in his favourite study of British history, he received encouragement from Thomas Godwell, Bishop of St Asaph, Sir Henry Pecham, and Sir Francis Englefield, formerly privy councillors to Queen Mary'. None of these three Englishmen wrote any books as far as I know, but the lives of at least two of them are well documented. Thomas Goldwell (not Godwell) was born about 1500, presumably in Kent, and entered All Souls College, Oxford, in 1520. He became an exile for the faith and left England in 1538 for Rome. He was for several years Chaplain to Cardinal Reginald Pole. He became Bishop of St Asaph in 1555, but after the death of Queen Mary and of Cardinal Pole in November 1558, he soon decided it was more prudent - indeed necessary - to return to Rome. He took part in the Council of Trent in 1561, and was appointed Master of the English Hospital at Rome. In 1580 we find him briefly at Rheims, and he died in Rome on 3 April 1585 in his 85th year.[6]

On Sir Francis Englefield (1522-96) there is a very good biographical chapter in Albert J. Loomie's book, *The Spanish Elizabethans: the English exiles at the court of Philip II* (London, 1963), pp. 14-51. Englefield's circle included the two devout priests, William Allen and Nicholas Sanders. He was in Spanish service from 1568, and he visited Rome with Allen in 1576. He died in Spain.

Apart from the reference in Dodd's *Church History*, I have found no account of Sir Henry Pecham (Peacham or Peckham). He was clearly not nearly as eminent a person as the other two.

It is said that White maintained a regular correspondence with the great scholar in Rome, Cardinal Cesare Baronio (1538-1607), author of the great *Annales ecclesiastici*; but in the three volumes of Baronio's correspondence published in Rome in 1770 which I have consulted, I find only two letters from White, dated from Douai on 6 December 1600 and 8 January 1601, both dealing with bigamy.

The only other book by White to be published before the end of the 16th century is the collection of five orations printed at Arras in 1596. It cannot be said, as the British Library catalogue claims, that the book was edited by Christopher Johnson, whose preface is dated from Winchester on 1 March 1565; this is the preface to Johnson's edition of White's first book, the two orations in 1566, 30 years earlier. In any case, Johnson was not on the Continent, and the Arras book begins with a short note to the reader from Thomas White, explaining that his father was too modest to prepare his own book for the press; he was, however, finally persuaded to add the copious notes, which have provided us with the best biographical details about this reticent man. The true editor is his son, Thomas White.

Perhaps I should mention that Father Thomas Francis Knox, who edited the first and second Diaries of the English College, Douai, in 1878, distinguishes between two persons named Richard White, both from Winchester, who were ordained at Douai respectively in 1581 and 1587. Of these the first was sent on a mission to England on 31 May 1582, while the second was sent to England in 1587. Neither of them can be identified with the subject of this essay, who was not ordained until after 1592. It is difficult to believe that there were three persons at Douai named Richard White, all of whom came from Winchester; but let us not forget that the use of pseudonyms was very common at this period, for obvious reasons.

In 1609, Richard White published at Douai a small book entitled *Breuis explicatio priuilegiorum iuris, et consuetudinis, circa venerabile Sacramentum Eucharistiae.* He shows that in 1583 he had been ill, and again in 1608: the Peter White who introduces the book with a brief note to the reader may be yet another son. In 1607 we note that Richard White was thanked for the first ten books of his *Histories* by William Gifford, on 2 April 1606 from Lille, and by Matthew Kellison, on 16 July 1607 from Rheims. William Gifford (1554-1629) was Archbishop of Rheims in 1622, after having been Dean of the Church of St Peter at Lille. Matthew Killison (1560?-1642) was appointed in 1601 Regius Professor of Divinity at Rheims, and was President of the English College at Douai for 27 years from 1613 to 1641, when he died on 21 January 1641/42.

In 1610, at the age of 71 years, White published at Douai a book of 79 pages, consisting of only 18 pages of text, all the rest being his notes, entitled: *Breuis explicatio martyrii Sanctae Vrsulae et vndecim millium virginum Britannarum.* The historical uncertainty and mystery of this story is duly emphasised by the *Encyclopedia Britannica*; but Richard White, being so passionately interested in ancient British history, could not help writing about it with conviction.

Richard White's death seems to have occurred in 1611, at the age of 72, although certain unreliable authorities have placed it in 1602 or 1612. He was buried in the church of St Jacques at Douai.

We end with one more unsolved problem. In 1621 an anonymous book was published without imprint, but we know that it was a product of the English College Press at St Omer.[7] Its title is *Of the author and substance of the Protestant Church and religion, two books. Written first in Latin by R.S., and now reviewed by the author, and translated into English by W. Bas.* It is known that the author was Richard Smith, Bishop of Chalcedon, and his Latin version was first published in Paris in 1619. For some reason unspecified, the British Library catalogue has identified the translator, 'W. Bas.', as Richard White of Basingstoke. This cannot possibly be true, since White had died at least eight years before the Latin book had been published: and indeed he was not in the habit of translating books from Latin into English. The true identity of 'W. Bas.', the translator, may never be revealed, and could well be in the nature of a name such as William Bassett, rather than an abbreviation for Basingstoke.

How are we to sum up the life and works of this strange man, Richard White? If the Douai bibliographer H. R. J. Duthilloeul in 1842 dismisses his vast *Histories* as unimportant, we cannot but admire the enormous industry, patient research and erudite scholarship that went into them. No wonder he published virtually nothing else for 30 years. He never indulged in religious controversial writing, restricting himself to history and law, more harmless and unprovocative exercises.

It has been my aim to concentrate on the biography of White, which I find fascinating, rather than to analyse his works in detail. Certainly there are some obscure passages in his life which it would be most interesting to illuminate further, if only we could fill in the missing details. Even if Richard White is not a person of supreme importance in 16th-century history, at least Basingstoke is not likely to have produced a more intriguing character or one who, in his day, lived a more unusual life. He deserves our respect.

### Notes

*This essay is a slightly enlarged version of a talk which I gave at Basingstoke on 31 March 1982 to the local branch of the Hampshire Archaeological Society. I am grateful to Mr Peter Heath for his kind hospitality at Basingstoke, and for permission to print my text here.

1. *STC* 13376 and 13377. The title is *A consolatorie epistle to the afflicted catholikes.*

2. A. L. Rowse, *The England of Elizabeth* (London: Reprint Society, 1953 – first published 1950), p.572.

3. T. F. Kirby, *Annals of Winchester College* (London, 1892), p.276.

4. This John Rastell was a Jesuit, and must not be confused with the printer of that name, who specialised in music-printing, and whose dates are somewhat earlier.

5. *STC* 25403.

6. Revd Thomas F. Knox, 'Thomas Goldwell', being chapter IX of *The True Story of the Catholic Hierarchy deposed by Queen Elizabeth*, by Revd T. E. Bridgett and Revd T. F. Knox (London, 1889), pp.208-63.

7. *STC* 22812.

# Helen Wallis

## *Intercourse with the Peaceful Muses*

I am grieved that your country is so disturbed, nay torn to pieces, that you have hardly any hope of seeing it recover its original greatness and liberty. I advise those who have intercourse with the peaceful Muses, and who possess the excellent monuments of the most noble and useful arts, to seek for themselves and their relatives some temporary place of refuge, against the present raging fury of war.

The London-born geographer John Dee (1527-1608), writing from Mortlake on 16 January 1577, sent these words of encouragement and advice to the Dutch cartographer Abraham Ortelius, whom he had visited in Antwerp in 1571.[1] Close ties of friendship and professional collaboration existed between English and Dutch geographers and mapmakers at that time. It was a period of constitutional and religious revolution; and from 1565 the Netherlands were in revolt against their Catholic Habsburg ruler King Philip II and his representatives.

Despite the background of political and social instability, the Netherlands was becoming a leading centre of the arts and sciences. At the University of Louvain, from about 1535, Gemma Frisius, astronomer and mathematician, was promoting the study of a scientific geography unequalled elsewhere in Europe. His friend and most famous pupil, four years his junior, was Gerard Mercator, described by Ortelius as 'Nostri Saeculi Ptolemaeus', the Ptolemy of our age. Dee himself studied at Louvain. In May 1547, then a Fellow of Trinity College, Cambridge, he 'went beyond the sea … to speake and conferr with some learned men and chiefly Mathematicians, as Gemma Frisius, Gerardus Mercator, Gaspar à Mirica, Antonius Gogava, &c.'[2]

In England Queen Elizabeth's accession to the throne in 1558 and the restoration of Protestantism encouraged Englishmen to take up the cause of the Dutch patriots and dissidents. The Dutch, on their side, applauded at first the English ventures on voyages and travels overseas, which challenged the monopolistic claims of Spain and Portugal. Ortelius and Mercator in particular eagerly awaited news of English discoveries in order to prepare or revise their maps, charts and atlases.

A record of the exchange of news and comment is preserved in the correspondence of Ortelius[3] and Mercator,[4] and the results of their cooperative enterprises with Englishmen are found in a wide range of publications. Aspects of this collaboration are documented in recent works, such as the series of atlases in facsimile, 'Theatrum Orbis Terrarum', published from 1963 onward by Nico Israel, Meridian Publishing Co, Amsterdam. R. A. Skelton, my predecessor as Superintendent of the Map Room at the British Museum, supplied introductions in the form of Bibliographical Notes to many volumes in this series.

Major carto-bibliographies which document Dutch publications include Cornelis Koeman's *Atlantes Neerlandici. Bibliography of terrestrial, maritime and celestial atlases …published in the Netherlands,* 6 vols, 1967-85. Discoveries of atlases and maps hitherto unknown have provided new source material. Günter Schilder has been indefatigable in seeking Dutch maps through the libraries of the world, and since 1986 has been editing a new series, *Monumenta Cartographica Neerlandica,* published by Canaletto at Alphen aan den Rijn. Antoine de Smet of the Royal Library, Brussels, has been outstanding in publishing the achievements of the Renaissance map makers of the southern Netherlands, from Gemma Frisius and Mercator onwards.[5]

Mercator established his reputation as the greatest cartographer of the day with a series of wall maps and his pair of globes, the terrestrial published in 1541, the celestial in 1551. Partly in response to a personal experience of religious persecution in 1544, and also to take up appointment as court cosmographer to Duke Wilhelm of Cleves, he had moved in 1552 from Louvain to Duisburg. Two years later he published his wall map of Europe. He was particularly concerned with the delineation of the northern regions where English expeditions had ventured. He was corresponding therefore with Dee, then the leading expert on the north-east passage.

The first expedition in search of the passage, that of Sir Hugh Willoughby and Richard Chancellor, had sailed in 1553, under the direction of the Muscovy Company, to which Dee was advisor. Chancellor reached the White Sea and had gone overland to Moscow. Other expeditions followed in 1555 and 1556, and the fourth, 1557-58, was accompanied by Anthony Jenkinson travelling as the first English ambassador to Russia. From Moscow in April 1558 he went eastward via Nijni-Novgorod and Astrakhan to the Caspian Sea, and on to Bokhara, before returning to England in 1560.

Mercator was keeping abreast of these developments. In February 1569 he applied for an Imperial licence, intending to revise the northern parts of his map of Europe in the light of the English discoveries.[6] On the revised map of 1572 he justified the need for the new edition in the legend referring to English voyages to northern Russia[7].

Mercator's second wall map, that of the British Isles, was published in 1564. In the address to the reader, Mercator explained that the original was sent to him by a friend. Walter Ghim, his friend and neighbour in Duisburg, describes in his life of Mercator, 1595, how 'a distinguished friend sent Mercator from England a map of the British Isles which he had compiled with immense industry and the utmost accuracy, with a request that he should engrave it …'[8] Skelton suggested John Elder or Laurence Nowell as a possible author of the original. John Elder was a clerk and a Highland Scot, who sent a map of Scotland (now lost) to King Edward VI in about 1550. Laurence Nowell was an antiquary and map maker, and probably the cousin of the Dean of Lichfield of the same name, with whom he was previously confused. His maps of 1560-65 are preserved in the British Library.[9] The Library has now also acquired Nowell's miniature map of the British Isles, c.1563, which Sir William Cecil, later Lord Burghley, carried around with him in his pocket atlas.[10] This appears to be a reduced version of a large map, one which may have been the prototype for the map sent to Mercator. It is significant that both show Cardigan Bay for the first time.

Fig.1    Polar map by Gerard Mercator, published in his *Atlas*, 1595; a later version of the inset map on his world chart of 1569.

Another English mapmaker has recently come to light who might have been Mercator's distinguished friend, namely John Rudd, prebendary of Durham Cathedral.[11] The Queen had granted Rudd two years' leave of absence in 1561 to travel across the country and so improve the 'platt of this our Realme', which he had 'taken some payn in making'. Records of April 1570 show him as the master of Christopher Saxton, author of the first atlas of England and Wales, 1579.[12] It is possible therefore that Saxton's county maps derived some of their material from Rudd's survey. As none of Rudd's works appear to survive, any connection with Mercator remains speculative.

In 1569 Mercator published the third of his great wall maps, the first world chart on the projection which bears his name, and for which he gained lasting fame.[13] It displays a circular inset of the north polar regions, which mark the magnetic pole as a high black rock (fig.1). This depiction prompted Dee to ask Mercator to explain his sources. The reply, dated 20 April 1577, is transcribed and translated in Dee's manuscript 'Volume of Great and Rich Discoveries'.[14] Mercator names two manuscripts (both now lost), the history of the voyage of Jacobus Cnoyen Buschoducensis throughout all Asia, Africa and the North, and the work entitled 'Inventio Fortunatae'. This was a description of polar regions by a 14th-century Franciscan, which is now known only from references by 15th- and 16th-century authorities, including Mercator's.

Mercator's large maps were ordered in some quantity by London booksellers. They made their transactions through Antwerp, where Christopher Plantin had established the leading book publishing and printing business of the period (1555-89). His firm had the monopoly of sales of Mercator's maps in the Low Countries. In the year 1566, orders from London included four copies of Europe, 1554, and twelve copies of the British Isles, 1564. Plantin's ledgers between 1558 and 1576 record the sale of 868 copies of the wall map of Europe. The many references in England to the world map of 1569 suggest a considerable import. Martin Frobisher took with him on his voyage in search of the north-west passage in 1576 the 'great mappe universall of Mercator in prente'.[15]

Mercator was known in the 1560s and early 1570s primarily for these wall maps and his globes. Ortelius on the contrary made his name with the issue of the *Theatrum Orbis Terrarum*, 1570, the first modern atlas. Yet Ghim comments that long before Ortelius, Mercator had formed the idea of publishing further particular and general maps of the world in a small format – in other words, of making an atlas. Since Ortelius was an intimate friend, Ghim continues, Mercator held up the enterprise until Ortelius had sold a large quantity of his atlas. While this reflected the friendly spirit between the men,[16] Mercator could never have been ready with his atlas by 1570. The publication of his world atlas, which first introduced this title for a collection of maps, had to wait until 1595, a year after his death.

In the light of Ghim's remark, it is significant that an atlas made up of the sheets of Mercator's world map of 1569, and believed to have been put together by Mercator himself, has survived and is now in the Maritiem Museum Prins Hendrik, Rotterdam. It comes from the Von Mirbach family library at Castle Harff.

That a second composite atlas of Mercator's maps is now known is one of the most exciting cartographic discoveries of recent years. A Dutch schoolmaster looking for old prints of Amsterdam in the summer of 1967 found the atlas in a print shop in

Brussels. It comprises an atlas of Europe evidently put together by Mercator, probably between 1570-72. Nine maps have been formed by pasting together pieces from several copies of his 15-sheet wall map of Europe. Six maps are similarly made up from his wall map of the British Isles, 1564, and two maps are taken from his world chart of 1569. To supplement these maps Mercator has included 30 maps from Ortelius's *Theatrum*, making a total of 51 maps in 46 sheets.

The wall map of Europe so constructed is unique, for what was thought to be the last known copy of Europe was destroyed in Breslau in 1945. There are only three other known copies of the map of Great Britain, in Rome, Paris and Perugia.

Two manuscript maps in the Mercator atlas are of even greater interest. These have been identified by A. S. Osley as in Mercator's hand, and they rank as the only MS maps by him now known.[17] One is of Ancona, the other of part of Lombardy. It is significant that in a letter to Ortelius of 22 November 1570 Mercator made serious criticisms of existing Italian maps, declaring that they were 'sine ordine, sine proportione, sine discretione tam falsas et depravatus quam genuinas et veras descriptiones in unum corpus congerunt, uti in multis videre est tabulis quae ex Italia nobis prodeunt...'[18]

There is an impressive body of evidence to suggest that Mercator made the atlas for Werner von Gymnich, who had close connections with Mariawald, where the atlas was preserved in 1771 at the Cistercian monastery, as recorded in a manuscript note on the verso of the first page. The atlas bears the book plate of Carl Otto von Gymnich, Werner's descendant.

Werner von Gymnich was land bailiff at Jülich where the Mariawald monastery is situated. He was a close friend of Mercator, and was a notable official at the court of the Duke of Cleves. On 14 July 1578 Mercator wrote a letter as follows to Von Gymnich to accompany the gift of a copy of his Ptolemy atlas of 1578: 'as a small gift... I am now preparing the new geography of all lands... Italy I have divided into nine sections and one general map... I ask that anything new from Italy that geographers may have published be shown me... so that I may publish the most perfect work... when I have completed this book. I shall send you that also'.[19] A significant link between this atlas of Europe and the world atlas in the Maritiem Museum Prins Hendrik arises from the fact that the Von Harff and Von Mirbach families intermarried with the Von Gymnich family several times.[20]

Through the vicissitudes of the sale room, a full study of the atlas of Europe has yet to be made. It was purchased at Sotheby's on 13 March 1979 for the sum of £376,720 (including premium and VAT), a record price for a cartographic item. The buyer, who made the successful bid by telephone, has remained anonymous and nothing more has been seen of the atlas.[21]

Unlike Mercator, Ortelius was more of a map editor than an original cartographer. He obtained from the best authorities maps and information for the compilation of his atlases and maps. His world map of 1564 on a cordiform projection, published at Antwerp by Gerardus de Jode, was his first major cartographic work.[22] The map was particularly influential in England on account of its depiction of the north-west passage as an open seaway to the Pacific. Sir Humphrey Gilbert included a miniature version of the map in *A Discourse of a Discoverie for a New Passage to*

*Cataia*, 1576. Gilbert's map ranks as the earliest printed English world map.

Ortelius's world map of 1564 was to a large extent superseded by Mercator's of 1569. In the *Theatrum Orbis Terrarum*, 1570, Ortelius adapted Mercator's chart to an oval projection in reduced format, and this became the most popular map of the 16th century. From the English point of view it was notable in showing the north-west and north-east passages to be of more or less equal length and difficulty. The 'Fretum Trium Fratrum' which Gemma Frisius had shown on his terrestrial globe, 1536, and which Ortelius had opened out to a wide passage on his map of 1564, was replaced by a long strait oriented from west to east between the arctic lands and America. The map therefore encouraged a continuation of the search for the north-east passage.

Both Mercator and Ortelius had been gently chiding Dee and his associates for not pursuing that search with greater energy. The Muscovy Company had been diverted from exploration into exploiting the Russian trade. This trade provided Ortelius with one of his most important maps, 'Russiae, Moscoviae et Tartariae descriptio'. As Ortelius stated in his cartouche, the map was based on that of Anthony Jenkinson, whose name also features in Ortelius's catalogue of authors.[23]

Jenkinson made his map of Russia on his return to England in 1560. It was published in 1562, after he had set out (in May 1561) on his second voyage to Russia.[24] The original map was long believed to be lost, but has now come to light in Poland. Krystyna Szykula of Wrøclaw University Library announced the discovery in June 1989 at the 13th International Conference on the History of Cartography, Amsterdam. She had heard about the map while visiting the library of Wrøclaw Cathedral, and the University Library was able later to acquire it.[25]

Jenkinson's map was edited by Clement Adams, author of the Latin text of Richard Chancellor's first voyage. Adams is well known also as the engraver of Sebastian Cabot's world map of 1549. Sir Henry Sidney (1529-86), to whom the map of Russia is dedicated, was a leading government official under Edward VI and Elizabeth I, and a patron of cartography. The engraver was a Londoner, Nicholas Reynolds, who later engraved the map of Hertfordshire for Christopher Saxton's county atlas, 1579.

In an undated letter to Ortelius, Reynolds (Nicolas Reinoldus) says that at the request of Reynold Wolff, the royal printer, he has sent 25 copies of the map of the province of Moscow.[26] 'One copy he asked me to give you as a present, which I have gladly done on account of your kindness to me when I was with you at Antwerp.' The letter must be referring to Jenkinson's map, and the suggested date of about 1573 should be corrected to 1562/63. Peter Barber is now investigating the possibility that Reynolds may also have been the author of the map of the British Isles sent to Mercator.

Two other Dutch derivatives of Jenkinson's map and bearing his name are known.[27] Gerard de Jode made a version larger than Ortelius's, entitled 'Moscoviae maximae amplissimique Ducatus chorographica descriptio', engraved by the brothers Johannes and Lucas à Deutecum, and published in his *Speculum Orbis Terrarum*, 1578, Vol.II, no.6b. The other, 'Regionum Septentrionalium Moscoviam... nova description', was also engraved by the Deutecum brothers and appears to date from before 1572. It is known in only one example, preserved in the Dashkow collection in Leningrad.

The publications of Mercator and Ortelius on the one hand, and the increasingly active exploring ventures under Elizabeth I on the other, stimulated a vigorous correspondence between the Dutch and English geographers in the 1560s and 1570s. Both Mercator and Ortelius had family connections with England. Mercator's youngest son Rumold, who was an agent of the Cologne bookseller Birckmann, was often in London, and Ghim writes of Rumold's prolonged stay there. Ortelius's cousin Emmanuel van Meteren and his nephew Jacob Cole (known as Ortelianus) lived in London, and Ortelius himself came on a visit in 1577. These contacts, as well as a widening circle of friends, kept Mercator and Ortelius informed of English ventures overseas, and especially, the search for the passages to eastern Asia.

Dee favoured the north-east passage, encouraged by Mercator's maps as well as his own researches. He set out his conclusions in his great geographical tetralogy, *General and Rare Memorials pertayning to the Perfect Art of Nauigation.* Only the first volume of this work was published, in 1577. The second volume is lost, and the third part survives as his manuscript treatise 'The Great Volume of Famous and Riche Discoveries'. This mainly comprises an account of the north-east passage and the advantages for England in its discovery. 'I trust with one or two complete surveys, after this to be performed by my travail... that all the northern part of Asia, with the two principal cities thereof, Cambala and Quinsay, will become to the Brytish natural inhabitants of this Monarchy so well known, as are the coasts of Denmark and Norway and their periplus.'[28]

In a letter of 16 January 1577 to Ortelius, Dee expounded these ideas. He asked questions about features shown in the northern parts of Ortelius's maps. 'Tell me on what authority you have placed the "Cape of Paramantia" and "Los Jardines" on the northern coast of the Atlantic, and of all the other things, which you are the first and only one to place in that region.'[29] These two names were marked on the north coast of North America on Ortelius's map of 1564.

Ortelius's source must have been a chart by Diego Homem, the emigré Portuguese cartographer, or his kinsman André Homem, cosmographer to Charles IX of France. Both mark the Sea of Parmentier in the north-east Pacific. Presumably their source was Pierre Crignon, the Dieppe cosmographer, who had sailed as pilot on Jean Parmentier's expedition to Sumatra in 1529-30. In a eulogy commemorating Parmentier's death at Sumatra in 1529, Crignon had hoped that the name of Parmentier would be given to the waters of the Pacific, and on his own charts (now lost) he must have inscribed Parmentier's name, to fulfil this end. Dee himself does not appear to have consulted the atlas made by Diego Homem in 1558 for Queen Mary, then in the Royal Library. The chart of North America marks 'Mare le paramantium'.[30]

The answer to Dee is not known, but on 12 March 1577 Ortelius visited Dee at Mortlake, after meeting the historians William Camden and Richard Hakluyt in London. Shortly after this Dee asked Mercator about the sources of the north polar inset on his world chart of 1569, and received the long reply of 20 April.

These questions about the Arctic were urgent since the search for the north-west passage was now in progress. Martin Frobisher had sailed on his first voyage in 1576 and was away on his second voyage. Ortelius and Mercator were anxious to obtain a report of Frobisher's discoveries as soon as possible. Hakluyt was later to report that

Ortelius came to England in 1577 'to no other end but to pry and look into the secrets of Frobisher's voyage'. The Dutch would have been interested themselves in north-west discovery, Ortelius told Hakluyt, 'if the War of Flanders had not been'.[31]

Mercator wanted to know if Frobisher's observations confirmed his own theories about magnetic variation. Mercator's scientific theories had provided the impetus for English efforts in devising methods of determining variation and in making compass observations.[32] William Borough's chart of 1576, drawn for Frobisher to mark his discoveries, has inked additions recording the landfalls of the expedition and observations of magnetic variation.[33] Mercator's chart of 1569 had been designed to aid navigators such as Frobisher, since a rhumb line course could be laid down as a straight line on the chart. The distorted outlines in high latitudes were, however, a disadvantage, and partly for this reason William Borough described the chart as 'more fitte for suche to beholde, as studie in Cosmographie, by readying aucthours upon the lande, then to bee used in nauigation at the sea'.[34]

Whereas Mercator, Dee and Jenkinson were advocates of the north-east passage, Frobisher's ventures to the north-west had been inspired by the rival authority, Sir Humphrey Gilbert. He wrote his *Discourse* in 1566, and it was published in 1576 as an encouragement to Frobisher's first voyage. His map shows an open passage to the north, complete with the 'C. de Paramania' (*sic*) on coast. The north-east passage (as on Ortelius's map) is conveniently cut off by the border.

Frobisher's first voyage, on which he discovered in Baffin Land the strait which bears his name, raised great hopes of a passage, as Dee recorded in his 'Famous and Riche Discoveries'(1577). The second expedition, 1577, was diverted into a treasure hunt for gold. The third, 1578, led to the discovery of Hudson Strait and gave new hope of a passage. The ore, however, had proved worthless, and Frobisher's backers, the Company of Cathay, chartered in 1577, became bankrupt.

Despite the financial failure of the enterprise, Frobisher's discoveries encouraged the belief in the north-west passage. They became widely known through a number of publications. Dionyse Settle's accounts of the second voyage, published in 1577, and George Best's *True Discourse*, 1578, covering the three voyages, were best-sellers, and Settle's was translated for foreign editions.

The account of the Eskimos was of special interest. One was brought home from Frobisher's first voyage in 1576 and three from the second, 1577. Their appearance encouraged the belief in the north-west passage. Michael Lok, the main financial backer, described the first Eskimo, as 'much like to the tawny Mores; or rather to the Tartar Nation whereof I think he was'.[35] In 1578 he referred to the Eskimo as Frobisher's 'strange man of Cathay'. The idea that the Eskimos were Asiatic prompted a protest from Moscow that Frobisher had carried off Russian subjects.[36]

The Eskimos became well known in Europe through a number of drawings made of the captives and of scenes on the second voyage. Cornelis Ketel, a Flemish painter living in London, made pictures of the 1576 captive.[37] The only drawing of that Eskimo known today, perhaps derived from a now lost drawing by Ketel, is a water colour by Lucas de Heere, another emigré Flemish artist, a friend of Ortelius who lived in London as a Protestant refugee from 1566 to 1577. His Eskimo is found in his book of fashion plates, preserved in the Ghent municipal archives.[38]

PICTVRA VEL DELINEATIO HOMINVM NVPER EX ANGLIA AD-
vectorum, una cum eorum armis, tentoriis, & naviculis.

Fig.2    Eskimo scene in Dionyse Settle's account of Frobisher's second voyage, 1577, from a Latin edition published in Nuremburg in 1580. Kalicho, Arnaq, and her baby Nutaaq are depicted on the shore. BL 790.b.1

Other Eskimo drawings relate to the 1577 expedition. John White, the artist of Raleigh's Virginia colony of 1585, evidently sailed on Frobisher's second voyage. An eye-witness scene of a skirmish with the Eskimos in Baffin Land, drawn after White, is the accepted evidence that he was present.[39] White's watercolours of the three captives brought to London in 1577, the man Kalicho, the woman Arnaq and her baby Nutaaq, became known through woodcuts published in the Latin and German editions of the account of the second voyage[40] (fig.2). Ketel also painted them and presented several pictures to the Queen.

Through these publications Frobisher's Eskimos gained ethnographical significance as the stereotype of exotic peoples. As William Sturtevant and D. B. Quinn have commented, they are rare examples of known named individuals whose portraits ended as typifying whole populations.[41] Philipp Galle the Flemish engraver and map maker, friend of Ortelius and Mercator, featured the three Eskimos in his engraving entitled 'America', from a now lost drawing of Marcus Gheeraerts the Elder.[42]

The disappointing results of Frobisher's voyages in terms of immediate profits gave a new impetus in 1580 to the search for the north-east passage after a break of over ten years. An attempt was now to be made by Arthur Pet and Charles Jackman in two ships of the Muscovy Company, with scientific instructions prepared by Dee and Borough. Richard Hakluyt the Elder, the younger Hakluyt's cousin, advised them to take 'Ortelius booke of maps with you ... to present the same to the great Cam [the Great Khan], for it would be to a Prince of marvellous account'.[43]

More letters crossed the North Sea, as Hakluyt sought the advice of Mercator in a letter received on 19 June 1580. Mercator replied on 28 July 1580, expressing his regret that his answer would arrive too late, for the ships had departed on 1 July:

The voyage to Cathaio by the East, is doubtless very easie and short, and I have oftentimes marvelled, that being so happily begun, it hath bene left of, and the course changed into the West, after that more than halfe of your voyage was discovered.

He suspected that the Emperor of Russia and Muscovie might have hindered the proceedings.[44] Mercator in return asked for information about currents in the seas towards Tabin, which he depicted as the north-easterly cape of Asia.

All was in vain. The ships were beset by ice in the Kara Sea, and Jackman was lost with his ship on the return voyage. This setback led England to abandon further attempts on the north-east passage until 1675. The Dutch in their turn took up the search, and Willem Barents made three epic and equally unsuccessful voyages in 1594, 1595 and 1596.[45]

In 1580 Mercator and Ortelius were seeking news of a more sensational exploit, Francis Drake's 'famous voyage', as it became known. Drake had returned to England on 26 September 1580 from his three-year voyage round the world. It was soon public knowledge that he had navigated the Strait of Magellan and travelled up the west coast of America, but the fact that he had circumnavigated the globe was kept a closely guarded secret. In a letter of 12 December 1580 to Ortelius, Mercator speculated about Drake's route home and the reason for secrecy.[46] The reason in fact was political. Drake had broken into the Spanish and Portuguese overseas domains, threatening a diplomatic crisis with Philip II, who in 1580 united the two thrones (fig.3).

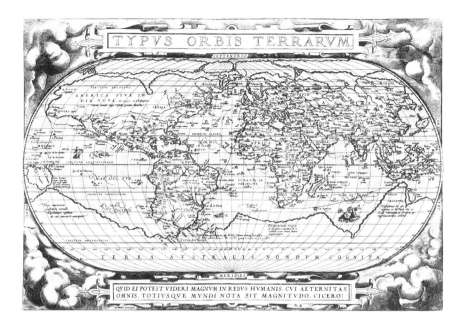

Fig.3    World map by Ortelius, 1570, with the track of Drake's circumnavigation added in manuscript. BL Maps 920.(327).

Within a week of the *Golden Hind*'s return, Queen Elizabeth had summoned Drake to court ordering him to bring 'some specimens of his labours'. He spent more than six hours in audience with the Queen early in October 1580, and presented her with 'a diary of everything that happened during the three years he was away and a very large map'.[47] This is the earliest reference to the chart of Drake's voyage which Samuel Purchas was to describe in *Purchas his Pilgrimes*, 1625, as 'still hanging in His Majesties Gallerie at Whitehall near the Privie Chamber'.[48] Two other maps were presented, one by Drake to the Archbishop of Canterbury and one by the Queen to Henry of Navarre, later Henry IV of France.[49] Both these maps have disappeared.

The Queen's map is also lost. It was presumably burnt in the fires which destroyed the Palace of Whitehall in 1697-98. However, three derivative maps are known. Of these two were engraved and have links with the Netherlands.

The map which appears to be closest to the Queen's (as described by Purchas) is a manuscript, now known as the Drake-Mellon map.[50] The text is in Latin, and the map displays not only the track of the *Golden Hind* around the world but also Drake's route on his West Indian voyage of 1585-86, indicating a date not earlier than 1586. The map's authorship and provenance are unknown.

The earlier of the printed maps is entitled 'La Herdike [*ie* Heroike] Enterprinse faict par le signeur Draeck d'avoir cirquit toute la terre'. It bears the engraver's inscription 'Nicola van Sype f.' A statement claims that the map was seen and corrected by Drake ('Carte veuee et corige par le dict siegneur drack'). This legend was presumably displayed on the original and was copied by Van Sype. An oval portrait of Drake, aged 42, is evidently derived from the miniature by Nicholas Hilliard, 1581, and suggests a date of 1582 or 1583 for the completion of the map. No other work by Nicola van Sype is known, but the place of publication is believed to have been Antwerp. A later version, known in two states, was published probably in Antwerp in about 1585, and has text in French and Dutch.

The third derivative became famous as the double hemispheric world map of Jodocus Hondius, published in Amsterdam about 1595. The map marks the tracks of the circumnavigations of Drake and of Thomas Cavendish, 1586-88. There is evidence that the map was printed, perhaps in London, as early as 1590.[51]

Up to 1588 the prohibition on publications relating to Drake's voyage remained in force. Richard Hakluyt who from 1582 was publishing works on America as an encouragement to English enterprise, nevertheless contrived to insert Drake's discoveries on maps used to illustrate his texts. In his edition of Peter Martyr's celebrated work *Decades of the New World* (1587), he included a map 'Novus Orbis', which marks the islands Drake discovered to the south of South America, and on the north-west coast of North America Drake's 'Nova Albion'. The dates are given erroneously as 1579 and 1580, instead of 1578 and 1579. The map was engraved by 'P. G.', who was probably Philipp Galle. It provides one of the best depictions of America for its date.

There was more news of Drake to report in 1586. William Camden wrote to Ortelius from London on 31 January: 'Here everybody is agitated by naval expeditions. Sir Francis Drake has sailed for America, but we have not heard of him since he left Lanzarote among the Fortunate [Canary] Islands, where last December he remained a few days. He is reported, however, to aim at somewhere between Nombres de Dios and Panama. Sir Richard Grenville is preparing for a voyage to Winandichoa, also called Virginia, where last year he left a small colony of Englishmen.'[52]

Under the auspices of Sir Walter Raleigh, the Virginia colony had been established in 1585 at Roanoke in what is now North Carolina. Drake returning from his raid on the Spanish settlements in the West Indies called there with reinforcements in June 1586. While he was on shore, a storm blew up, and the colonists elected to return home. An Italian artist, Baptista Boazio (*fl.*1585-1606), who was serving in Drake's fleet as an attendant of the lieutenant-general Christopher Carleill, made a set of maps of the voyage which were used to illustrate the narrative of the voyage, *A Summarie and True Discourse of Sir Francis Drakes West Indian Voyage*, by Walter Bigges, London, 1589. Latin and French editions had already been published at Leiden in 1588, but without the general map. This map may have been omitted for security reasons, as the location of the Roanoke colony was kept secret, for fear of a Spanish attack.

This secrecy explains questions in Ortelius's correspondence with Jacob Cole in London. In a letter of 30 September 1586, Ortelius thanks Cole for the 'hand-drawn coloured pictures by him that had arrived safely in Antwerp'. 'That geographical map will sometime be of use to me. As to this district is it that which the English discovered, in the true sense of that word – Virginia, or one different from that? If another, I should like to know by what name this is called.' Cole informed Ortelius that the district was called Wigandecua, and Ortelius duly inserted this name (as Wigandekoa) on the map of America engraved in 1587.[53]

Hakluyt provided the first narrative account of Drake's circumnavigation. 'The famous voyage of Sir Francis Drake into the South Sea, and there hence about the whole Globe of the Earth' appeared in six unnumbered leaves between pages 643 and 644 in his one volume collection, *The Principall Navigations, Voiages and Discoveries of the English Nation* (London, 1589). Hakluyt had decided to include this text at the last minute when the book was almost ready for publication.

Despite Hakluyt's earlier efforts to map Drake's discoveries, he did not provide a graphic record to accompany the text. Instead he contented himself (to use his own words) 'with inserting into the worke, one of the best generall mappes of the world onely, until the coming out of a … terrestriall Globe… composed by M. Emmerie Mollineux…' The general map was a copy of a world map engraved for Ortelius in 1587, with no indication of Drake's discoveries.

With the end of the official restriction on publication Drake, aided by Mercator's family, seized the opportunity to commemorate his circumnavigation. The voyage was depicted on a silver map or medal. Its connection with Mercator was recorded by Purchas: 'My learned friend Master Brigges told me, that he had seene this plot of Drakes Voyage cut in Silver by a Dutchman (Michael Mercator, Nephew to Gerardus) many yeeres before Scouten or Maire intended that Voyage'.[54] Master Brigges was Henry Briggs the mathematician.

The similarity of the silver map to the map of America by 'P. G.' in Hakluyt's *Decades* led some historians, such as Miller Christy, to suggest that the 1587 map was based on the medal and that the two works were by the same engraver.[55] In April 1967, however, a medal turned up with an inscription which reads 'Micha: Merca: fecit extat Londi: prope templum Gallo: An° 1589'. The legend may be translated as 'Michael

Fig.4   Silver medal commemorating Drake's circumnavigation, made in London by
Michael Mercator in 1589. The unique example inscribed with the author's legend, now in
the Library of Congress, Washington DC.

Mercator made [this]. It is available in London near the French Church, 1589' (fig.4).

The medal had appeared in Christie's salerooms as the property of the Earl of Caledon. Immediately after the sale it was brought to the Map Room of the British Museum for investigation of its authenticity. The possibility that a forger had made the medal in the light of Purchas's reference to Michael Mercator could not be ruled out; yet an inscription with such specific details had the ring of truth. Following up the clue of 'templum Gallo', we identified this as a French Protestant church, namely the Huguenot Church in Threadneedle Street. In the Public Record Office, London, an entry under S. Benet Fink includes the following: 'Michael Mercator servaunte to Baptista ... iiijd', with the date 18 June of the 32nd year (of Queen Elizabeth's reign), *ie* 1590.

Michael Mercator is identified as the son (1567-1614) of Arnold Mercator. He was the grandson (not nephew) of Gerard Mercator, the great cartographer. These records show Michael Mercator to be in London from 1589 to 1590 as the guest of one Baptista. The word following 'Baptista' is rubbed and cannot be deciphered, but definitely is not 'Boazio', disproving the natural conjecture that Mercator's host might have been Baptista Boazio the artist on Drake's West Indian voyage.

This documentary evidence of Mercator's visit to London authenticated the medal, which therefore ranks as the earliest dated map depicting Drake's track and voyage, and the first map of the voyage published in England.

The inscribed medal was presumably the prototype.[56] The omission of the author's legend on the later medals, of which eight exemplars are known, was probably done for commercial and patriotic reasons, since the legend gives prominence to Mercator and only passing reference to Drake. By following the map engraved by 'P. G.', 1587, Mercator repeated the incorrect dates of 1579 and 1580.

Yet another version of the silver map has come to light. In the collection of the shoemaker, book collector, and antiquary John Bagford (1650-1716), which came to the British Museum Library (now the British Library), there is preserved a unique paper impression of the silver medal, showing the eastern hemisphere only. It has been identified as a counter impression of the silver medal in the Department of Coins and Medals of the British Museum (registration, 1882.5.7.1.). The paper impression shows not only the *intaglio* lines of the medal map, but also the various accidental imperfections on the surface of this example of the medal.[57]

Raleigh's Roanoke colony was another English enterprise which was slow to gain an appropriate record in print. Thomas Harriot, the scientific adviser to the expedition, 1585-86, published in 1588 his *Briefe and true report*, as a prospectus for the future development of Virginia, where the Roanoke colony had been re-established in 1587 under the governorship of John White the artist. Harriot's book was a summary pending the preparation of a 'large discourse', in the manner of the chronicle. White and Harriot had brought home some hundreds of drawings and many manuscripts to illustrate the country of Virginia and the lives of its inhabitants. Their plans for publication were influenced by a remarkable coincidence of events, culminating in a major illustrated work, published in 1590, Theodor de Bry's *America*, vol.I.

De Bry was a native of Liège who as a Protestant refugee had established a printing house in Frankfurt am Main. He came to England in 1587 to engrave Thomas Lant's

Fig.5   Revised edition (1603) of the terrestrial globe by Emery Molyneux, engraved by
Jodocus Hondius, and first published in 1592 in London. Preserved in the library of the
Middle Temple, London.

drawings of Sir Philip Sidney's funeral of February 1587. During his visit Richard Hakluyt showed De Bry Harriot's *Report* and the paintings of John White and also those of Jacques Le Moyne illustrating René de Laudonnière's Huguenot colony in Florida, 1564-5. Through the good offices of Hakluyt, De Bry agreed to publish *Virginia* first. White prepared the drawings, and Harriot supplied descriptive notes in Latin (translated by Hakluyt for the English edition). Simultaneous editions of the work were supplied with text in English, French, German and Latin. This first volume of 'De Bry's Voyages' (as they became known) gave Europeans their first real picture of life in America. The Algonquians of Roanoke, as depicted by White and De Bry, became for over a century the stereotypes of the North American Indian.

The map of Virginia, as engraved by De Bry, ranks as one of the best depictions of any part of America in the 16th century. The original map by White, which owed much to Harriot's skills as a surveyor, was deficient only in the lack of a scale of latitude.[58] This was presumably a deliberate omission to keep the exact position of the colony secret. In 1590 the need for secrecy persisted, and De Bry's map also gave no indication of latitude.

Another enterprise in Anglo-Dutch collaboration resulted in the publication of Molyneux's globes in 1592, the event heralded by Hakluyt in 1589. These were the first globes to be made and printed in England, and the first by an Englishman (fig.5). Their engraver was Jodocus Hondius who was born at Wakken in Flanders in 1563, and brought up at Ghent where he must have known Lucas de Heere and his family.[59] In 1583-84 he came to London as a refugee, and his skills as an engraver soon brought him important commissions which gave him privileged access to geographical intelligence. The pair of globes by Emery Molyneux with the Drake map are his outstanding achievements during his ten years in England. He returned to the continent in about 1593 to settle in Amsterdam.

Some time between March or April 1596 and June 1597 Molyneux with his wife also moved to Amsterdam, and he died there between June 1598 and April 1599. A letter of Petruccio Ubaldini, reporting to his master the Grand Duke of Tuscany in Florence, 1591, may explain why Molyneux chose to emigrate. Ubaldini, who visited Molyneux in his workshop in Lambeth, wrote 'he betrays a strong desire to make himself known abroad for these globes of his and takes down the names of several princes, both Italian and German, intending to present his work in person'.[60]

These presentations would be more conveniently undertaken from Amsterdam. Molyneux, moreover, would require the services of Hondius to revise the globes. Ubaldini commented particularly on the dedication of the terrestrial globe to Elizabeth. The wording contained a political message, indicating that the Queen could see at a glance how she could control the seas by means of her naval forces. For presentations to foreign princes, the globes would have needed new dedications.

The fate of the plates, however, is not clear. In about 1596 or 1597 the terrestrial globe was extensively revised, as is evident from a comparison of the Petworth globe of 1592 with the second edition of 1603 preserved with its celestial partner (1592) at the Middle Temple, the Inn of Court in London.[61]

If the plates remained in England, the author of the revision was probably Edward Wright, who is named as another of Molyneux's collaborators. Wright's world map, published in Hakluyt's *Principal Navigations*, 1599, is similar to the Molyneux globe, and

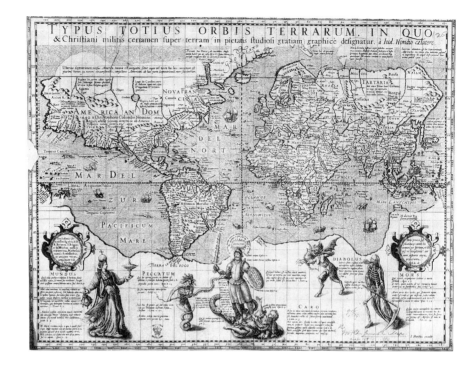

Fig.6    The 'Christian Knight' world map by Jodocus Hondius,
published in Amsterdam in about 1598.

Fig.7    (opposite) Detail of the Christian Knight, Henry of Navarre,
Henry IV of France.

Blanco

SPIRITUS

Si Spiritu actiones corporis mortificetis, vivetis. Quotquot enim Spiritu Dei aguntur, ii sunt filii Dei. Rom. 8. 15.

Recipite gladium Spiritus, hoc est verbum Dei. Eph. 6. 18.

Galeam salutis

State

State igitur

Ecce pono
in Sion la:
pidem in
imo angulo,
electum, pre:
tiosum: in que
qui credit, ne:
quaquam pu:
defiet. Vobis
igitur est ho:
nori qui creditis.
1. Pet. 2. 6. et

non intererit. Marc. 9

non
est
uta
ns
it. 1

until recently was attributed, mistakenly, to Molyneux himself. It is the first world map made in England on Mercator's projection, for which Wright had worked out an improved mathematical formula.[62]

Hondius profited from his association with Wright, who lent him his manuscript text on the projection. On returning to the Netherlands, Hondius used the projection for his so-called 'Christian Knight' world map of about 1598 (figs.6 and 7). He dedicated the map to the English mathematicians Robert Brewer, Henry Briggs, and Edward Wright, but did not acknowledge Wright's projection. For this he incurred Wright's censure, causing a breach of friendship.

Hondius's map has a further interest as an elaborate allegory. As Peter Barber has shown, the Christian Knight ('Spiritus'), fighting the forces of darkness – Death ('Mors'), the Devil ('Diabolus') and Sin ('Peccatum') – is none other than Henry of Navarre, afterwards Henry IV of France. The map was designed to rally the Protestants of England against Spain and the Catholic powers of Europe.[63]

On his return to the continent Hondius used to good effect the professional experience he had gained in England. His setting up in business in Amsterdam reflected the changed fortunes in the Netherlands. After the sack of Antwerp in 1576, many printers and publishers had moved to Amsterdam, which was soon to succeed Antwerp as the map publishing capital of Europe.

In Amsterdam Hondius established himself as a craftsman in type-cutting, engraving, and globe making.[64] He purchased in 1604 the plates of Mercator's atlas from the heirs of Mercator. As Mercator's successor he then embarked on atlas production on the grand scale. The Mercator-Hondius atlas, published by Hondius and his heirs, was to dominate the market for many years. Hondius also maintained his links with England; he was the engraver of the maps in John Speed's *Theatre of the Empire of Great Britaine* (London, 1611-12), the first printed atlas of the British Isles.

The popularity of Ortelius's *Theatrum* decreased through competition with Mercator's atlas. Furthermore, on Ortelius's death in 1598 his estate passed to his sister Anna Ortels, and on her death in 1600 to the three children of his other sister Elisabeth Cool (or Cole), then settled in London.[65] His favourite nephew Jacob Cole as a Protestant dared not venture to the Spanish Netherlands. The plates and rights of the *Theatrum* were sold to Jan Baptist Vrients of Antwerp in 1601.

The inheritance of Jacob Cole included Ortelius's letters, which later came into the possession of the Dutch Church of Austin Friars in London. The original letters were divided into lots and sold at Sotheby's in 1955. Hessels's publication of 1887 now remains the unique printed record of Ortelius's remarkable network of correspondents.

Ortelius's *Album Amicorum*, which also came to Jacob Cole, is now in Pembroke College, Cambridge.[66] The volume contains graceful tributes from Ortelius's many friends throughout Europe. Contributors from England were William Camden, Jacques Cools (Jacob Cole), John Dee, the botanist Richard Garth,[67] and the diplomat and antiquary Daniel Rogers, a kinsman.

The works of Ortelius and Mercator were adopted as part of the English heritage. Robert Burton wrote in *The Anatomy of Melancholy* (Oxford, 1621), 'To some kind of men it is an extraordinary delight to study, to looke upon a Geographicall mappe, and to behold, as it were, all the remote Provinces, Townes, Cities of the world, and never to goe forth of the limits of his study … What greater pleasure can there now be then to view those elaborate Maps of Ortelius, Mercator, Hondius, &c … such is the excellency of those studies, that al those ornaments and bubbles of wealth are not worthy to be compared to them.'[68]

## Notes

1. *Abrahami Ortelii … et vivorum eruditorum et eundem et ad J. Colium Ortelianum epistolae,* edited by Joannes Henricus Hessels (Cambridge, 1887), p.158. Translated from the Latin.

2. 'The compendious rehearsall of John Dee, Anno 1592, November 9,' in *Autobiographical Tracts of Dr John Dee,* edited by J. Crossley (Manchester, 1851), p.5.

3. The original collection was preserved by the Dutch Church, Austin Friars, in London. The Department of Manuscripts of the British Museum, now British Library, acquired the microfilm in 1955, reference M/457.

4. M. van Durme, *Correspondence Mercatorienne* (Antwerp, 1959). R. A. Skelton, 'Mercator and English Geography in the 16th century', *Duisburger Forschungen herausgegeben von Stadtarchiv Duisburg,* Bd.6, 1962, pp.158-70.

5. See *Album de Smet* (Brussels, 1974), for which I was honoured to be invited to write the introduction.

6.p Van Durme, 1959, pp.96-7.

7. H. Averdunk and J. Müller-Reinhard, *Gerhard Mercator und die Geographen unter seinen Nachkommen* (Gotha, 1914), p.60. See also R. A. Skelton, 'Mercator and English Geography', pp.159-60.

8. Walter Ghim's Life of Mercator was published in the first edition of Mercator's *Atlas* (Duisburg, 1595). See also A. S. Osley, 'Walter Ghim's Life of Mercator', in *Mercator: a Monograph on the Lettering of Maps, etc. in the 16th Century Netherlands* (London, 1969), p.187.

9. BL Cotton MS Domitian XVIII art 13. ff.97-123.

10. BL Add.MS 62540. See Peter Barber, 'A Tudor Mystery: Laurence Nowell's Map of England and Ireland', *The Map Collector,* no.22 (March, 1983), pp.16-21.

11. Sarah Tyacke and John Huddy, *Christopher Saxton and Tudor Map-making* (London, 1980), p.9.

12. David Marcombe, 'Saxton's apprenticeship: John Rudd, a Yorkshire cartographer', *Yorkshire Archaeological Journal,* 50, 1976, pp.171-75. See also Ifor M. Evans and Heather Lawrence, *Christopher Saxon, Elizabethan Map-maker* (Wakefield, 1979), p.6.

13. A summary account of the map is given by R. W. Shirley in *The Mapping of the World: Early Printed World Maps 1472-1700* (London, 1983), pp.137-42.

14. BL Cotton MS Vitellius C.VII. See E. G. R. Taylor, 'A letter dated 1577 from Mercator to John Dee', *Imago Mundi,* XIII (1956), pp.56-68. Also Van Durme, 1959, no.112, 114b, 115, pp.131-41.

15. Skelton, 'Mercator and English Geography', 1962, p.160.

16. Osley, *Mercator,* 1969, p.105.

17. A. S. Osley, 'Calligraphy, a cartographic tool?', *Imago Mundi,* XXIV, 1970, pp.70-75.

18. Van Durme, 1959, pp.101-2.

19. Van Durme, 1959, pp.150-51. Translated by Peter Scott and John Goss; see below note 20.

20. Peter Scott and John Goss, 'Important Mercator Discovery under the Hammer', *The Map Collector,* no.6 (March, 1979), pp.27-35. *Sotheby Catalogue,* 13 March 1979.

21. 'Mystery buyer for Mercator atlas', *The Map Collector,* no.7 (June, 1979), p.35.

22. Cornelis Koeman, *The History of Abraham Ortelius and His Theatrum Orbis Terrarum* (Lausanne, 1964), pp.13-14. Two copies of the

map are known today, one in the British Library, Maps C.2.a.6., the other in the Öffentliche Bibliothek der Universität Basel, which Günter Schilder has reproduced in facsimile in his *Monumenta Cartographica Neerlandici*, II, (Alphen aan den Rijn, 1987), pp.3-5, 33-51, plate I.

**23.** *A. Ortelii Catalogus Cartographorum*, edited by Leo Bagrow, I, (Gotha, 1928), pp.120-21. See also Samuel H. Baron, 'William Borough and the Jenkinson map of Russia', *Cartographica*, 26, 1989, pp.72-85.

**24.** Johannes Keuning, 'Jenkinson's Map of Russia', *Imago Mundi*, XIII, 1946, 172-5.

**25.** Krystyna Szykula, 'The newly found Jenkinson's map of 1562', in *XIIIth International Conference on the History of Cartography, Amsterdam and the Hague, June 26 to July 1, 1989. Abstracts.* [Amsterdam 1989], pp.109-11. Valerie G. Scott, 'Map of Russia revealed at conference', *The Map Collector*, no.48 (Autumn 1989), pp.38-39, including additional information from Peter Barber. 'The Jenkinson map' (with illustration), *The Map Collector*, no.52 (Autumn, 1990), p.29.

**26.** BL Add.MS 63650 Q. Hessels, 1887, no.43, pp.103-4.

**27.** Keuning, 1946, pp.172-73.

**28.** BL Cotton MS Vitellius C.VII. f.79ᵛ.

**29.** Hessels, 1887, p.158.

**30.** BL Add.MS 5415.A. Chart no.10.

**31.** Richard Hakluyt, 'Discourse of Western Planting', in E. G. R. Taylor, *The Original Writings and Correspondence of the Two Richard Hakluyts* (London, 1935), Vol.2, p.102.

**32.** Skelton, 'Mercator and English Geography', 1962, pp.164-5.

**33.** The chart is preserved at Hatfield House. See R. A. Skelton and John Summerson, *A Description of Maps and Architectural Drawings in the Collection Made by William Cecil First Baron Burghley Now at Hatfield House* (Oxford, 1971), p.69, pl.6.

**34.** William Borough, *A Discours of the*

*Variation of the Cumpas,* published with Robert Norman, *The newe Attractive* (London, 1581), sig.F.iii.

**35.** Michael Lok's notes on Frobisher's voyage, BL Cotton MS Otho E. VIII, f.54, printed in E. G. R. Taylor, *Tudor Geography* (London, 1930), p.271.

**36.** State papers, Foreign, Russia, Public Record Office, SP91/1, 13. Quoted in William C. Sturtevant and David B. Quinn, 'This New Prey: Eskimos in Europe in 1567, 1576, and 1577', in *Indians and Europe*, edited by Christian F. Feest (Aachen, 1987) pp.84-5.

**37.** Sturtevant and Quinn, 1987, p.75.

**38.** Another volume of costume figures and text by Heere, all relating to the British Isles, completed c.1580, is in BL Add.MS.28330.

**39.** British Museum, Department of Prints and Drawings, LB.3 [13].

**40.** White's originals are in the British Museum, Department of Prints and Drawings, LB.2(11) and LB.1(30), with derivatives.

**41.** Sturtevant and Quinn, 1987, p.119.

**42.** Sturtevant and Quinn, 1987, p.93.

**43.** Richard Hakluyt, *The Principall Navigations... of the English Nation* (London, 1589), p.464.

**44.** Hakluyt, *Principall navigations*, 1589, pp.483-5. See also Van Durme, 1959, no.143, pp.157-61.

**45.** Helen Wallis, 'England's Search for the Northern Passages in the Sixteenth and Early Seventeenth Centuries', in Louis Rey, Claudette Reed Upton, and Marvin Falk (eds.), *Unveiling the Arctic* (Calgary, 1984), p.457.

**46.** Hessels, 1887, no.99.

**47.** Letter of Don Bernardino, the Spanish ambassador in London, to King Philip II of Spain, 16 October 1580, BL Add.MS 28420, f.30. Printed in English translation in *Calendar of Letters and State Papers relating to English Affairs preserved in the Archives of Simancas, vol.III. Elizabeth, 1580-1586* (London, 1896), item 44, p.55. The reference to a large map (using the word 'carta') was mistranslated as a 'long letter' when the document came to be published. This important evidence of the cartographic records of Drake's voyage thus came to be overlooked. Patricia M. Higgins of the Department of Manuscripts, British Library, made the discovery. See the catalogue of the British Library exhibition, *Sir Francis Drake. An Exhibition to Commemorate Francis Drake's Voyage around the World 1577-1580* (London, 1977), item 99, p.98.

**48.** Samuel Purchas, *Purchas his Pilgrimes* (London, 1625), III.iii, p.461.

**49.** Helen Wallis, *The Voyage of Sir Francis Drake Mapped in Silver and Gold* (Berkeley, Calif, 1979), p.7. Also Helen Wallis, 'The Cartography of Drake's Voyage', in *Sir Francis Drake and the Famous Voyage, 1577-1580*, edited by N. J. W. Thrower (Berkeley, Los Angeles and London, 1984), pp.121-63.

**50.** The map is in the collection of Mr and Mrs Paul Mellon.

**51.** The life of Hondius set out in the Mercator-Hondius atlas of 1636, states that while in London Hondius 'drew many fine draughts, and master pieces, as S<sup>r</sup> Francis Drakes voyage about the world'. See Wallis, *Drake*, 1979, p.19.

**52.** Hessels, 1887, no.145, pp.334-5.

**53.** BL Harleian MS 6994, f.39. Translated from the Latin in Helen Wallis, *Raleigh & Roanoke: the First English Colony in America, 1584-1590*. British Library exhibition. (Raleigh, North Carolina, 1985), p.57, item 57.

**54.** Purchas, 1625, III,iii, p.461.

**55.** Miller Christy, *The Silver map of the World* (London, 1900), pp.44-5.

**56.** The medal passsed into the Drake Collection of H. P. Kraus, now in the Library of Congress.

**57.** *Sir Francis Drake: an Exhibition*, 1977, items 74 and 96.

**58.** John White, 'La Virginea Pars', British Museum, Department of Prints and Drawings, 1906-5-9-1(3). White's map of eastern North America from Florida to Chesapeake Bay, 1906-5-9-1(2), does include a

scale of latitude. See also Helen Wallis, 'Emigré map-makers of the late 16th century and the Protestant New World', *Proceedings of the Huguenot Society of London*, Vol.24, 1985, pp.210-20.

**59.** Lionel Cust, 'Foreign artists of the reformed religion working in London from about 1560 to 1660', *Proceedings of the Huguenot Society of London*, Vol.7, 1905, pp.45-50.

**60.** Anna Maria Crinò found Ubaldini's papers in the State Archives at Florence. See Anna Maria Crinò and Helen Wallis, 'New researches on the Molyneux globes', *Der Globusfreund*, no.35-37, 1987, pp.11-20, figs.1-5. See also Helen Wallis, 'Opera Mundi: Emery Molyneux, Jodocus Hondius and the first English globes', in Ton Croiset van Uchelen, Koert van der Horst and Günter Schilder (eds.), *Theatrum Orbis Librorum. Liber Amicorum presented to Nico Israel* (Utrecht, 1989), pp.94-104.

**61.** Helen Wallis, 'The first English globe: a recent discovery', *Geographical Journal*, vol.117 (1951), pp.275-90; 'Further light on the Molyneux globes', *ibid*, vol.121 (1955), pp.304-11. R. M. Fisher, 'William Crashawe and the Middle Temple globes 1605-15', *ibid*, vol.140 (1974), pp.105-12. Bob Ward has recently drawn attention to major changes to the plate realigning the north-west coast of North America ('Lost harbour found! The truth about Drake and the Pacific', *The Map Collector*, no.45 (Winter, 1988), p.8).

**62.** See Helen Wallis, 'Edward Wright and the 1599 World Map', in D. B. Quinn, ed., *The Hakluyt Handbook* (London, 1974), Vol.1, pp.69-73. A manuscript map which appears to be derived from that of Wright (who died in 1615) and is revised to about 1618, was preserved in the collections of the Duke of Northumberland, and was purchased at Sotheby's by the British Library in December 1990.

**63.** Peter Barber, 'The Christian Knight, the Most Christian King and the rulers of darkness', *The Map Collector*, no.52 (Autumn, 1990), pp.8-13.

**64.** Peter van der Krogt, *Old Globes in the Netherlands* (Utrecht, 1984), pp.148-54.

**65.** R. A. Skelton, 'Bibliographical Note', *Abraham Ortelius The Theatre of the Whole World, London 1606*, (Amsterdam, 1968), p.v.

**66.** It has been published in facsimile: Jean Puraye (ed.), *Abraham Ortelius, Album Amicorum* in *De Gulden Passer*, Jrg.45-46, 1967-68.

**67.** A senior clerk in Chancery. See R. T. Gunther, *Early British Botanists and Their Gardens* (Oxford, 1922), pp.237-38.

**68.** Robert Burton, *The Anatomy of Melancholy* (Oxford, 1621), Part 2, Sect.2, memb.4, sig.Z.

Acknowledgement: I am grateful to Mary Alice Lowenthal, Tony Campbell and Peter Barber for valuable help with this paper.

Bert van Selm

# Dutch book trade catalogues printed before 1801 now in The British Library

## Introduction

The value of old book trade catalogues is increasing rapidly. Apart from the fact that their commercial value rises, catalogues are more and more appreciated as important documents for the study of cultural history. Scholars in the field of the history of ideas or the history of science, the history of art or literature, and above all the history of books or libraries will eagerly consult these catalogues, since they form an abundant source of information. The private libraries of scholars, authors or artists are in most cases only known through auction catalogues. Many bibliographers use antiquarian and auction catalogues to recover the origin of manuscripts or special copies of printed books, and sometimes these are the only sources from which the existence of certain books is known.[1]

These catalogues, by their contemporaries usually considered as commodities of temporary importance, are also subject to growing interest from institutional libraries. Although many were lost forever, in a few old libraries precious collections have been preserved. In recent years this printed matter, often unsightly and awkward to describe, was not, or only very defectively, registered in library catalogues. The alphabetically arranged catalogue is not very suitable to make book trade catalogues accessible and, therefore, a few libraries have found a different way. The Royal Library in The Hague, for instance, provides the visitor with a separate registration of extant auction catalogues in the Rare Book Department. Other libraries have published printed catalogues of their catalogue holdings. As these have set excellent examples, I here mention the Royal Library Albert I in Brussels, where Mrs Jeanne Blogie has published three volumes containing Belgian, French and English catalogues up to now, and the inventory of Ghent University Library compiled by Vandenhole.[2] The Library of Zealand in Middelburg has published a catalogue in which, additionally, reproductions of the informative title-pages of the catalogues are included.[3]

For some years now I have been working on a bibliography of book sales catalogues, separately printed within the borders of the Republic of the United Netherlands before 1801. Consequently, I do not include the catalogues printed as back matter of books from the last decades of the 17th century onwards. These lists, issued as part of a larger unit, cannot be traced systematically at the moment. This will change in the near future, since the compilers of the *Short-Title Catalogue Netherlands*

(*STCN*) always indicate the presence of these lists. Once the *STCN* is completed it will be quite easy to produce a special bibliography of this kind of book catalogue.[4]

Within the scope of my extended research project I am attempting to trace and describe Dutch book trade catalogues in many Dutch and foreign libraries. This article concentrates on the collection of The British Library. Before I turn to some particular problems which the bibliographer of this kind of ephemeral printing will encounter, I will give an indication of the nature and size of this collection. Finally, I will give some examples of the kind of assistance the specialist can offer to come to a better description and a higher accessibility of the old catalogues, and of questions that can only be answered after the completion of the project.

### A survey of the collection

The number of Dutch book trade catalogues printed before 1801 now in the BL I estimate at slightly more than 300. About half of these date from the 17th century, the other half from the 18th. The oldest one is the auction catalogue of the Leiden clergyman Lucas Trelcatius, dated 1607.[5] The collection in the BL is smaller than that in the Herzog August Bibliothek in Wolfenbüttel (approximately 800, of which 700 are printed before 1701), the Bibliothèque Nationale in Paris (c.700) and the Library of the Dutch Book Trade Association in Amsterdam (c.900, of which c.825 from the 18th century). The collection in the BL is expected to be of a similar size to the one in the Royal Library, The Hague. However, the number of 18th-century catalogues is substantially larger in The Hague (c.280). Without a doubt, the London collection is much more extensive than those in other Dutch libraries. Formerly, catalogues were regarded as of temporary value in the Netherlands and were not incorporated in library collections.

The importance of the BL collection appears when one considers its holding of unique items. According to my registration (as of June 1989), 15 seventeenth-century and 36 eighteenth-century auction catalogues in the BL are unique copies. Moreover, the BL has 10 unique publisher's catalogues and four unique stock catalogues from the 17th century, and respectively two and 15 of these from the 18th century.

Some specific examples will render a clearer insight into the importance of the BL collection. The collection contains two tract volumes (s.c.1 and s.c.117) with unique and precious catalogues. The fourth item of s.c.1 is an intriguing publisher's catalogue of Hendrik Wetstein (1649-1726) from 1685, the oldest one known of this important Amsterdam bookseller. Wetstein ran his own bookshop from 1676 onwards, after having been apprenticed to Daniel Elzevier.[6] He also visited the Frankfurt Book Fairs and, most likely to support his trade at Frankfurt, he published a list of new publications every year. The BL also possesses a unique copy of his publisher's catalogue of 1686 (s.c.1(5)). Both of these catalogues consist of only one gathering and so it is understandable that his other publisher's catalogues have been lost. For printed matter of this kind in particular the bibliographical rule applies: 'The less there are, the more there were'.[7]

Another important source is the publisher's list of Joannes Maire from 1654. Maire was one of the leading booksellers of Leiden in the first half of the 17th century. He took over the bookshop of his father in 1603 and from that year up to 1657 he published about 450 editions. He auctioned his stock as early as 1661, although he did not die before 1666. In April 1990 Dr O. S. Lankhorst located a copy of his oldest known publisher's catalogue of 1639 in the Bibliotheca Angelica at Rome.[8] A copy of Maire's publisher's catalogue of 1645 has been preserved in the Royal Library at Copenhagen, while the only known copy of the edition of 1654 (Shelf-mark s.c.117.(7)) can be found in the BL. These catalogues unquestionably provide worthwhile sources from which to trace all books published by Maire.

For research into the list of the Amsterdam bookseller Johannes van Ravesteyn (1618-81), a visit to the BL is indispensable. This bookseller learned the trade from Joannes Blaeu before he established himself as an independent bookseller in 1650 among the other important traders in the centre of Amsterdam.[9] His oldest known publisher's catalogue dates from 1656; copies can be found in the Niedersächsische Landesbibliothek at Hannover and in the BL (s.c.117.(9)). The ensuing publisher's catalogue of 1658 is only to be found in Hannover, whereas the publisher's catalogues of 1663 and 1670 are solely known thanks to existing copies in the BL.[10]

In general only few books in the English language were in stock in the shops of the Dutch Republic. The exceptions do, in view of Anglo-Dutch cultural relations, deserve to be studied more thoroughly. Accordingly, I wish to draw attention to the catalogue of the stock auction of Jacob van der Velde. This Amsterdam bookseller was born in that city in 1651 or 1652, and was buried there on 11 May 1709. Publications with his imprint are known dating from 1680 up to 1704 in Dutch, Latin and French. He translated various works of the Labadists and some medical and physical books from English himself. According to the *Amsterdamse Courant* of 30 July 1709, the books of the deceased would be auctioned on 20 August 1709.[11] The BL has a copy of the auction catalogue, shelf-mark s.c.165, but the title-page does not give the date of the auction. This catalogue contains 191 numbers in folio, 565 numbers in quarto, 894 numbers in octavo, 421 numbers in duodecimo and, finally, a section of 'Unbound Books, that will be sold amongst Booksellers' ('Ongebonden Boeken, die onder de Boekverkopers zullen verkoft worden'), with 567 numbers. Amongst these are numerous items in English, of which I only quote folio no.145: 'the Works of our ancient and learned Poët G. Chaucer. 1598'.

### Some problems for the bibliographer of book catalogues
The most important issue for the bibliographer is how to find all the old catalogues in the holdings of a library. Unfortunately, it is impossible to trace them all systematically in the BL. Over 100 Dutch catalogues are not incorporated in the Sale Catalogues collection (shelf-marks s.c.). Therefore, I eagerly await the publication of the *General Catalogue of printed books to 1975 on CD-ROM*. This publication will render it possible to search efficiently on catchwords such as 'Catalogus', 'Bibliotheca', and 'Index', in combination with places of publication such as Amsterdam, Leiden and The Hague, and with dates of publication. Naturally, the condition must be met that all the catalogues that are present are described in the *General Catalogue of Printed Books to 1975* (hereafter referred to as *BLC*).[12]

Here the bibliographer might run into difficulties. As mentioned above I restrict myself to the registration of separately issued catalogues. Consequently, every now and then the question arises whether or not a certain catalogue has been issued separately.[13] Moreover, a catalogue in a certain volume or following the main text of a certain book might have been overlooked when the description was made. The catalogues that can be found in the edition of Thomas More, *Utopia*, translated into French by Nicolas Gueudeville (Leiden, Pierre vander Aa, 1715.12°. BL: 233.b.20) supply a significant illustration of these problems. This duodecimo edition includes a 'Catalogue de quelques livres, cartes geographiques, &c. nouvellement imprimées chez Pierre vander Aa, à Leide' on pp.364-72 of the last gathering Q (ff.Q8v-Q12v), following the 'Tables des matières' on pp.349-63. This undoubtedly is a publisher's catalogue, a list of books printed and distributed by Pieter vander Aa himself. It is unlikely that this catalogue was issued separately as well, since it is part of the last gathering. The catalogue that in all known copies succeeds the former one directly is a different case.[14] This concerns an intriguing stock catalogue of 48 pages: 'Catalogue de livres, de cartes géographiques, des villes, chateaux &c. de l'univers, tant en plan qu'en profil; publiés en France, en Allemagne, en Angleterre & ailleurs, qui se trouvent tout nouvellement à Leide, chez Pierre vander Aa, marchand en livres, en cartes geographiques & autres tailles douces, demeurant à présent dans l'Academie.' This catalogue of Pieter (I) van der Aa (1659-1733) is not dated, but as it includes titles from 1714 (see pp.33, 34 and 37) and because this catalogue always follows the More edition with a privilege dated 17 May 1715, this stock catalogue has to date from 1715 as well.

This separately signed catalogue of Pieter van der Aa should be included in my bibliography, but the copy in More's *Utopia* 1715 is not registered in the *BLC*.[15] Consulting the entry 'Aa (Pierre van der)', however, will reveal the surprising existence of a separate copy of the stock catalogue in the BL (shelf-mark 011899.e.5)![16] Obviously, it is desirable that there is mutual reference.

### Additions to the descriptions of Dutch sales catalogues

On the one hand the bibliographer should describe the catalogues in the BL as thoroughly as possible. On the other hand he may complement and improve the descriptions in the *BLC* in some instances with the help of catalogues found elsewhere. I can supply some examples of those instances here, although my bibliography is far from being completed.

The title-page of copy s.c.34 of the auction catalogue of J. Rutgerus is cropped, which makes the year of publication unreadable. The *BLC* mentions '[1692?]'.[17] Another copy of the catalogue can be found in the Herzog August Bibliothek at Wolfenbüttel, shelf-mark Bc Sammelband 16 (2), and the imprint says: 'Lugd. Batavorum, Ex officina Joan. du Vivie 1692'. It appears that the question mark following the year 1692 in the *BLC* can be omitted.

In a considerable number of old catalogues space is left open in order to leave room for the date of the auction which was filled in later in handwriting. This has been done in the catalogues of the books of the clergyman Vincentius Snellius, auctioned at Leiden on 8 June 1667 (s.c.846.(4.)), and of the books of the clergyman Aegidius van de Kellenaer, auctioned at Leiden on 28 September 1667 (s.c.846.(3.)). Both catalogues are unique.

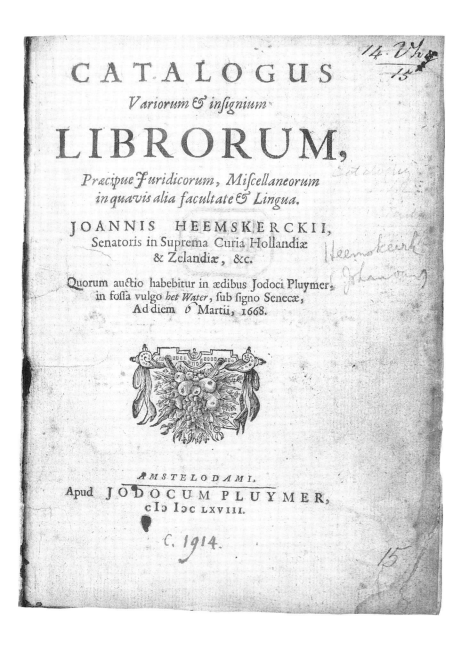

# CATALOGUS
## *Variorum & insignium*
# LIBRORUM,

*Præcipue Juridicorum, Miscellaneorum
in quavis alia facultate & Lingua.*

## JOANNIS HEEMSKERCKII,
### Senatoris in Suprema Curia Hollandiæ
### & Zelandiæ, &c.

Quorum auctio habebitur in ædibus Jodoci Pluymer,
in fossa vulgo *het Water*, sub signo Senecæ,
Ad diem 6 Martii, 1668.

*AMSTELODAMI,*
Apud JODOCUM PLUYMER,
cIɔ Iɔc LXVIII.

Fig.1    The title-page of the auction catalogue of Johan van Heemskerck (BL, s.c.954).

The BL also has copies of catalogues without the date in handwriting, presumably because the date of the auction was set at a very late stage, after some copies were already dispatched. The first day of auction would then be advertised in the newspapers. In the copy of the Appendix of the auction catalogue of Petrus Scriverius, shelf-mark s.c.921.(6.), the date is omitted, but from other copies it is known that these books were auctioned on 8 August 1663.[18] In some instances two copies of the same catalogue give a different date. According to the copy in the Herzog August Bibliothek, Be Kapsel 3 (9), Hendrik de Swaef auctioned an anonymous collection of books at The Hague on 24 January 1656, whereas, according to the handwritten date in the copy of the BL, s.c.462.(4), this occurred on 7 February 1656.

It is not always easy to identify with any certainty the deceased owner of a particular library. In the BL a unique copy (shelf-mark s.c.954) is preserved of the 'Catalogus variorum & insignium librorum, praecipue juridicorum, miscelaneorum[!] in quaevis alia facultate & lingua. Joannis Heemskerckii, Senatoris in Suprema Curia Hollandiae & Zelandiae, &c. Quorum auctio habebitur in aedibus Jodoci Pluymer, in fossa vulgo het Water, sub signo Senecae, ad diem [6, in hand] Martii, 1668. [ornament] Amstelodami. Apud Jodocum Pluymer, 1668. 4°.'[19] The question arises whether or not this Joannes Heemskerck is indeed the same one as the author of the *Batavische Arcadia*.[20] The auction catalogue is not mentioned in D. H. Smit's dissertation on Johan van Heemskerck. This Van Heemskerck was, successively, a lawyer and a barrister to the city of Amsterdam, alderman of Amsterdam and, from 1645 onwards, councillor of the Supreme Court (Hoge Raad) in The Hague. He died as a wealthy man at The Hague on 27 February 1656. His wife died of consumption in January 1657.

Not a single reference book, nor the genealogical tree of the Van Heemskerck family published by D. H. Smit, mentions another Johan van Heemskerck that could match the description.[21] Moreover, the advertisement in the *Oprechte Haerlemse Courant* of 28 February 1668 announcing the auction seems to point to the Van Heemskerck known to us: 'On March the sixth, the books of the deceased Councillor Iohannes van Heemskerck on Law and other faculties and all languages will be sold in the shop of Ioost Pluymer, bookseller at Amsterdam, the catalogue [!] of which are to be obtained at Gerrit Amelingh's at The Hague, at Salomon Wagenaer's at Leyden, at Johannes Ribbius's at Utrecht and at Arnout Leers's at Rotterdam.'[22] Considering all available information we have to assume that we are dealing with the library of the lawyer and Dutch author Johan van Heemskerck (1597-1656). The reasons why his books were auctioned as late as 12 years after his death are unknown. In any case, the catalogue deserves closer research.

Who was the owner of the Bibliotheca Rotheana (s.c.453)? This concerns a relatively large scholar's library from the 17th century. The collational formula of the catalogue in-quarto is: π 1, A-H⁴ I², Aa-Ii⁴ Kk1, 72 ff. The date of the auction is omitted in the London copy, but we know that the auction started on 8 October 1669 from the copy in the Herzog August Bibliothek, Bc 1864. One has to consult the newspapers in order to find out more about an auction and, in this particular case, to identify the former owner. An advertisement in the *Oprechte Haerlemse Courant* of 3 August 1669 announces the auction of the books of 'D. Iohannis Rhoteus, P. M.', to be held in September. The only Johannes Rothe that I could find is a religious fanatic, born 2 December 1628 at Amsterdam in a patrician family originally from Danzig. This Rothe led an adventurous life before he died in Amsterdam on 18 March 1702.[23] When the prosperity of his family and the contents of the library are taken into consideration, this Rothe might well have been the owner. The addition P. M. (Piae Memoriae) to his name in the newspaper of 1669 obviously fails to fit the year of death 1702. However, it is quite conceivable that this is a slip in the advertisement. It was common practice for auctions to be held after the owner's death and the compositor might have added the letter automatically, even though they were not in his copy. In any case, this addition does not appear on the title-page of the catalogue itself. This leads us to believe that the bigoted fanatic Johannes Rothe sold his library during his lifetime, possibly to meet financial demands.

Auction catalogues lacking their title-page are even harder to identify. The possibility that the title-page disappears in the course of time is not at all inconceivable, since quite often the title-page of an auction catalogue is a separately added leaf, and not, as with ordinary books, part of the first quire. It was convenient to add the title-page at the last moment, when the complete catalogue was already printed, so that the right date of the auction could be stated on the title-page.[24] Thus it is understandable that many large libraries possess catalogues without a title-page. Thorough descriptions of catalogues will allow identification of these incomplete ones. With the help of the recorded facts in my database my assistant E. Hofland established the fact that the catalogue without a title-page under shelf-mark s.c.117.(2.) – *cf BLC*, vol.56 (1980), p.130 – is a copy of the auction catalogue of Saphaeus ab Heemstra from 1692. This recognition was largely due to the extraordinary differences in the size of the gatherings: $8°:*^2$, A-B$^8$ C$^6$ D$^8$ E$^4$ F$^8$ G$^6$ H-L$^8$ M-N$^2$, 82 folios. The auction was held on 25 September 1692 and the following days at the shop of Pieter van der Aa in Leiden. The fact that this is the right identification is very easy to check for any visitor to the BL, because the BL also possesses a complete copy of this catalogue (shelf-mark s.c.57.(2.)). The deceased owner of the library was the Frisian Feye van Heemstra, who was born on 7 January 1630 at Coevorden and who died on 7 March 1690 at Emden.[25] Like his father and his father-in-law before him, he was a senior military officer serving under the Frisian stadtholders. From 1678 until his death he was a colonel and commander of Emden. The size and quality of his library was rather extraordinary for a military commander in those days.

## Unsolved questions

Unfortunately, I have not been able yet to identify a number of catalogues. One of these is a catalogue under shelfmark s.c.117.(1.), of which the title-page A1 is missing. It must be an auction catalogue from 1690 or slightly later. An extremely interesting case is s.c.853.(3.), a catalogue in 4° of no less than 176 folios with titles in two columns a page (*cf BLC*, vol.56 (1980), p.130). This has to be a stock catalogue or a stock auction catalogue of an important Dutch bookseller, published after 1652. To my sincere regret I cannot yet offer an identification to Anna, who has devoted herself for such a long time to improving the descriptions of the Dutch books in the *BLC*.

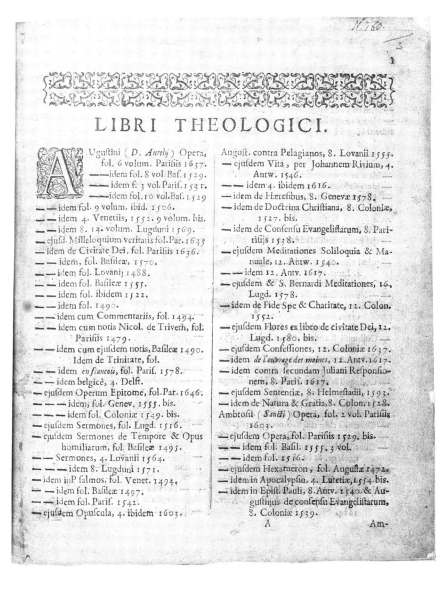

# LIBRI THEOLOGICI.

Uguftini ( D. Aurelij ) Opera,
fol. 6 volum. Parifiis 1637.
——idem fol. 8 vol. Baf. 1529.
——idem f. 3 vol. Parif. 1531.
——idem fol. 10 vol. Baf. 1529.
——idem fol. 9 volum. ibid. 1506.
——idem 4. Venetiis, 1552. 9 volum. bis.
——idem 8. 14. volum. Lugduni 1569.
——ejufd. Milleloquium veritatis fol. Par. 1645
——idem de Civitate Dei, fol. Parifiis 1636.
—— idem, fol. Bafileæ, 1570.
—— idem fol. Lovanij 1488.
—— idem fol. Bafileæ 1555.
—— idem fol. ibidem 1522.
—— idem fol. 1490.
—— idem cum Commentariis, fol. 1494.
—— idem cum notis Nicol. de Triveth, fol.
Parifiis 1479.
—— idem cum ejufdem notis, Bafileæ 1490.
Idem de Trinitate, fol.
—— idem en fiançois, fol. Parif. 1578.
—— idem belgicè, 4. Delft.
—— ejufdem Operum Epitome, fol. Par. 1646.
—— —— idem, fol. Genev. 1555. bis.
—— —— idem fol. Coloniæ 1549. bis.
—— ejufdem Sermones, fol. Lugd. 1516.
—— ejufdem Sermones de Tempore & Opus
homiliarum, fol. Bafileæ 1495.
—— —— Sermones, 4. Lovanii 1564.
—— —— idem 8. Lugduni 1571.
—— idem inP falmos, fol. Venet. 1494.
—— —— idem fol. Bafileæ 1497.
—— —— idem fol. Parif. 1542.
—— ejufdem Opufcula, 4. ibidem 1603.

Auguft. contra Pelagianos, 8. Lovanii 1555.
—— ejufdem Vita, per Johannem Rivium, 4.
Antw. 1546.
—— —— idem 4. ibidem 1616.
—— idem de Hærefibus, 8. Genevæ 1578.
—— idem de Doctrina Chriftiana, 8. Coloniæ,
1527. bis.
—— idem de Confenfu Evangeliftarum, 8. Pari-
rifijs 1538.
—— ejufdem Meditationes Soliloquia & Ma-
nuale, 12. Antw. 1540.
—— —— idem 12. Antv. 1617.
—— ejufdem & S. Bernardi Meditationes, 16.
Lugd. 1578.
——idem de Fide Spe & Charitate, 12. Colon.
1552.
—— ejufdem Flores ex libro de civitate Dei, 12.
Lugd. 1580. bis.
—— ejufdem Confeffiones, 12. Coloniæ 1637.
—— idem de l'ouvrage des moines, 12. Antv. 1617.
—— idem contra fecundam Juliani Refponfio-
nem, 8. Parif. 1617.
—— ejufdem Sententiæ, 8. Helmeftadii, 1593.
—— idem de Natura & Gratia, 8. Colon. 1528.
Ambrofii ( Sancti ) Opera, fol. 2 vol. Parifiis
1603.
—— ejufdem Opera, fol. Parifiis 1529. bis.
—— —— idem fol. Bafil. 1555. 3 vol.
—— —— idem fol. 1516.
—— ejufdem Hexameron, fol. Auguftæ 1472.
—— idem in Apocalypfin. 4. Lutetiæ, 1554. bis.
—— idem in Epift. Pauli, 8. Antv. 1540. & Au-
guftinus de confenfu Evangeliftarum,
8. Coloniæ 1539.

A                    Am-

Fig. 2   First page of an unidentified stock catalogue or stock auction catalogue of a Dutch
bookseller (BL, s.c.853(3)).

Nevertheless, it can already be stated that this is a source of the utmost importance for the history of the Dutch book trade.

The copy registered under shelf-mark s.c.848 also lacks its title-page; in this instance a title-page on a separate leaf. Considering the collation 4°: A-L⁴ (-L4; blank?) and the contents (separate headings with Libri medici; Libri philisophici; Philologi, Poetae etc; Mathematici etc; Cosmographici etc) this has to be the second part of a large auction catalogue. The first part should then contain the Libri Theologici and the Libri Juridici. We are possibly dealing here with a copy of part two of the rare auction catalogue of Adriaan Pauw of 1657. This assumption might prove to be justified when it is compared to the copy in the Royal Library at Copenhagen.[26]

It requires even more book-historic research to solve other questions sufficiently. For instance, the following entry can be found in the *BLC*: 'DU MARTEAU (Pierre): Livres qui se trouvent à Cologne chez Pierre Marteau. [Cologne?] 1698. 12°.' The question mark following 'Cologne' is undoubtedly justified. I believe that this is a publisher's catalogue of an Amsterdam publisher, possibly the Huguetan firm. This belief might be scientifically proved if the titles that are listed in this catalogue are identified. However, research of that nature will be relatively time-consuming.

**Conclusion**

Of the approximately 300 Dutch catalogues in the BL, about 200 are available on microfilm. It is often extremely troublesome for the scholar to work with microfilm. In order to establish if s.c.57.(2.) and s.c.117.(2.) are both copies of the catalogue of Feye van Heemstra of 1692, one has to place two microfilm viewers side by side. It is impossible to establish either the format of a book or the collational formula showing the physical construction of the book on the basis of a microfilm.

Nevertheless, it is irresponsible to let visitors consult the vulnerable old documents any longer. Even recently unique information has been lost permanently, such as the title-page of the auction catalogue of Carolus Beronicus from 1733, of which the BL possesses the only known copy (11902.b.32.). This title-page has vanished without a trace and now we only recover through Kossmann that this extensive library – the catalogue has 264pp. – was auctioned by Johannes Swart at The Hague on 7 September 1733 and the following days.[27] It is desirable to have the remaining 100 catalogues on microfilm, so that any more losses might be prevented.

The funds that will be available in the near future for research in the field of humanities have to be spent as efficiently as possible. Only few young scholars can be enabled to do long-term research into important sources in foreign libraries. However, a considerable amount of research might as well be done by studying copies of the original documents. Therefore, it is essential that old book trade catalogues, which have to be consulted for numerous purposes in historical research, are available in the main research libraries. The more people that are able to use old catalogues in their scientific work, the more rapidly will our knowledge of this category of sources increase. At any rate, it will take a considerable amount of exertion before the problems of the copies of the BL are solved satisfactorily.

## Notes

1. *Cf* Archer Taylor, *Book Catalogues: their Varieties and Uses.* 2nd edition revised by Wm P. Barlow Jr (Winchester, 1986) and B. van Selm, *Een menighte treffelijcke Boecken: Nederlandse boekhandelscatalogi in het begin van de zeventiende eeuw* (Utrecht, 1987).

2. Jeanne Blogie, *Répertoire des catalogues de ventes de livres imprimés* (Brussels, 1982- ; 3 vols. published). The announced vol. IV will contain the *Catalogues de ventes néerlandais.* F. Vandenhole, *Inventaris van veilingcatalogi 1615-1914 met topografische, alfabetische en inhoudsindexen [aanwezig in de] Centrale Bibliotheek van de Rijksuniversiteit Gent.* 2 vols. (Ghent, 1987).

3. *Veilingcatalogi Zeeland 1731-1925: Verzameling catalogi van in Zeeland geveilde boeken, handschriften, prenten, instrumenten en andere goederen.* Samenstelling Zeeuws Documentatiecentrum: Marian Bogers [et al] (Middelburg, 1987).

4. *Cf* B. van Selm, 'Een nieuwe toekomst voor oud "handelsdrukwerk": de bibliografie van Nederlandse boekhandelscatalogi gedrukt vóór 1801', in *Open*, 22 (1990), pp.334-39. J. A. Gruys, P. C. A. Vriesema & C. de Wolf, 'Dutch National Bibliography 1540-1800: the *STCN*', in *Quaerendo*, 13 (1983), pp.149-60.

5. *Cf* Van Selm, op cit (n.1) p.162, no.28.

6. I. H. van Eeghen, *De Amsterdamse boekhandel 1680-1725.* 5 vols. (Amsterdam, 1960-1978), vol.4, pp.169-73.

7. Oliver M. Willard, 'The survival of English books printed before 1640: a theory and some illustrations', in: *The Library*, 4th series, vol.23 (1943), pp.171-90, esp. p.173.

8. Until recently the existence of this publisher's list was only known from the catalogue of the library of Martin Fogel, which was auctioned in Hamburg on 13 August 1678 and the following days; *cf* Hans Dieter Gebauer, *Bücherauktionen in Deutschland im 17. Jahrhundert* (Bonn, 1981), p.71, ill.10; and from Antoine Teissier, *Catalogi auctorum qui librorum catalogos, indices, bibliothecas,... scripts consignârunt* (Genevae, 1705; copy Leiden UL, 181 C 25), p.159: 'Ioannes Maire, Catalogus Librorum Officinae Joannis Maire, continens Libros, qui cum ejus typis & impensis, tum etiam ex Officinâ Plantinianâ Raphelengii prodierunt. Lugduni-Batavorum, 1639. in 4.'

9. J. W. Enschedé, 'Johannes van Ravesteyn', in: *NNBW*, vol.2 (Leiden, 1912), cols.1169-71.

10. Van Ravesteyn's publisher's list 1663: s.c.117.(13.) Latin books and (14.) Dutch books; his publisher's list 1670: s.c.1 (8.) Latin books and (9.) Dutch Books. Unfortunately the last one is incomplete: pages 9-16 are missing.

11. About Jacob van de Velde: Van Eeghen, op cit (n.6), vol.4, p.152.

12. *The British Library General Catalogue of Printed Books to 1975.* 360 vols. (London [etc], 1979-87).

13. *Cf* Robert Winans, *A Descriptive Checklist of Book Catalogues Separately Printed in America 1693-1800* (Worcester, 1981), p.VII. See also Archer Taylor, op cit (n.1), pp.83-5.

14. *Cf* the description of the edition by R. W. Gibson, *St Thomas More: a preliminary bibliography of his works and of Moreana to the year 1750* (New Haven [etc], 1961), pp.280-30, no.22a. The copy at Leiden, UL, 703 F 27, with a different imprint, probably belongs to the issue described by Gibson as no.22b.

15. *BLC*, vol.324 (1986), p.235.

16. *BLC*, vol.1 (1979), p.74. This publisher's catalogue is also present in other libraries as a separate book, for instance in Amsterdam, Library of the Dutch Book Trade Association (unfortunately, this copy is missing) and in Leiden, UL, Coll. BN 20077 A5. Although the last copy consists of identical matter to that which is found in the More edition of 1715 (copy Leiden, UL, 703, F 27), the quires are differently signed: $\pi 1$, $4S^8$, $4T^4$, $4V^8$ ($-4V8$), $4X^4$. Considering this signing of the quires this issue has to be a section of an extensive book. I have not yet established the nature of this edition.

17. *BLC*, vol.286 (1985), p.27.

18. Copies in Leiden UL, 1366 C 27; Paris BN, Q 2192; Uppsala UL and Wolfenbüttel HAB, Bc Sammelband 5.

19. Collational formula: π1, A-E⁴, F1, 22 ff. The year '1688' in the *BLC* vol.143 (1982) p.355 is incorrect!

20. *Cf* Johan van Heemskerck, *Inleydinghe tot het ontwerp van een Batavische Arcadia*, edited by P. E. L. Verkuyl (Deventer, 1982) ( = *FELL* 1).

21. D. H. Smit, *Johan van Heemskerck 1597-1656* (Amsterdam, 1933).

22. Quoted in translation from the copy in Haarlem, Stichting Museum Enschedé.

23. W. P. C. Knuttel, 'Johannes Rothe', in: *NNBW*, vol.1 (Leiden, 1911), cols.1443-6 and R. B. Evenhuis, 'Johannes Rothe', in: *Biografische lexicon voor de geschiedenis van het Nederlands protestantisme*, vol.1 (Kampen, 1978), pp.297-8.

24. *Cf* Van Selm, op cit (n.1), p.83.

25. W. M. C. Regt, 'Feye (5) van Heemstra', in: *NNBW*, vol.10 (Leiden, 1937), col.346; *Nederland's Adelsboek* vol.[6] (1908), p.156 and vol.40 (1942), p.412.

26. *Cf* H. Krol, 'Adriaan Pauw als verzamelaar van wapens, kunst en boeken: de Bibliotheca Heemstediana', in H. W. J. de Boer, H. Bruch [et al], *Adriaan Pauw (1585-1653) staatsman en ambachtsheer* (Heemstede, 1985), pp.71-90, esp. p.90 about the auction catalogue.

27. E. F. Kossmann, *De boekhandel te 's-Gravenhage tot het eind van de 18de eeuw* (The Hague, 1937), p.388.

Gervase Hood

# A Netherlandic Triumphal Arch for James I

In *Ten Studies in Anglo-Dutch Relations* Anna Simoni published an essay on the English edition of Jacob de Gheyn's *Wapenhandelinghe* (1607-08) using it to illuminate a particular moment in Anglo-Netherlandic cultural exchange in the reign of James I. The present essay focuses on a near-contemporary printed book *Beschryvinghe vande her-lycke Arcvs Trivmphal… ter eeren… Coninck Iacobo* (1604-05) which was designed to celebrate and strengthen Anglo-Netherlandic relations in a period of insecurity. It is offered as a 75th birthday tribute to Anna Simoni.[1]

Traditionally English monarchs processed in state from the Tower of London to Westminster at the time of their coronations. The new monarch was presented to the people of his capital in a procession of great visual display. The City of London in reply expressed its loyalty, by dramatising aspects of the sovereign's relationship with his subjects in festive architecture, symbolic paintings and statues, allegorical scenes of dramatic action, orations, and inscriptions. The form was not confined to English coronation entries, and indeed it was much more highly developed on continental Europe, especially in the southern Netherlands.[2]

The Corporation of the City of London reduced its expenditure upon the entries by making companies of foreign merchants resident in London responsible for individual pageants. The foreign merchants thus had an opportunity (albeit a slightly involuntary one) to protest their loyalty to the new monarch, and to cooperate with the civic authorities. The involvement of foreign merchants in the organisation of the entries, and on some occasions, of foreign courtiers in the processions,[3] provided a means whereby architectural and iconographic influences could be disseminated across Europe. The exigencies of national and civic pride created a competitive awareness of entries in other cities, and often the printed records of continental entries were aimed at an international readership.

James I was crowned on 25 July 1603, and work had begun preparing the pageants for this occasion. However the entry had had to be postponed until the following year on account of the severity of the plague. The entry took place on 15 March 1604, with seven pageants in the form of triumphal arches erected in the City of London. Five were paid for by the City, and the other two were the responsibility of the Italian merchants in London and the Netherlandic community respectively. Although all the arches set up within the City were under the control of the Corporation, and the programmes displayed on them were subject to ideological constraints, it is clear that

Fig.1    The engraved title-page of the *Beschryvinghe*. (Royal Library, Brussels.)

for this entry the foreign communities had considerable autonomy in devising their programmes. Furthermore no aesthetic control was exercised over their arches and no attempt was made to coordinate the different pageants of the entry.

This lack of formal unity is evident in the different English texts printed to mark the entry. Thomas Dekker, the dramatist, had overall responsibility for the City's five arches and his pamphlet, *The Magnificent Entertainment*, celebrates the entry in a eulogistic tone, summarising for a semi-popular audience the programmes that adorned the seven arches. Dekker's text was preceded in print by Ben Jonson's, *His Part of King James his Royall and Magnificient Entertainement.* Jonson's work was designed to preserve in print the learned and intellectually sophisticated programmes that he had devised for two of the arches and for a third pageant outside the City boundaries. He sets out in austere and precise detail the images, inscriptions, and orations of his programmes, and their relationship to one another and to his conception of the purpose and meaning of pageant display. This statement contains an implicit attack on Dekker's conception and an assertion of independence from Dekker's management. The third text, *The Arch's of Trivmph*, was written by Stephen Harrison, who was responsible for the architectural form and physical construction of the City's five arches. Harrison's book draws extensively upon Dekker's and Jonson's, but it also contains engraved plates by William Kip illustrating the seven triumphal arches. Although Harrison's work has a provincial gaucheness set beside the lavishly illustrated books that recorded contemporary continental entries, it is the first book with engravings of English pageant architecture, and it reflects an awareness of continental achievements.[4]

The texts of Dekker, Jonson and Harrison have been much studied. However the published account of the Netherlandic triumphal arch, the *Beschryvinghe*, has received very little attention, and it is hoped that the preliminary account in the present essay may be instrumental in bringing it to a wider audience.

The *Beschryvinghe* appears to survive in a single copy now in the Royal Library in Brussels.[5] This copy comes from the library of Charles van Hulthem. In his manuscript notes at the front of the volume Van Hulthem records how he had long been aware of the existence of the work from a reference to it in Emanuel van Meteren's history of the Low Countries, but he had never seen a copy until he acquired his from a Ghent bookseller.[6] Van Meteren's reference to the work is almost certainly the first printed citation of it. Subsequently the work was included in Muller's *De Nederlandsche geschiedenis in platen*, and it has been noticed briefly in several 20th-century academic publications.[7]

Before Van Hulthem acquired his copy it was dismembered and mounted in a volume of blank sheets. The cut-down leaves of the engraved title-page (fig.1), the letterpress title-page, and the text were suspended over holes made in some of the leaves of the volume and pasted in around their edges. An engraved plate showing the arch's groundplan was pasted in and two very large engravings (figs 2 and 3) showing the front and rear elevations were sewn in.

The letterpress title-page and the text were printed by Richard Schilders in Middelburg and comprise two quires of a folio in fours:

$2°$ : A – B$^4$ [\$3 signed (-A1)], 8 leaves.

Fig.2    MD's engraving of the front elevation of the arch.

At some stage it was envisaged that there would be only one plate as the text refers the reader to a plate at the beginning of the narrative.[8] Where the three plates showing the groundplan and the two elevations were inserted before the Brussels copy was broken up, it is now impossible to say. However the dimensions of the two plates showing the front and rear façades are so large that they must have been inserted as folio sheets and they were probably folded around their edges. The dismembering and mounting of the leaves of the book was designed to display these plates to maximum advantage and protect them from damage.[9]

Schilders was a religious refugee from Hainault, who worked in London from *c*. 1567 to 1580, before settling in Zeeland as the province's official printer. He is best known for printing, sometimes surreptitiously, works of Protestant polemic, psalms and prayer books for the English market, and Dutch translations of English official publications. He printed three editions of the congratulatory address delivered by the French and Dutch Protestant churches in England to James I on his accession, and in 1606 he published *Den Staet van London in hare groote peste*, a poem on the plague of 1603 by Jacob Cool. Cool was a leading intellectual among the Netherlanders in London and a central figure in the composition of the programme displayed on their triumphal arch.[10]

Schilders was therefore a central figure in Anglo-Netherlandic intellectual relations and well placed to supply both book markets. However, illustrated works are very rare among his imprints and a folio work like the *Beschryvinghe* with its engraved title-page and three other plates has a lavishness alien to the closely printed quarto and octavo pamphlets that comprise the greater part of his production.

The letterpress title-page states simply that the book was printed by Schilders in 1605. The engraved title-page by contrast is a proclamation of the artistic aspirations of Conrad Jansen for whom the book was printed and who was the architect of the arch. It is in the form of an architectural wall monument, with the title in the space enclosed by the monument:

*BESCHRYVINGHE*/VANDE HERLYCKE ARCVS/TRIVMPHAL OFTE EERE POOR:/ te vande Nederlantshe Natie opghe:/recht in Londen/*TER EEREN*/*Den Hoochgheborenen Coninck Iacobo Coninck van Enghe*:/*lant Schotlant Vranckryck ende Irelant den. 15.en.*/*Merte.* 1603. *stylo Angliae.*/Ghedruckt tot Middelburgh voor Conraet/Iansen by Richard Schilders Drucker/Der Staten VAn Zeland. 1604.[11]

The wall monument is surmounted by a cartouche containing the image of a hand measuring a scale with a pair of compasses. The compasses are accompanied by a scroll with the legend LABORE ET CONSTANTIA, on either side of them are the initials CI, and between the compasses what appears to be a craftsman's mark. In a cartouche pendent from the bottom of the monument are the words:

*Men vintse te coope int Corte*/*Suyt werck inden vergulden*/*Passer ten huyse van*/CONRAET IANSEN./*Tot*/*Londen.*

The allusion to the Plantin Press is obvious.[12] However compasses were also traditional emblems of joiners, and Jansen, a joiner by trade, adapted the Plantin device by adding the measuring scale and what was presumably his craftsman's mark. The same

Fig.3    MD's engraving of the rear elevation of the arch.

device and motto appear on the two plates of the elevations, with the inscription '*Coenrardus Iansen.* ARCHIT:'.

Jansen came to England from 's Hertogenbosch in 1567 as a Protestant refugee and was denized in 1571. He married the widow of another Netherlandic refugee and five children were baptised in the London Dutch Church in the 1570s. As a joiner he seems to have prospered, employing four English employees in 1593. His wife was buried on 26 February 1607 and on 26 April he married Elizabeth Garland at the church of St George the Martyr, Southwark. Whether or not this marriage was contrary to the wishes of the Consistory of the London Dutch Church is not known as the relevant minute book is not extant. However accounts recording regular contributions of members of the church are extant for the period from 1609 and Jansen's name does not appear. He may however have died by this date. He was 61 at the time of the coronation entry.[13]

Of his intellectual and artistic achievements there are only the records of this entry. The *Beschryvinghe* however is suggestive about Jansen's aspirations and status. Firstly it informs us that he began by sketching his designs for the elevations and groundplan, regretting that the narrow site prevented him from realising his conception in full. In the context of contemporary architectural theory this is an assertion that intellectual design preceded physical construction, that Jansen was a practitioner of the learned and liberal art of architecture, and not a manual craftsman. Secondly Jansen is described as 'des Conincx Dienaer'. This may indicate that Jansen worked for the Office of Works, the department responsible for royal building, and the predominant source of patronage for English architecture.[14]

Although the engraved title-page of the *Beschryvinghe* states that the book was printed for Jansen neither it nor the letterpress title-page identify him as the author and the text refers to him in the third person. However there is another source which supplies information about the authorship of the programme displayed on the arch, and this is relevant to the question of the *Beschryvinghe*'s authorship.

Symeon Ruytinck, a minister of the London Dutch Church from 1601 to 1621, wrote three manuscript histories of the Netherlandic community in England. Two of these contain substantial accounts of the 1604 triumphal arch, and one of them records that:

D'inventeurs syn voornemelyck gheweest Christopherus de Stuer ende *Assueros Regemorterus*: die t met dichten verciert hebben waeren Monsieur *Thorius, Iacobus Coolius*, ende *Rutingius*.[15]

An iconographic programme consists of a basic concept, or set of concepts, expressed in inscriptions and visual images. Ruytinck informs us that Assueros Regemorter and Christopher de Stuer devised the basic concepts. Regemorter was the senior minister of the London Dutch Church. He died in the plague in September 1603, and could have had no part in any modifications to the programme made after that date.

The Latin oration delivered from the arch, in addition to being recorded by the *Beschryvinghe* and Ruytinck, survives in a manuscript volume of verse by Raphael Thorius. Thorius, a Flemish emigré, was a distinguished physician and a Neo-Latin poet, and friend of many Protestant northern European intellectuals.[16]

The other author identified by Ruytinck, Jacob Cool, has already been mentioned as the writer of a poem on the 1603 plague printed by Schilders. Cool was born in Antwerp in 1563, the nephew of Abraham Ortelius. He was brought up in London, but maintained close links with continental humanist scholarship, both by travel and by correspondence. He published a Dutch verse translation of the psalms, a treatise on botany, and meditation on death.[17] His Latin verse and classical learning were praised by his contemporaries and he wrote two manuscript treatises on classical numismatics.[18] He collected coins and annotated a copy of his correspondent Adolph Occo's *Impp. Romanorum numismata* (Antwerp, 1579) with the details of his own and Ortelius's collections.[19]

The Netherlandic triumphal arch bore two types of inscription. Firstly each image (or set of images) was accompanied by an epigrammatic motto designed to explicate its significance. Such mottoes on this arch, and on many pageant artifacts in Renaissance Europe, are analogous to the mottoes that accompanied printed emblems. They are succinct Latin phrases, often quotations from poetry and often of a proverbial nature. The second type of inscription on the Netherlandic arch may be called the epigraphic inscription. There were two of these, occupying central positions on the front and rear façades. The *Beschryvinghe* informs us that the epigraphic inscription on the front was composed from the titles of honour the Romans used on their triumphal arches and coins, and indeed it adopts the structure of the principal inscriptions on the arches of Septimus Severus and Constantine, and it imitates the highly compressed and conventionally abbreviated style of expression cultivated by epigraphists.[20]

Cool's hand as a poet and scholar of numismatics and epigraphy therefore can be detected behind both types of inscription. Ruytinck also claimed responsibility for the 'dichten' on the arch, and Thorius may have contributed to the inscriptions as one of the motto inscriptions appears in his volume of verse.[21] The translations of the verses Ruytinck says were the work of himself, Cool, and De Stuer. The texts of almost all the inscriptions and of the oration are followed in the *Beschryvinghe*, and in Ruytinck's two manuscript accounts, by translations into Dutch. The translations of the oration and the epigraphic inscription on the front elevation are substantially the same in the *Beschryvinghe* and in Ruytinck's accounts, but some of the translations of the motto inscriptions differ, and Ruytinck provides a verse translation of the epigraphic inscription on the rear of the arch while the *Beschryvinghe* gives only a prose one. In 1612 Ruytinck published in Dutch an iconoclastic work which includes verse descriptions of the legends associated with different saints of the Catholic Church.[22] It is not difficult to imagine men like Ruytinck and Cool offering different translations of the Latin mottoes and perhaps competing to produce the most elegant and epigrammatic versions.[23]

The *Beschryvinghe* however makes no mention of any of the authors identified by Ruytinck. Instead it describes Jansen's role as being of central importance and identifies some of the joiners and carpenters who assisted him.[24] It is most unlikely that men of the standing of Cool and Ruytinck would have written the *Beschryvinghe* to promote Jansen, and there are telling differences between Cool's accounts of the plague and Ruytinck's exposition of the front elevation and those given in the *Beschryvinghe*.[25] If the *Beschryvinghe* was not written by Jansen it was written at his commission.[26]

It is also highly likely that Jansen commissioned the four engraved plates. The two plates of the elevations are signed 'MD sculpsit', and a comparison of the letter forms and architectural details on these plates, with those on the engraved title-page and groundplan makes it seem likely that the same engraver was responsible for all four engravings. No engraver with the initials MD has been identified working in the Low Countries in this period, but the initials may be those of Michael Droeshout. Michael Droeshout learnt to engrave in Brussels and came to England *c.*1590. He was a member of the London Dutch Church and almost certainly the brother of Martin Droeshout, a painter who worked on the arch.[27]

If the plates were engraved by Michael Droeshout in London it is possible that they were also printed there, for there is no reason to suppose that Schilders owned a rolling press. The difference in paper size between the sheets used for the engravings and those used by Schilders, and the discrepancy between the dates on the two title-pages, strengthen the supposition that the plates were made, and probably also printed, in London. It is not uncommon for an early 17th-century book printed in London to have illustrations made from plates engraved in the Low Countries, and which sometimes had also been printed overseas. The *Beschryvinghe* may be a very rare instance of a book printed overseas, but with plates engraved and printed in England.

The classical learning displayed by the authors of the programme and by Jansen was designed both to honour James I by relating him to the idealised world of antiquity and also to express the interests of the body that organised and paid for the arch. The *Beschryvinghe* tells us that a committee of 12 was appointed to organise the Netherlandic arch, and it is highly likely that this committee was established under the auspices of the London Dutch Church, as the equivalent committee was for Charles I's coronation entry.[28] The Church permeated every aspect of the Netherlandic community's life, and, as we have seen, the authors of the programme included ministers and influential members of it.[29]

The London Dutch Church was founded in 1550 as an institution independent of the reformed Church of England. It was hoped in English radical Protestant circles that it would serve as a model for the Church of England to follow. At the beginning of Elizabeth's reign however it was placed under the superintendence of the Bishop of London so that its influence could be restricted and religious heterodoxy among the immigrant population might be controlled. The Netherlandic community attracted sympathy as persecuted Protestants who had fled Spanish tyranny to preserve their faith, but the principal attraction of the community to the Elizabethan government was an economic not an ideological one. The foreigners' skills could be used to revitalise English industries and reduce dependence upon imports. The government and Church cooperated to exploit this advantage to their mutual benefit, the Church giving the government the names of skilled workers so that they might be freed from the legal restrictions that beset strangers' trading activities, or sent to economically depressed provincial towns to revive local economies.

However the economic activities of the immigrant communities provoked xenophobic hostility among some sections of the indigenous population, who accused the Netherlanders of prospering at their expense. This hostility became especially marked after the great influx of refugees following the fall of Antwerp in 1585 and perhaps reached its zenith in 1593. In this year the Netherlanders were the victims of organised violence and malicious lawsuits reviving moribund restrictions on their trading activities. They came under vehement attack in the House of Commons and a bill to prevent the strangers selling by retail was passed, although it never completed its passage through Parliament. This bill had the support of the City of London. In the months after the coronation entry a bill to restrict the economic rights of strangers' children came before the Commons.[30]

This is the context behind the Netherlandic community's expensive self-promotion at James I's coronation entry. The community was protesting its loyalty to the king and making its contribution towards the cost of the entry to the City. It hoped to persuade both the king and the City authorities that it was worth protecting against its many enemies.

The programme on the front elevation was directed to praising James as a Prot-estant ruler. Surmounting the arch was a statue of Providence, and underneath this two sceptres joined in an imperial crown, indicating that the unification of the king-doms of England and Scotland, which had been brought about by James's accession to the throne of England, had been achieved through the workings of Providence. The arch was constructed on three levels, and in the middle of the highest level James was portrayed with personifications of Religion and Piety. On either side were statues of Justice and Fortitude.

On the central level were painted images of four kings who were presented as James's spiritual ancestors and models for him to emulate. On one side were the Old Testament kings David and Josiah, David as the godly king of the Jews and Josiah as the king who restored purity of worship by his ferocious attacks on idolatry.[31] On the other side were Lucius, according to antiquaries the first Christian king of England, and Edward VI, who had given the London Dutch Church its legal status and who represented to its community the English Reformation in its purest phase. Between the two pairs of model kings there was arranged a tableau of 17 maidens representing the provinces of the Low Countries, each with the appropriate coat of arms. They were positioned above the principal inscription on the front façade which besought James to continue Elizabeth's policy of protecting the refugee community and praised him as the bringer of peace and the defender of the word of God.

On the lowest level of the arch over the central archway there was a model of a phoenix, representing James as the reincarnation of Elizabeth. On either side there were two allegorical paintings, one depicting tame animals disporting themselves under the sun, the other showing wild beasts attacked by thunder and lightning. The former represented the condition of the godly and peaceloving under James, the latter his treatment of the godless and rebellious.

When James succeeded to the English throne an image of a wise and learned peacemaker was promoted.[32] He had united England and Scotland without conflict through his rule of both kingdoms, and he was pursuing a policy of making peace abroad. In a new departure from Elizabeth's policy he was making peace with Spain. In the months following the coronation entry the Peace of London was negotiated and the English agreed formally to cease supporting the Dutch revolt in the Netherlands. The programme on the Netherlandic arch did praise James as a peacemaker, but not as a reconciler of conflicting nations and parties. Instead he was praised as the bringer of peace to the loyal and godly. It would be achieved by militant Protestantism's rout of the godless. Thus the programme on the arch praised James as a peacemaker, but the image was reinterpreted adroitly to present an almost antithetical view of the king's role in the world, while simultaneously he was reminded of the Netherlanders' status as refugees from Spanish persecution.

The rear of the arch was addressed primarily to economic issues. A statue of Prudence crowned the arch, and beneath it there was an imperial crown, pierced by an olive and a laurel branch, representing triumphant peace. A Latin motto alluded to the peaceful unification of the kingdoms. Below Prudence there were statues of Sincerity and Time, and in the centre of the highest level were painted images of Diligence, Industry, and Labour. Concrete evidence of the interdependence of these three qualities was provided in three large paintings set in the central level, which showed fishing off the English coast, and merchants trading on the quays of London and Middelburg. On the lowest level two paintings depicted the farming of flax and spinning 'op de Neerlandtsche wyse'.[33] The principal inscription described how the well-governed and peaceful condition of Britain allowed trade to flourish, skills to be cultivated, and transnational friendships to develop.

In the most recent study of the London Dutch community in the Stuart period O. P. Grell argues that by the early 17th century the settler mentality was superseding that of the refugee. The immediacy of contact with the Low Countries was diminishing as the United Provinces became more secure from the Spanish threat, and new waves of immigrants ceased to come to England. The community, Grell shows, was dominated by the richest merchant members who tended to be conservative in social outlook and theology. The Church invariably deferred to the crown's dictates in matters of religious doctrine and discipline.[34]

The programme on the arch represents the way that the leaders of the community chose to present it in 1604, and therefore to some extent how they perceived themselves. As might have been expected on a traditional occasion such as a coronation entry when the basic relationships between the ruler and the ruled were being expressed, the community represented itself in terms of its origins, that is, as a gathering of exiles from the 17 provinces, rather than as a settler group in England. The emphasis on the community's involvement in international trade perhaps underlines Grell's arguments about the dominance of the merchant members over the skilled artisans, and it would not have been diplomatic to have reminded the civic authorities that the immigrants possessed superior skills to those held by the indigenous population. The king himself had mentioned in May 1603 the economic benefit of the immigrant community in his reply to the congratulatory address of the foreign churches on his accession.[35] Nevertheless the view that peace was a product of Anglo-Netherlandic trade rather than royal diplomacy, and the attempt, albeit one disguised in the imprecision of imagery and epigraphical allusion, to place James as the heir to a tradition of radical Protestantism, was not the expression of a conservative submissiveness but a carefully poised attempt to redirect the king's foreign policy. However James's lack of interest in pageant displays is well attested and Dekker implies that he rode on past the Netherlandic arch without pausing to listen to the oration.[36]

It is of course not very likely that a programme presented on a temporary triumphal arch and an unheard oration would, by themselves, influence the king's religous or diplomatic policies. The Hampton Court Conference of January 1604 had already dashed the hopes of Calvinist reformers within the Church of England. In the months after the entry James concluded peace with Spain, and in 1605 he allowed the Archduke Albert, ruler of the Spanish Netherlands, to recruit in England. At the end of his reign leading members of the London Netherlandic community were harshly prosecuted for the alleged export of bullion in a barely disguised attempt to seize as much of the wealth of the immigrant community as possible for the crown.[37]

The major importance of the Netherlandic triumphal arch is in terms of its contribution to artistic and intellectual life. The impact of Netherlandic artists on English cultural life in the 16th and 17th centuries has been often studied. The triumphal arch provided an opportunity for leading London Netherlanders to patronise artists among their own community and to exhibit the achievements of Antwerp painters. The allegorical and large-scale paintings appear to have been the work of Daniel de Vos and Paul van Overbeke, brought over from Antwerp, with their assistants, and of Adrian van Sond and Martin Droeshout, both already resident in England. The woodwork was painted by Daniel Papeler, with the aid of native English painters.[38] None of the English arches in the entry displayed large-scale paintings; they were confined to allegorical figures and *tableaux vivants*.

The information that the *Beschryvinghe* furnishes about the painters employed on the arch extends our picture of the dependence of English visual culture in this period on Netherlandic art, but it is obviously of little significance when compared to the influence of Van Dyck or to Rubens's visit to England in 1629-30. In the area of architecture however the *Beschryvinghe* should perhaps modify our perceptions about early 17th-century English culture. Per Palme has stated that in architectural terms 'James's triumphant passage through [Stephen] Harrison's arches led on to the Banqueting House of Inigo Jones', because Harrison's arches were the first structures in England to be published as having been built in accordance with Renaissance principles of the harmonic relation of the parts to the whole. It is doubtful however whether Harrison fully understood these principles, for he appears to have believed that they were expressed in Kip's perspective engravings.[39] In practice Harrison's arches belong not with classical architecture but with the flamboyant achievements of Jacobean monumental joinery such as the hall screens at Audley End and Knole.[40]

Conrad Jansen however did understand classical architecture. His corinthian arch with its detached columns manifests the influence of the Arch of Constantine, which he probably studied in Serlio. In its upper levels it is indebted to the classically inspired pageant arches erected in the Spanish Netherlands from the time of Philip of Spain's entries in 1549.[41]

It has been suggested above that Jansen may have worked for the Office of Works. The influence of Serlio on the early Jacobean Office is evident in the recently analysed plan for a temporary auditorium at Christ Church, Oxford in 1605.[42] In the context of these works, and indeed of the Italian arch in the entry, our view of pre-Jonesian classical architecture in England needs modifying, and Inigo Jones should no longer be seen as devoid of precursors in the first years of James I's reign.

There were serious exponents of classical architecture in England in the years immediately before Jones undertook his earliest commissions.

Throughout the 16th century the medieval form of the royal entry was adapted to conform to the Renaissance conception of the Roman imperial triumph, and the self-conscious classicism of Cool and Jansen in devising the London Netherlandic arch was part of this process. In the same entry Ben Jonson was concerned to align his programmes to classical prototypes by the precision of his classical allusion and his theory of the relationship between the visual image and the motto inscription. The addition of an oration to the image and motto made Jonson's programmes structurally analogous to the emblem.[43] Modern scholars of English Renaissance culture have seen the emblem as a central genre in a culture that aspired to the ideal of 'ut pictura poesis', to make verse speaking pictures and painting silent poetry.[44] However to Cool and antiquaries of his background the classical coin with its combination of image and inscription provided a more direct access to antiquity, and as Renaissance emblematists identified the antecedents of their genre in the supposed Egyptian hieroglyphs of Horapollo, so Occo, Cool's correspondent in numismatics, traced the origins of the coin to the same source.[45]

However the *Beschryvinghe* does not cite particular coins as sources for images on the arch, a practice adopted by the devisers of the programme for the Cardinal-Infante Ferdinand's entry into Antwerp in 1635, and, under that influence, Charles II's entry into London in 1661.[46] Indeed contrary to the trend in 16th- and 17th-century European pageantry the Netherlandic programme of 1604 employed allegorical personifications to depict abstract virtues, rather than mythological figures embodying those forces. The rear of the arch is presided over by Prudentia, not by Mercury, god of commerce. It is very likely that in the intellectual world that Cool and his fellow devisers inhabited, the study and composition of inscriptions had greater weight than the selection and delineation of images and attributes. In a 17th-century treatise on epigraphy the principal inscription on the rear of the Netherlandic arch was cited for its simplicity and brevity, and it is this praise that they would have valued.[47]

The Netherlandic arch for James I then was the product of men who combined devout Calvinism with classical erudition. The *Beschryvinghe* was addressed to their fellows in the European republic of letters as much as to the English crown and civic authorities. The patronage that the leaders of the Netherlandic community could offer their writers and artists was obviously less significant than that which the court and great nobility could extend to Jonson, Jones, and Van Dyck. However the creative patronage of a merchant like Cool, using his knowledge of Roman triumphs and coins to adorn Jansen's corinthian arch, is a precursor of the movement that inspired the Earl of Arundel to collect statuary and inscriptions and make them available for Jones and Van Dyck.[48]

## Notes

1. Anna E. C. Simoni, 'A Present for a Prince', in *Ten Studies in Anglo-Dutch Relations*, edited by Jan van Dorsten (Leiden, 1974), pp.51-71.

In the course of working on the Netherlandic community in London I have incurred many debts to a large number of people: the most extensive of these are to the editor of this volume, to Rachel Stockdale, and to T. Y. Tjia.

2. The best introduction to English pageantry is Sydney Anglo, *Spectacle, Pageantry and Early Tudor Policy* (Oxford, 1969). For European see, eg, Roy Strong, *Art and Power: Renaissance Festivals, 1450-1650* (Woodbridge, 1984).

3. In 16th-century London these occasions were the entries of Katharine of Aragon, 1501, the Emperor Charles V, 1522, and Philip of Spain, 1554.

4. *The Magnificent Entertainment*, in *The Dramatic Works of Thomas Dekker*, edited by Fredson Bowers, 4 vols (Cambridge, 1953-61), 2, pp.229-309. *The King's Entertainment*, in *Ben Jonson*, edited by C. H. Herford and Percy and Evelyn Simpson, 11 vols (Oxford, 1925-52), 7, pp.65-109. Stephen Harrison *The Arch's of Trivmph* (London, 1604), *STC* 12863. For Jonson's attack on Dekker, see D. J. Gordon, 'Roles and Mysteries', in *The Renaissance Imagination*, edited by Stephen Orgel (Berkeley, 1975), pp.3-23.

5. Shelf mark CL.14. 543$^b$ C LP. Copies do not survive in either the Old Royal Library, now in the British Library, or in the Dutch Church library. The book does not appear in *A Catalogue of Books, Manuscripts, Letters, &c, belonging to the Dutch Church, Austin Friars, London* (London, 1879), which records the Church's holdings before the sales of the twentieth century.

6. The *Beschryvinghe* is not included in *Bibliotheca Hulthemiana*, 6 vols (Ghent, 1836-37). Van Hulthem's manuscript note is printed in the catalogue of the sale at which the Royal Library acquired its copy, *Catalogue des livres de la bibliothèque de feu Monsieur De Bremmaecker, provenant en grande partie de celle de Monsieur Ch. van Hulthem* (Ghent, 1845), pp.171-72.
   Van Meteren's description of the Netherlandic arch first appears in the 1609 edition of his history (*STC* 17845.3, sig.Qqqq6$^{r-v}$). Van Meteren's description is largely dependent upon that given in the *Beschryvinghe*: it concludes by referring the reader to the printed 'beschrijvinghe met conterfeytsels'.

7. F. Muller, *De Nederlandsche geschiedenis in platen*, 4 vols (Amsterdam, 1863-82), 4, no.1190. Irmengard von Roeder-Baumbach, *Versieringen bij Blijde Inkomsten gebruikt in de Zuidelijke Nederlanden gedurende de 16e en 17e Eeuw* (Antwerp, 1943), pp.19, 129, 131-32. George R. Kernodle, *From Art to Theatre* (Chicago, 1944), p.236. Edward Croft-Murray, *Decorative Painting in England, 1537-1837*, 2 vols (London, 1962-72), 1, pp.194, 213; 2, p.215. Ole Peter Grell, 'The French and Dutch congregations in London in the early 17th century', in *Proceedings of the Huguenot Society of London*, 34 (1987), pp.362-77, 368 and n. 44, and *Dutch Calvinists in early Stuart London* (Leiden, 1989), p.91.

8. sig.B3.

9. The engraved title-page measures 285 × 176mm. It has been trimmed within the platemark. The leaves of the letterpress title-page and the text are 260mm high and vary in width from 170 to 177mm. The plates of the groundplan, and the front and rear façades measure respectively 245 × 175mm, 543 × 320mm and 544 × 320mm.

10. J. Dover Wilson, 'Richard Schilders and the English Puritans', in *Transactions of the Bibliographical Society*, 11 (1909-11), pp.65-134. Dingeman van Wijnen, 'Richard Schilders: printer to the protestants', unpublished dissertation, University of Leiden, 1980. On Cool see below n.17.

11. In this transcript the long *s* and large initial capitals have not been indicated. The superscript *en* in *15.en.* has been lowered to the line.

12. Leon Voet, *The Golden Compasses*, 2 vols (Amsterdam, 1969-72), 1, p.31.

13. *Returns of Aliens... from the reign of Henry VIII to that of James I*, edited by R. E. G. Kirk and Ernest F. Kirk, Publications of the Huguenot Society of London, 10 (in 4 parts) (1900-08), 2, pp.108, 291, 312, 328, 379, 413, 445, 455, 473: 3, pp.1, 74. *Letters of Denization and Acts of Naturalization for Aliens in England, 1509-1603*, Publications of the Huguenot Society of London, 8 (1893), p.132. *The Marriage, Baptismal, and Burial Registers, 1571-1874, ... of the Dutch Reformed Church...*, edited by William John Charles Moens (Lymington, 1884), pp.146, 38.

*Returns of Strangers in the Metropolis, 1593, 1627, 1635, 1639*, edited by Irene Scouloudi, Publications of the Huguenot Society of London, 57 (1985), p.185. Burial register, St Olave Southwark, Greater London Record Office, R627. Marriage register, St George the Martyr, in the incumbent's custody. Dutch Church accounts, Guildhall Library MS 7390/1. I have not been able to trace any record of Jansen's burial or will.

14. *Beschryvinghe*, sig.A2ᵛ. John Summerson, *Architecture in Britain, 1530 to 1830*, seventh edition (Harmondsworth, 1983), pp.28, 53-60. No evidence has yet been found to document Jansen's hypothetical connection with the Office of Works.

15. Guildhall Library MS 9621, pp.135-40, p.135. (In my quotation abbreviated words have been expanded silently.) This manuscript has been published, although the edition omits the Dutch translations of the arch's Latin verses and oration: *Gheschiedenissen ende Handelingen die voornemelick aengaen de Nederduytsche Natie ende Gemeynten wonende in Engelant*, edited by J.J. van Toorenbergen, Werken der Marnix- Vereeniging, serie 3, deel 1 (Utrecht, 1873), pp.189-93. Ruytinck's other manuscript accounts of the arch are Guildhall Library MS 9620, ff.87ᵛ-90, and Guildhall Library MS 10,055, f.27.

16. Thorius's text in British Library (BL) Sloane MS 1768, f.39, is annotated with revisions most of which appear in the *Beschryvinghe* and in Ruytinck's two accounts, and some of which appear in Dekker's *Magnificent Entertainment*, ll.624-662. Dekker and Sloane MS 1768 also contain 14 lines omitted by the *Beschryvinghe* and Ruytinck. On Thorius see *DNB*, and Mark Pattison, *Isaac Casaubon, 1559-1614*, second edition (Oxford, 1892), pp.280, 304, 412, 467-69.

17. *Ecclesiae Londino-Batavae Archivum*, edited by J.H. Hessels, 3 vols (Cantabrigiae, 1887-97), I. Jacob Cool, *Den Staet van London in hare groote peste*, edited by J.A. van Dorsten and K. Schaap (Leiden, 1962). J.A. van Dorsten, ' "I.C.O.": The Rediscovery of a Modest Dutchman in London', in *The Anglo-Dutch Renaissance*, edited by J. van den Berg and Alaistair Hamilton (Leiden, 1988), pp.8-20.

18. Cambridge University Library (CUL) Gg

vi 9ᶠ. See *A Catalogue of the Manuscripts preserved in the Library of the University of Cambridge*, vol.3 (Cambridge, 1858), pp.217-18.

19. CUL, Adv.d.3.22. I owe this reference to David McKitterick. See also his *Cambridge University Library, A History: The Eighteenth and Nineteenth Centuries* (Cambridge, 1986), p.134, and Hessels, I, nos.320, 324.

20. *Beschryvinghe*, sig.A4. The inscriptions on these Roman arches were widely available to humanist scholars in a variety of sources including Occo, sigs h1ᵛ, z3.

21. Sloane MS 1768, f.39ᵛ.

22. *Gulden Legende vande Roomsche Kercke* (London, 1612) (*STC* 21471).

23. Little is known of De Stuer (or Steur), an emigré merchant. He presented two books to the Dutch Church library in 1609. He had died by 1617. (Guildhall Library MS 20, 185/4, p.11, *Returns of Aliens*, 3, pp.29, 45, 97, 124, 150.)

24. sigs A2ᵛ, B4.

25. Cool in *Den Staet* is concerned to give the precise number of persons recorded as having died of the plague in different areas and at different stages. The *Beschryvinghe* is much vaguer. Ruytinck's accounts in Guildhall Library MSS 9620 and 9621 are more economical and cogent than that in the *Beschryvinghe*.

26. Some students may detect in the different accounts of Ruytinck and the *Beschryvinghe* evidence of the conventional conflict between literary and visual artists in the production of pageants and related entertainments. See D.J. Gordon, 'Poet and Architect: the Intellectual Setting of the Quarrel between Ben Jonson and Inigo Jones', in *The Renaissance Imagination*, pp.77-101.

27. *Returns of Strangers*, p.172. A.M. Hind, *Engraving in England in the 16th and 17th centuries*, 3 vols (Cambridge, 1952-64), 2, pp.341-43. *Beschryvinghe*, sig.A2ᵛ. As the engraved title-page in the Brussels copy has been trimmed an engraver's signature may have been lost.

28. *Beschryvinghe*, sig.A2ᵛ. Grell, *Dutch Calvinists*, pp.91-92. The corresponding Consistory minutes and account books are not

extant for the first years of James I's reign.

**29.** The best recent accounts of the Church are Grell, and Andrew Pettegree, *Foreign Protestant Communities in Sixteenth-Century London* (Oxford, 1986).

**30.** Pettegree, pp.291-92; *Returns of Strangers*, pp.57-66; Grell, p.17–18.

**31.** II Kings 22-23.

**32.** See eg Graham Parry, *The Golden Age restor'd: the culture of the Stuart Court, 1603-42* (Manchester, 1981), pp.1-39.

**33.** sig.B2$^v$.

**34.** Grell, pp.8, 27-33, 43-72.

**35.** Hessels, 2, no.272; 3.1, no.1556.

**36.** Arthur Wilson, *Life and Reign of King James the First* (London, 1653), sigs C2$^v$-C3 (Wing w288). Dekker, ll. 705-10.

**37.** Grell, pp.15, 149-75. Geoffrey Parker, *The Dutch Revolt* (Harmondsworth, 1977), p.237.

**38.** *Beschryvinghe*, sig.A2$^v$. On these artists see Croft-Murray, 1, pp.194, 213-15; 2, p.215. On Van Sond (or Vanson), see also Lorne Campbell, *The Early Flemish Paintings in the Collection of Her Majesty the Queen* (Cambridge, 1985), p.xxxiii.

**39.** Per Palme, 'Ut Architecture Poesis', in *Idea and Form: Studies in the History of Art*, Figura, nova series 1 (Stockholm, 1959), pp.95-107, 105. It is necessary to use an orthogonal projection to express visually and measurably the metrical relationships of the parts of a façade.

**40.** Eric Mercer, *English Art, 1553-1625* (Oxford, 1962), pp.120-21.

**41.** The closest parallels to Jansen's arch in Netherlandic pageant architecture are to be found in the arches erected in Ghent in 1549: F. van de Vandle, *Arcus trivmphales Quinque a S.P.Q. Gand. Philippo Austrie Caroli imp. principi* (Antwerp, 1549), reproduced in M. Lageirse, 'La Joyeuse Entrée du Prince Héritier Philippe à Gand en 1549', in *Ancien Pays et Assemblées d'Etats / Standen en Landen*, 18 (1959), pp.31-46.

**42.** John Orrell, *The theatres of Inigo Jones and John Webb* (Cambridge, 1985), pp.24-38, *The human stage: English theatre design, 1567-1640* (Cambridge, 1988), pp.119-29.

**43.** Jonson, ll.243-67. See Gordon, 'Roles', (cited above n.4), pp.11-14, and 'Poet and Architect' (cited above n.26), pp.79-81.

**44.** The most valuable account of Renaissance inconographic theory is E. H. Gombrich, '*Icones Symbolicae*: Philosophies of Symbolism and their Bearing on Art', in his *Symbolic Images: Studies in the Art of the Renaissance* (Oxford, 1972), pp.123-95. For an indication of recent trends in emblem studies see eg Peter M. Daly, 'The Cultural Context of English Emblem Books', in his *The English Emblem and the Continental Tradition* (New York, 1988), pp.1-60.

**45.** Adolph Occo, *Impp. Romanorum numismata* (Antwerp, 1579), sig.*2.

**46.** Jan Casper Gevaerts, *Pompa Introitus honori Serenissimi Principis Ferdinandi…* (Antwerp, [1641-42]). John Ogilby, *The Entertainment of His Most Excellent Majestie Charles II*, introduced by Ronald Knowles (Binghampton, New York, 1988).

**47.** Christian Weise, *De Poesi Hodiernorum Politicorum sive de Argutis Inscriptionibus Libri II* (Weissenfels, 1678), p.90.

**48.** David Howarth, *Lord Arundel and his Circle* (New Haven and London, 1985), pp.108-14, 156-61.

Elly Cockx-Indestege

# Poems by Cornelis Kiliaan on engravings by Theodor Galle

In the early years of the 17th century the Latin poetry written by the Antwerp humanist Cornelis Kiliaan was collected and copied in a manuscript, which is still preserved in the Museum Plantin-Moretus (Shelf-mark M 14.2*). In 1880 the collection was published by Max Rooses, first curator of the Museum after the Officina Plantiniana was bought by the city of Antwerp.[1]

When collecting material for the bibliography of Kiliaan,[2] I was struck by the fact that hardly any of these poems seemed to have been published during his lifetime. A few of them appeared in the preliminaries of works by other authors.[3] The majority however were never collected in book form (until Rooses's edition) but remained hidden as a humble accompaniment to engraved scenes. A hunting-party in some 20 printrooms in and outside Belgium yielded some good results.[4] Nevertheless, a number of these poems, preserved in the Antwerp manuscript, have not yet emerged in contemporary prints; on the other hand, other ones, unknown to Rooses, have been discovered.

Cornelis Kiliaan (1530?-1607) is above all known for his philological work. His *Dictionarium Teutonico-Latinum*, published for the first time in 1574 by Christopher Plantin, is the first dictionary on a scientific base, to be considered as a standard in the history of the Netherlandic language.[5] Kiliaan served as a proofreader in the Officina Plantiniana and was encouraged by Christopher Plantin himself to do research in the field of lexicography. In 1777 the last 'old' edition was published. Kiliaan is known also for two important translations, one from the French and one from the Italian into his native tongue: Philippe de Commines (1445-1509) and Ludovico Guicciardini (1523-89).

In his spare moments however Kiliaan exercised himself as a part-time Latin poet: compositions in honour of a friend or a famous writer, or as a 'laudatio post mortem', or whatever else came to his mind. He seems to have taken pleasure in writing shorter poems, often just a few lines, to 'illustrate' engravings. This kind of harmless pastime is not at all uncommon among Low Countries humanists in the second half of the 16th and the first half of the 17th century.[6] Famous artists and engravers, among them members of the Galle family, joined these circles and were probably more than once looking for poets willing to spin off a distich or a quatrain as an explanation of (mostly) biblical or mythological scenes.[7]

Poetry of this kind generally has only seldom caught the attention of bibliographers: actually most of these 'lucubratiunculae' still remain hidden in collections of

84 . Elly Cockx-Indestege

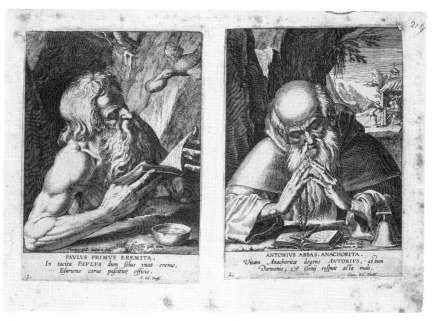

Fig. 1                                          Fig. 2

Figs 1-6, Basel, Kupferstichkabinett

HILARION EREMITA, MONACHVS .
HILLARION uvenis deserta petit loca: carnem
Edomat, in Domino demoriturq; senex.

ABRAHAMIVS CONFESSOR, EREMITA.
Cælatus ostensi secessum ABRAHAMIVS antri
Incolit, a turbis dum procul esse cupit.

Fig. 3                Fig. 4

MALCHVS CAPTIVVS, MONACHVS.
A Sarracenis captus MALCHVS, fit ouilis
Custos: fit Monachus, sicut et ante, redux.

IOANNES AEGYPTIVS, MONACHVS.
Inuia IOANNES sub rupe latendo, dolosas
Mundi fallacis defugit illecebras.

Fig. 5                Fig. 6

engravings, without having been published in book form during their author's lifetime; moreover, they often do not rate highly. On the other hand, art historians and
curators in charge of drawings and engravings have rarely paid attention to the texts
underneath the representations – although now fortunately a changing attitude is
emerging.[8] Even if the literary value of this poetry is not that high, it seems equitable
to render unto Caesar what is due to him.

The very nature of this writing activity makes it clear that lists of engravings with
texts by a specific poet will rarely be complete. Since our bibliography of Kiliaan was
published, new items have been amassed. Some important copies of his dictionary
were brought to our attention,[9] as well as a couple of pre- and postliminary poems
hidden in the works of other people,[10] and no doubt a few more will come to light. As
to Kiliaan's contributions to the projects of his friends in the artistic circles in
Antwerp, we found many more copies or states or editions of engravings already
described.[11] The harvest also included engravings, only now linked to Kiliaan. One set
of these will be presented here.[12]

## [Solitudo sive Vitae patrum anachoritarum]

A series of six (?) numbered engravings (145 × 115mm), drawn and engraved by Theodor Galle, published by Philip Galle. The praying hermits are represented down to
the waist in various attitudes, in a landscape; below follow their names and a distich.
(See figs.1-6.) Each plate is signed *C. Kil. Duffl.* (pl.2: *Corn. Kil. Duffl.*). At the bottom, to
the left, appears a numbering in Arabic numerals. The text, not in Rooses' edition,
runs as follows:

1. PAVLVS PRIMVS EREMITA
In tacita PAVLVS dum solus viuit eremo,
Esuriens corui pascitur officio.

In the silent desert, Paul, the first of hermits,
is fed by a raven.

2. ANTONIVS ABBAS, ANACHORITA
Vitam Anachoritae degens ANTONIVS, astum
Daemonis, & Genij respuit acta mali.

Abbot Anthony is the anchorite fighting all
his life against the Devil and the Bad Genius.

3. HILARION EREMITA, MONACHVS
HILLARION iuvenis deserta petit loca: carnem
Edomat, in Domino demoriturq[ue] senex.

The monk Hilarion came young to the desert;
he subdued the Flesh and died in old age.

4. ABRAHAMIVS CONFESSOR, EREMITA
Coelitus ostensi secessum, ABRAHAMIVS antri
Incolit, à turbis dum procul esse cupit.

Withdrawn in a cavern, Abraham the confessor
desires to live far away from tumult and turbulence.

5. MALCHVS CAPTIVVS, MONACHVS
A Sarracenis captus MALCHVS, fit ouilis
Custos: fit Monachus, sicut et ante, redux.

Taken captive by the Saracens, the monk Malchus
was made a shepherd, and later a monk again.

6. IOANNES AEGYPTIVS, MONACHVS
Invia IOANNES sub rupe latendo, dolosas
Mundi fallacis defugit illecebras.

Living in a cave, John of Egypt could resist
the betrayal of the fallacious world.

It is however not to be ruled out that the engravings are part of a larger series, possibly
published with a title-page, as was the *Solitudo, sive vitae foeminarum anachoritarum*, a
similar series of 24 numbered engravings with a title-page.[13] There are, moreover,
more than just these six hermits! Indeed there happens to be another series, with a
completely different text, drawn by Maarten de Vos, engraved and published by
Johannes I and Raphael I Sadeler,[14] in which these six names appear in the very same
order, but are followed by 23 other desert Fathers.[15]

*Copies*
BASEL, Kupferstichkabinett, Inv.1857. II Bd. M 82 pp. 217-19, Galle, Theodor (the
plates are trimmed and pasted, two on one leaf, in a oblong 'Sammelband').
COBURG, Veste, Kupferstichkabinett, Galle T. VII, 117, 47-52.
FRANKFURT AM MAIN, Städelsches Kunstinstitut, Gr.Slg., Th.Galle 50032
(pl. 2 only).
MUNICH, Staatliche Graphische Sammlung, Galle J. & Th.560, 37877-80 + 102145-
46.

## Notes

1. *Kilianus Latijnsche gedichten*, edited by Max
Rooses, Maatschappij der Antwerpsche
Bibliophilen, 6 (Antwerp, 1880).

2. Lode van den Branden, Elly Cockx-
Indestege and Frans Sillis, *Bio-bibliografie van
Cornelis Kiliaan*, Bibliotheca Bibliographica
Neerlandica, II (Nieuwkoop, 1978).

3. *Bio-bibliografie*, nos.30-42.

4. *Bio-bibliografie*, nos.43-83.

5. For the use of 'Dutch', 'Flemish', and
'Netherlandic' see O. Vandeputte, P. Vincent

and T. Hermans, *Dutch: the language of twenty
million Dutch and Flemish people* (Rekkem, 1989).

6. Some other names are Caspar Barlaeus
senior (†1595) and Johannes Bochius (†1609),
both town clerks of Antwerp; Laurentius
Beyerlinck (†1627), a humanist priest in the
same city; Hugo Favolius (†1585), Victor
Giselinus (†1595), Hugo Grotius (†1645),
Willem van Haecht (†1603) and Cornelis
Schonaeus (†1611).
    Recently a lesser known poet was studied
by A. Hamilton and C. L. Heesakkers,
'Bernardus Sellius Noviomagus (*c.*1551-93),
proof-reader and poet', *Quaerendo*, 19 (1989),
pp.163-224.

7. See E. Cockx-Indestege, 'Hugo Favolius ludebat: woord en beeld op Vlaamse prenten uit de 16de en 17de eeuw' in *Liber amicorum Leon Voet*, edited by F. de Nave, De Gulden Passer, 61-63 (1983-85), (Antwerp, 1985), pp.505-17.

8. See *eg* the excellent monograph by Ilja Veldman, *Maarten van Heemskerck and Dutch humanism in the sixteenth century* (Maarssen, 1977) and volumes of Hollstein's *Dutch and Flemish etchings, engravings and woodcuts ca.1450-1700* (Amsterdam, 1949-) where at least the incipits of the verses are included).

9. A copy of the *Etymologicum* of 1613 (*Bio-bibliografie*, no.16d, Sint-Andriesabdij, Bruges) had been prepared for a new edition by the Utrecht lawyer C. A. van Wachendorff (1737-1810), to be published by P. van der Eyk at Leiden and F. Houttuin at Amsterdam. See W. Couvreur, 'C. A. van Wachendorffs vermeerderde Kiliaanuitgave: een bijdrage tot de studie der XVIIIde-eeuwse leksikografie', *Studia Germanica Gandensia*, 7 (1965), pp.9-24; with thanks to Father J. D. Broekaert. H. Chr. van Bemmel gave some additions in *Dokumentaal*, 10 (1981), pp.90-91.

10. The late D. Grosheide, former director of Utrecht University Library, brought to my attention a 14-line poem 'In Bibliotheca Francisci Sweertii', published in the latter's *Athenae Belgicae sive Nomenclator* (Antverpiae, G. a Tungris, 1628, f.55); *cf. Kilianus Latijnsche gedichten* p.20. My colleague M. de Schepper came across a poem of 17 lines entitled 'D. Ricardo Verstegano viro cl. nationis et linguae veteris Anglicanae restauratori', published in Richard Verstegen, *A Restitution of decayed intelligence in antiquities, concerning the… English nation* (Antwerp, R. Bruney for I. Norton and I. Bill in London, 1605, f. ++4), *STC*, second edition, 21361. With thanks to both of them.

11. We had the opportunity, generously supported by the Ministry of Education, to visit between *c.*1976 and 1982 about 30 collections in The Netherlands, Germany, Switzerland, Italy, France, England and the United States. All this material will be presented later as a Supplement.

12. Not in Hollstein.

13. *Bio-bibliografie*, no.52.

14. Hollstein, XXI, 377-406: Solitudo sive vitae patrum eremicolarum.

15. Their names are: Theonas, Apollonius, Mutius, Helanus, Johannes, Paphnutius, Didymus, Helias, Spiridius, Eulogius, Apelles, Origines, Evagrius, Or, Copres, Macharius, Macharius Alexandrinus, Anub, Ciomus, Ammon, Onofrius, Piamon, Hieronymus.

A. F. Allison

# *Leonardus Lessius of Louvain and his English translator*

Of the many works listed in bibliographies under the Belgian[1] Jesuit theologian, Leonardus Lessius (1554-1623), one, his *Defensio potestatis summi pontificis*, 1611, has always been something of a mystery. The earliest bibliography to mention it, Philippe Alegambe's *Bibliotheca scriptorum Societatis Iesu*, 1643, simply quotes its title, with the comment: 'It was indeed printed but, up till now, has been for good reason suppressed'. Alegambe does not say where it was printed or what the reason was for suppressing it. Nathaniel Southwell, whose revised and enlarged edition of Alegambe, published in 1676, forms the basis of all subsequent bibliographies of the Society, merely repeats the comment without further explanation. About 60 years ago, two Belgian Jesuits published extracts from documents that throw some light on the mystery. Alfred Poncelet, in his history of the ancient Belgian provinces of the Society, published in 1926,[2] and Charles van Sull, in the enlarged French version of his life of Lessius, published in 1930,[3] drew upon letters from the Jesuit General at Rome to Belgian provincials at the time when Lessius wrote the work. From these it appears that the General stopped its distribution after it had been printed, in deference to the Jesuits of the neighbouring province of France who believed that it would provoke the French government into taking reprisals against them even though they themselves were not responsible for its publication. Since the time of Poncelet and Van Sull further evidence has come to light. Letters from King James I's agent at Brussels, William Trumbull, reveal that the original intention was to print the book at Antwerp, but the local authorities refused it a licence on the orders of the Archduke who feared the political consequences if it were allowed to appear. It was nevertheless put into print, though Trumbull was uncertain where; he believed it was sent to Germany for the purpose. Recently, several copies of the book have been found and an examination of the typography shows that it was produced at the press of the English Jesuits at their college at Saint-Omer which enjoyed special privileges in regard to licensing and censorship. The College printed, at the same time, an English summary of Lessius's work, and this was freely circulated, though the ban on the original was never lifted. In the present article I shall try to draw the various strands in the story together.

Lessius wrote the *Defensio* in 1609 as a contribution to the dispute arising out of James I's oath of allegiance of 1606. It is an answer mainly to the Scottish Catholic jurist, William Barclay, whose *De potestate papae* was published posthumously at

London in 1609 under English government auspices.[4] Barclay argued that there was no sound reason to regard as *de fide* the mediaeval doctrine of the papal deposing power which the oath required English Catholics to repudiate. According to this doctrine, the pope had some authority over secular princes even in temporal matters and could, in extreme cases where the good of the commonwealth demanded it, release a monarch's subjects from their allegiance to him, thereby paving the way for his removal and replacement. It is important to note, in this connection, that refusal to take the oath did not necessarily imply acceptance of the deposing power; some leading English Catholics, such as William Bishop who was later made bishop for England, rejected the doctrine but condemned the oath as unacceptable in the form in which it was presented. Nevertheless, although it was becoming increasingly unlikely that the pope would ever again invoke the power, the central Catholic tradition held that the doctrine could not be denied because popes and councils in earlier times had made pronouncements that rendered it *de fide*. To reinforce this tradition, Pope Paul V invited three eminent Jesuit theologians, Lessius, Bellarmine and Suarez, to enter the controversy.

The Jesuit General, Claudio Acquaviva, wrote to the Belgian provincial, François Fléron, on 29 August 1609, that the Pope himself wanted Lessius to write in defence of the papacy against King James.[5] Lessius set to work immediately and, by the beginning of 1610, sent to Rome for approval the manuscripts of two separate treatises. One, entitled *De Antichristo et eius praecursoribus*, dealt with James's claim, in the 'Praefatio monitoria' to the 1609 edition of his *Triplici nodo triplex cuneus*,[6] that the pope was Antichrist. *De Antichristo* was passed by the censors at Rome, sent back to Belgium, given an approbation by the public censor at Louvain, and printed early in 1611 by the firm of Moretus at the Plantin press at Antwerp.[7] The other treatise, answering Barclay and treating of the whole question of papal authority, spiritual and temporal, was the *Defensio potestatis summi pontificis*. This also was passed by the Roman censors and sent back to Belgium where it was given an approbation by the same Louvain censor before being passed for printing to Moretus at Antwerp. But at this point difficulties arose because of political interference by France. We learn about what happened from Trumbull's letters to the English secretary of state, Robert Cecil, Earl of Salisbury. Trumbull informed Salisbury on 10/20 April 1611[8] that the French Ambassador to the Archduke had lodged a complaint at the court at Brussels, and also with the Papal Nuncio, about a passage in the recently published *De Antichristo* deemed prejudicial to the sovereign rights of princes. Trumbull does not identify the passage in question. The Archduke, it seems, though he refused to have the book called in and the offending words excised, nevertheless took fright at allowing the *Defensio* to be published, as this dealt extensively with the same sensitive theme. Moretus was refused a licence to print it. On 28 August 1611,[9] Trumbull commented in a letter to Salisbury that the Belgian authorities, solidly Catholic though they were, had little enthusiasm for the doctrine of the deposing power. The *Defensio*, he said, had now been printed, but not in Belgium. 'Even in this nest of superstition,' he observed, it had proved impossible to obtain a licence for it, and so it 'was sent to Cologne or Mainz for that purpose and is forthwith to be divulged'. Trumbull was correct in reporting that the book was now in print but his surmise that it was sent to Germany for printing was, as I shall show, unfounded.

While these events were taking place in Belgium, the Jesuits in France, knowing that the *Defensio* was soon to be published, sent an urgent plea to Acquaviva to order its suppression. They feared that their government would take drastic reprisals against them if the book were allowed to appear. It must be recalled that the Jesuits had been readmitted to France as recently as 1603 after several years of banishment. King Henri IV had befriended the Society and, under his protection, it had rapidly regained its former influence, especially in the field of education. When Henri was assassinated, on 17 March 1610, the enemies of the Jesuits, and particularly the Parlement of Paris, accused them of complicity in the murder. The fact that the Jesuits had nothing to gain and everything to lose by the King's death counted for little in the hysterical atmosphere in Paris in the closing months of 1610. They became convinced that the Queen Regent, though she was personally friendly towards them, would find herself powerless to resist pressure to banish them once again and so undo at a stroke all that had been achieved in the previous six years. On 20 November, the Parlement publicly condemned Bellarmine's *Tractatus de potestate summi pontificis*[10] which had been written at the Pope's request and published at Rome earlier in the year. This, it seems, was the signal that finally prompted the French Jesuits to appeal to the General.

Acquaviva was in a difficult position. He well understood the threat to the Society in France, but on the other hand the Pope himself had asked Lessius to write the book. On 11 December,[11] he wrote to the Belgian Provincial, Fléron, praising the work as 'a magisterial defence of the dignity and authority of the Supreme Pontiff' but instructing him to suspend publication temporarily because of the situation in France. Two months later, for reasons undisclosed, he changed his mind. He wrote to Fléron on 5 February 1611,[12] giving him permission to proceed with printing. After another two months he changed his mind again, instructing Fléron on 16 April[13] that, notwithstanding the permission he had given earlier, publication must be halted. The Pope, he said, had agreed. But, by the time Fléron received this last letter, printing had already been completed and two copies of the book were on their way to Rome for final approval before publication. Acquaviva sent word to Lessius on 21 May[14] that he had given a copy to the Pope who had expressed himself well pleased with the work; nevertheless, it was not to be published for the time being, for reasons he had already given the Provincial. He repeated this instruction in a letter to Fléron of 28 May.[15] There is nothing in Acquaviva's letters to suggest that he knew about the difficulty Fléron had experienced in getting the book printed in Belgium. The Belgian Jesuits, at their provincial congregation of 1611, sent a request to the General to allow them to issue the book under a pseudonym, if that were thought desirable, but Acquaviva refused. He told Fléron, in a letter of 2 July 1611,[16] that it was better to delay publication until the book could appear under the author's real name, as his great reputation as a theologian would lend added weight to the arguments presented in it.

Until quite recently, no copy of the printed *Defensio* was thought to have survived. Poncelet and Van Sull, writing in the 1920s, were familiar with the text in a 17th-century manuscript version preserved in the Royal Library at Brussels, but the only copy of the printed version of which they had any record had been destroyed in 1914 when the Germans fired the old library of the University of Louvain. We now know that three copies are still extant, two of them in Italy (perhaps the two that Fléron sent to Rome in 1611)[17] and one at Lambeth Palace in London.[18] This last, as I shall show, appears to have been prepared for issue in 1613, two years after the date of printing. The title-page (as printed in 1611) reads as follows: *Defensio potestatis summi pontificis, aduersus librum regis Magnae Britanniae, Guilielmi Barclaii Scoti, & M. Georgii Blacuelli. Authore Leonardo Lessio Societatis Iesu sacrae theologiae professore.* Caesaraugustae, apud Christophorum Iouium. M.DC.XI. The collation is as follows: 4°.a-c⁴ A-Fff⁴. Pp.[i-xxiv] + [1] 2-416. The preliminaries (a-c⁴) include the approbation given by the Louvain censor on 14 September 1610 and a dedicatory epistle to the Emperor and the Christian princes of Europe to whom King James had directed his appeal in the 'Praefatio monitoria'.

The imprint 'Caesaraugustae, apud Christophorum Iouium' is plainly fictitious; there was no printer of this name at Saragossa. Types and ornaments used in the book show that it was printed at the press of the English Jesuits at Saint-Omer. The main typographical characteristics of that press are described and illustrated by the late Father C. A. Newdigate SJ, in an article he contributed to *The Library* in 1919.[19] Lessius's *Defensio* contains the following features described by Newdigate: the 58, 46 and 35 mm types (article, p.223), the 28 mm ornamental initials (article, p.224), and the very characteristic tailpiece in which the arabesque design has been cut on the block at a slight angle to the perpendicular, giving the whole figure a pronounced tilt to the right (article, p.227). Newdigate never saw the *Defensio* or he would certainly have included it in his list of books printed at the press (article, pp.230-42).

Fléron's motive in sending the book to Saint-Omer to be printed was undoubtedly to circumvent the Archduke's order without losing control over publication himself, as would have happened if he had sent it outside the boundaries of the Belgian province. The college press at Saint-Omer, set up in 1607, existed to serve the needs of the mission to England and, for this reason, was exempt from customary civil and ecclesiastical licensing regulations. The English Jesuits kept the local ordinary, the Bishop of Saint-Omer, informed about the books they intended to print and accepted his judgment on them, but otherwise were subject to no regional constraints.[20] The Bishop, at this period, was Jacques Blaise OFM, a close friend and great benefactor of the College. As regards relations with the Belgian Province of the Society, the English Jesuits, though more or less independent of it and subject directly to the General at Rome, were nevertheless bound by their regulations to cooperate with the Belgian Provincial in all matters overlapping his sphere of jurisdiction. The Vice-President of the English mission had his office at Brussels where he could keep in close touch with the Provincial. Moreover, as part of the policy of maintaining a smooth relationship with the Belgian Jesuits, the Rector in charge of the English community and pupils at the College at Saint-Omer was, at this period, always a Belgian.

The *Defensio* was not the usual type of book handled by the college press, but good reasons could be found for printing it there. The English Jesuits believed there was a practical need to have the book in print as a means of stopping the flow of Catholics in England who were being induced to take the oath of allegiance by the arguments of Barclay and others. As we shall see, they themselves were soon to publish a shortened version of the work in English which would serve as an introduction to the original. Printing the *Defensio* was not, in fact, the first incursion by the press into the controversy arising out of the oath. In 1608 it had reprinted Bellarmine's *Responsio* (answering supporters of the oath) from the Cologne edition of the same year,[21] and in 1610 the same work again, together with the author's defence of it, the *Apologia*, from the Rome edition of the two works together published in 1609.[22] Neither of these reprints discloses the true place of printing but both are attributable to the college press on typographical grounds, and, in the case of the second, there is corroborative testimony by Trumbull. Writing to Salisbury on 6 December 1609,[23] Trumbull reported that Bellarmine had sent the Archduke a copy of the Rome edition of the joint *Responsio* and *Apologia*, and he added: 'It is said here that the said book shall forthwith be printed [*ie* reprinted] at S.Omers'.

Acquaviva's injunction of May 1611 effectively prevented the *Defensio* from being generally distributed after it was printed. The stock was evidently moved from the college and kept somewhere under lock and key; later correspondence between the General and Belgian provincials seems to indicate that it was held in or near Antwerp. Just a few copies circulated privately among Jesuit houses and certain trusted individuals. But the English Jesuits had also printed at their press at Saint-Omer a shortened version of the work in English which they distributed among English Catholics, apparently without hindrance. It was entitled: *A briefe and cleare declaration of sundry pointes absolutely dislyked in the lately enacted oath of allegiance.* It bore the date 1611 but had no imprint.[24] Fr. Newdigate identified the place of printing from typographical evidence and included the book in his bibliography of the press.[25] Though the English compiler masks his identity under the initials I. H. (the precise significance of which is not known) all the early Jesuit bibliographers concur in identifying him as Anthony Hoskins. Their testimony fits in with what we know about Hoskins's life at this period from other sources. In 1609, after working for several years as a missionary priest in England, he was sent to Brussels as vice-prefect of the English Jesuit mission in Belgium, a post he held until early 1613[26] when he went to Madrid to succeed Joseph Creswell as vice-prefect in Spain. His official duties in Belgium took him on periodic visits both to Saint-Omer and to Louvain where the English Jesuits had their theologate, and at Louvain he may well have made the acquaintance of Lessius, though we have no firm evidence of this. It is certain, however, that at Brussels he was closely associated with the Belgian provincial, Fléron, who would have informed him about the Archduke's ban on the *Defensio*. We may assume that Hoskins, having read the work and recognised its importance, concurred with the idea of printing it at Saint Omer and also decided to prepare a shortened version of it in English and have that printed at the college press as well. Hoskins was a man of outstanding gifts, literary as well as administrative. While he was at Brussels he published at Saint-Omer for the benefit of English Catholics more than one translation which he himself had either made or supervised.[27]

*A briefe and cleare declaration* does not mention Lessius by name or give the title of the original Latin, but its preface addressed to English readers provides hints that some among them would certainly understand. Dated 1 April 1611 and signed H. I., it includes the following passages:

There is lately come to my hands a book, which both learnedly & largely treateth of this subject, in so solid and exquisite a manner, as were it to be had in England (which I think as yet is not) I doubt not, but by reading thereof, thou wouldst receive full satisfaction… The book itself is in Latin, and greater than can be translated in few days: and of the Latin copies I think few are yet to be had. That therefore thou mayest have some taste in the meantime of that, whereof thou shalt hereafter, as I hope, be able to satisfy thyself in more full manner; I send thee in as few words as I can the sum and substance of this work… And if by reason of the brevity which I intend I shall sometimes seem obscure: thou mayest shortly chance to have a view of the book itself, and from thence receive a more plain and clear explication of what thou desirest.

The English summary – a short book of only 56 pages – follows the order of the Latin fairly closely but treats some sections more fully than others. Lessius divides his work into two parts, the first dealing with the pope's primacy over the universal church, the second with his authority over princes in temporal matters. The résumé of part 1 merely states the main points briefly, adding that the author proves them from various authorities. In part 2, however, the summary becomes fuller, and throughout the last two sections of this part, where Lessius argues that the doctrine of the deposing power is *de fide* and that the oath of allegiance is utterly unacceptable, Hoskins paraphrases extensively and, in places, translates word for word. Thus, the very parts of the work which had caused the Latin to be suppressed were made freely available in an English version. The English Jesuits were not required to seek permission from Rome before printing books for use on the mission; they had been exempted from any such obligation in the regulations specially drawn up for them by Acquaviva himself. The words 'Permissu Superiorum' which are printed at the foot of the title-page of *A briefe and cleare declaration* merely indicate that it was passed by the local English Jesuit censors. If Acquaviva ever knew about Hoskins's version of Lessius, it would seem that he took no notice of it; I have found no reference to it in his extant letters to the English superiors. The early Jesuit bibliographers enter the work under Hoskins without mentioning that it is a translation or adaptation. Alegambe, for example, says of it simply that Hoskins 'wrote in English against the oath of allegiance imposed by the King on the Catholics of England', adding that it was printed at Saint-Omer in 4°.

The English summary was in circulation by 24 July 1611 when Trumbull reported to Salisbury that he had heard about it but not yet seen it.[28] On 28 August[29] he wrote to Salisbury again, saying that he had now seen it and could confirm that it was a 'compendium of a great volume written by one Lessius a father of that Society in Louvain'. On 3 October,[30] he reported: 'Lessius the Jesuit hath printed but not yet published his book of the Pope's authority in temporals whereof the English translation mentioned in my former letters (which before only by conjecture was esteemed to be his) is now indeed found to be a compendium. Those of his Society and their special friends have copies of the said book presented unto them for their private use, but others … are not permitted to have the view thereof'. It is not clear from this whether Trumbull had managed to see the original himself or was quoting from hearsay. Throughout October 1611 his agents at Antwerp scoured the city for a copy of it that he could send to Salisbury, but without success. On 10 November,[31] John

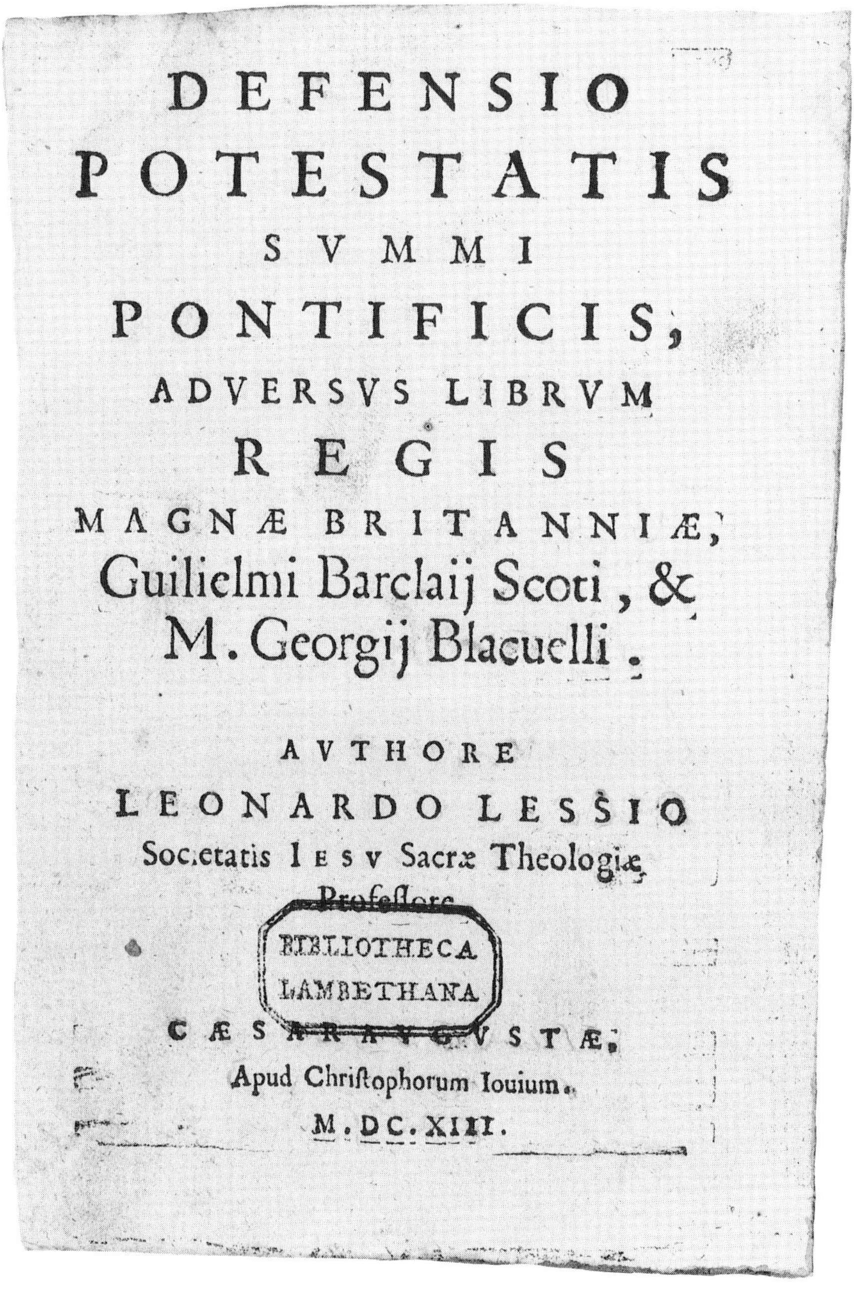

DEFENSIO
POTESTATIS
SVMMI
PONTIFICIS,
ADVERSVS LIBRVM
REGIS
MAGNÆ BRITANNIÆ,
Guilielmi Barclaij Scoti, &
M. Georgij Blacuelli.

AVTHORE
LEONARDO LESSIO
Soc.etatis I E S V Sacræ Theologiæ
Professore

CÆSARAVGVSTÆ,
Apud Chriſtophorum Iouium.
M.DC.XIII.

Fig.1   Lambeth Palace Library. H1810 L3. Showing the date in the imprint altered by pen
from M.DC.XI. to M.DC.XIII.

Brownlow informed him from Antwerp that it was not to be found. That is the last reference to the book that I have traced in Trumbull's extant letters and papers.

Hoskins's summary appears to have been sent to England as soon as it was published in 1611. Thomas Preston (alias Roger Widdrington), the English Benedictine who publicly supported the government over the oath, was familiar with it soon after it appeared. In his *Responsio apologetica* (a reply to an unpublished work by the English secular priest, Edward Weston),[32] which he completed before August 1612, Preston complained that a whole year had passed since the publication of the English summary which had promised its readers that they would soon have the Latin original. But the original, he said, was still not obtainable; it was not even available to Catholics in general but only to a few who had to pledge themselves not to pass it on to others. Here he seems to be echoing Trumbull's words and it is not clear whether he knew for certain that copies had found their way to England. The secular priest, Robert Pett, who lived at Brussels and sent from there a copy of Preston's *Responsio* to the clergy's agent at Rome, Thomas More, seems to have been of the opinion that Lessius's *Defensio* had already arrived in England. In his covering letter to More, dated 4 August 1612,[33] Pett remarks of Preston's work: 'You will perceive by it that he seemeth to take no knowledge that Lessius his book is come into England'.

Preston did not see the original before about the middle of 1613. He says in the preface to his *Disputatio theologica*, 1613 (answering several continental theologians who had attacked the oath),[34] that he first saw the Latin while his own work was in the press. This preface is dated 1 June 1613. He evidently saw the original in time not only to make numerous marginal references to it but also to introduce one or two short verbatim passages from it into his own text. It is not known how or where Preston obtained sight of the work, but all his references to it show one very marked peculiarity: though the page and section numbers that he cites correspond exactly to those in the printed edition we have been describing, he always refers to the work by the head-title which precedes the text on p.[1]: *Disputatio apologetica de summi pontificis potestate*, and never by the title-page title: *Defensio potestatis summi pontificis.* This suggests that the copy he saw lacked the title-leaf. If so, it has probably not been preserved. The only copy now known outside Italy is at Lambeth Palace in the collection formed by George Abbot, Archbishop of Canterbury (1562-1633), and this has the title-leaf. As there appears to be no record of Trumbull's having sent a copy to England, the probability would seem to be that Abbot acquired it during one of the many searches of Catholic property in England that he organised. Abbot's copy appears to have been prepared – or, at least, half-prepared – for issue in 1613. The date in the imprint has been skilfully altered by adding two digits in manuscript to the original printed figure, turning M.DC.XI. into M.DC.XIII. The preliminaries that followed the title-leaf have been removed. As these had consisted mainly of a dedicatory epistle to the Emperor Rudolf II who died in 1612, the excision was probably deliberate, and there may have been an intention to replace it with something else. Apart from the missing preliminaries, the copy is well preserved.

Acquaviva had intended the ban on the *Defensio* to be temporary, but it was never lifted, for the situation in France continued to deteriorate. In June 1614 the Parlement of Paris condemned and ordered to be publicly burned the work on the same topic by

Francisco Suarez which the Pope had also commissioned, *Defensio fidei Catholicae*, 1613 (reprinted 1614).[35] Before his death, Acquaviva issued fresh instructions forbidding members of the Society to publish books on the subject before submitting the text to Rome for approval. He died on 31 January 1615. In April, the Vicar-General, Ferdinand Alberus, reaffirmed the ban on Lessius's work, ordering the Provincial, Jean Herrenius, to have all copies of it that had found their way into Jesuit houses, together with any others in private hands that he could reach, called in and stored with the main stock.[36] The new General, Mutio Vitelleschi, elected in 1616, pursued the same policy. On 25 May 1624,[37] six months after Lessius's death, he wrote to the Flandro-Belgic Provincial, Florent de Montmorency, who had appealed to him to change his mind, that the *Defensio* could not be put into circulation without raising a storm against the Society in France; it was preferable, he said, to suppress a book, no matter how excellent, than to stir up such trouble. The condemnation by the Paris Parlement in 1626 of the *De omnipotentia pontificis* of the Italian Jesuit, Antonio Santarelli, which, in spite of the General's prohibition, had treated of the deposing power, confirmed Vitelleschi in his determination. He had the wholehearted support of the Pope. Urban VIII was less concerned than Paul V had been to insist on the rights of the papacy if that meant endangering the unity of the Church. Vitelleschi wrote to Montmorency on 25 July 1626[38] ordering him in the Pope's name to gather together any copies of the book still at large and to make sure that the stock was kept in a safe place under lock and key, and to allow no one to have access to it. Montmorency was to write and confirm that he had done this so that the Pope could be informed. The last reference to the book found in the General's letters is in a reply by Vitelleschi on 28 December 1641[39] to yet another appeal by Montmorency, now Gallo-Belgic Provincial. Reaffirming his refusal, Vitelleschi wrote: 'It is better that the book should be destroyed by worms and beetles, or even by domestic conflagration, than by officials of the state'. How long after this the stock was kept is not known. The *Defensio* was never published. By the middle of the century the circumstances that had caused it to be written belonged to the distant past. It was pointless to continue to insist on a doctrine which had lost all relevance to the realities of political life.

## Notes

The following abbreviations are used:

| | |
|---|---|
| AAW | Archives of the Archdiocese of Westminster. |
| A&R | A. F. Allison and D. M. Rogers, *A Catalogue of Catholic Books in English printed abroad or secretly in England, 1558-1640* (Bognor Regis, 1956). |
| ARCR | A. F. Allison and D. M. Rogers, *The Contemporary Printed Literature of the English Counter-Reformation between 1558 and 1640*. Vol.I. Works in Languages other than English (London, 1989). |
| HMC Downshire | Historical Manuscripts Commission. Report on the Manuscripts of the Marquess of Downshire. Vols.2–4. Papers of William Trumbull the Elder (London, 1936-40). |
| SP 77 | Public Record Office, London, State Papers, Flanders. |
| STC | A. W. Pollard and G. R. Redgrave, *A Short-title Catalogue of Books printed in England, Scotland, & Ireland and of English Books printed abroad, 1475-1640*. 2nd Edition, completed by Katharine F. Pantzer. 2 vols. (London, 1976, 1986). |

1. In this article the words 'Belgium' and 'Belgian' are used for convenience to refer to the whole of the former Spanish Netherlands. It must be remembered that the territory included at its southern extremity the province of Artois in which Saint-Omer was situated. Though Artois became part of northern France in 1659 and has remained so ever since, at the time when the events described here were taking place it was Spanish and governed from Brussels.

2. A. Poncelet, *Histoire de la Compagnie de Jésus dans les anciens Pays-Bas*, Académie Royale de Belgique. Classe des Lettres, etc, Mémoires, sér.2, tom.21, 21² (Brussels, 1926). Up to 1612 the whole of the Spanish Netherlands formed a single Jesuit province. On 10 May 1612 the territory was divided into two separate provinces, the Flandro-Belgic, with its centre at Antwerp, and the Gallo-Belgic, with its centre at Brussels.

3. C. van Sull, *Léonard Lessius de la Compagnie de Jésus*, 1554-1623, Editions du Museum Lessianum (Louvain, Paris, Brussels, 1930).

4. ARCR vol.1, nos.53.1-53.3. *STC* 1408, 1408.3.

5. Poncelet, ii 520. Van Sull, p.216.

6. *STC* 14401-2.

7. See note to ARCR vol.1, no.1534.

8. SP77/10 f.59.

9. SP77/10 f.109.

10. ARCR vol.1, no.1505.

11. Poncelet, ii 520. Van Sull, pp. 219-20.

12. Poncelet, ii 521. Van Sull, p.220.

13. Poncelet, ii 521.

14. Van Sull, p.220.

15. Poncelet, ii 521.

16. Poncelet, ii 521.

17. (1) Vatican Library. Barberini Stamp. G.VIII.128. (2) Naples, Biblioteca Nazionale, 12.K.14.

18. Shelf-mark: H 1810 L3.

19. 'Notes on the Seventeenth Century Printing Press of the English College at Saint Omers', *The Library*, 3rd series, vol.10 (1919), 179-90; 223-42.

20. See the report of Guido Bentivoglio, Papal Nucio at Brussels, 7 March 1615, in Raffaele Belvederi, *Guido Bentivoglio Diplomatico*, 2 vols (Rovigo, 1948), ii 345.

21. ARCR vol.1, no.1503.

22. ARCR vol.1, no.1492.

23. SP 77/9 ff.297-8.

24. A&R 405. STC 13840.

25. Newdigate, p.232.

26. For his life, see Henry Foley, *Records of the English Province of the Society of Jesus*, 7 vols. (London, 1875-83), iv, 392-94. Foley was unable to give the precise date of his departure from Belgium. Trumbull records that he left Brussels for Rome, en route to Spain, soon after 11 February 1613. SP 77/10 ff.259-61, 294-95.

27. A&R 349, 815.

28. SP 77/10 f.103.

29. SP 77/10 f.109.

30. SP 77/10 f.125.

31. HMC Downshire, iii 153,179.

32. ARCR vol.1, no.926.3. *STC* 25597. For the background to this work and for a qualification of the note in the ARCR entry, see A. F. Allison, 'The Later Life and Writings of Joseph Creswell S. J.', *Recusant History*, October 1979, p.112.

33. AAW A11 no.132.

34. ARCR vol.1, no.925.6. *STC* 25602.

35. ARCR vol.1, nos.1541-2.

36. Poncelet, ii 521. Van Sull, p.223.

37. Poncelet, ii 521-2. Van Sull, p.224.

38. Van Sull, p.224.

39. Poncelet, ii 522. Van Sull, p.225.

Theo Bögels

# The City of Leiden v Jan Claesz van Dorp, bookseller

In 1617 the annual festivities of 3 October celebrating Leiden's liberation after the Spanish siege in 1575 ended in a riot. Dissatisfied citizens started to challenge the soldiers hired by the city's magistrates, the *waardgelders*, who were standing guard in front of the city hall. They were only too pleased to answer these provocations with violence. In the ensuing skirmishes a bullet fired by a solider killed a man who was watching the fight in the street below from his window. The popular outrage was so great that the authorities resorted to military defence tactics. On 5 October strange wooden fences on both sides of the city hall blocked the thoroughfare of the town's main street. From then on visitors to the town hall had to pass through a narrow gate, where they were meticulously searched by the *waardgelders* before being allowed into the presence of the civic authorities.[1]

The highly exceptional presence of paid soldiers in the service of a town is indicative of the tense situation in the Dutch Republic of the second decade of the 17th century. The domestic politics of the early years of independence were marked by the struggle for supremacy between the two major factions. One group consisted of orthodox Calvinists who saw the civic authorities as subservient to the church. Their irreconcilable attitude towards the Catholics gave them the support of the people who regarded them as the victors in the rebellion against the king of Spain who had cruelly tried to suppress the Reformation in the Netherlands. The Twelve Years' Truce which had been concluded with Spain in 1609 was an abomination to them. The political faction, on the other hand, considered the state superior to the church. They found support among many of the wealthy merchants and the more liberal and tolerant Protestants who needed the state to protect their religious freedom against the incessant attacks of orthodoxy. When Arminius, one of the Leiden professors of theology, very carefully began to question the doctrine of predestination, a theological dispute ensued which very quickly turned into a political conflict of such proportions that it threatened to disrupt the young Republic.

After Arminius's death in 1609, a number of ministers presented a request to the States of Holland in which they expressed their dissatisfaction with the Dutch Confession and voiced the wish for its revision. The group supporting this remonstrance were to be called Remonstrants or Arminians and their opponents Contra-Remonstrants. The majority of the States of Holland, the richest and most powerful province under the leadership of Pensionary Johan van Oldenbarneveldt, were

Remonstrant, because they looked upon the growing influence of the church with envy. In the States General there was growing mistrust against the superior attitude taken by Holland. The tide turned in 1615 when Amsterdam, Holland's predominant city, felt threatened in its mercantile independence by Van Oldenbarneveldt's political aspirations and started to undermine his position by turning Contra-Remonstrant. From then on an internally divided Holland was fighting a losing battle.

The army of the Republic, with Prince Maurice as its supreme commander, was in the service of the States General. It is clear that the Prince was unhappy with the Truce with Spain. Now Holland also refused to pay for an army that did not obey her. The so-called Sharp Resolution was accepted in August 1617. It determined that the part of the army for which Holland paid was to obey her rather than the Prince and the cities were given permission to employ *waardgelders* to ensure public order.[2]

To the mostly Contra-Remonstrant population of Leiden the *waardgelders* were felt to be oppressors rather than protectors. They represented the power of the Remonstrant authorities and symbolised the insults they felt were being done to the Prince. When the soldiers marched into the city dressed in uniforms in the Leiden colours red and white, the citizens were reminded of the Spanish soldiers who had worn similar uniforms. The Leiden magistrates were compared to the former Spanish tyrants, especially after they had entrenched themselves in the town hall, protected by the wooden fences, sarcastically nicknamed 'the Arminian bulwark'. From the final months of 1617 until October 1618 the hostilities were often acrimonious, although the Remonstrants naturally complied more than their opponents with the authorities in whom they found protectors. Since Leiden was a university town there were many – in 1617-18 approximately 25[3] – printers and booksellers within its walls and the two factions used their facilities in the vitriolic pamphlet war with great expertise. Of course, writers, printers and disseminators of pamphlets were always very careful to remain anonymous, and usually with success. One bookseller, however, was caught and brought to trial. The proceedings are evidence of the way in which local authorities applied censorship to protect their interests.

On 3 May 1618 the assistant of the Leiden bailiff went to the bookshop of Jan Claesz van Dorp in the Donkersteeg[4] to tell him that he was expected at the town hall on Monday next, 7 May, at 10 am to appear before the Court of Justice. There he was to defend himself against the charge of the bailiff, Loth Huygensz Gael, that he had published seditious pamphlets

serving no other purpose than to misguide unknowing and unprovoked people and the common man and to bring them to error, schisms, seditions and actions against their lawful and loyal government. That, unless the afore-mentioned accused specifically identified the author, he was considered to have written these slanderous pamphlets as well, since they contained neither the authors' nor the printer's names.[5]

Van Dorp was warned that he was going to be made an example of and that the sentence demanded was four years' banishment from Leiden and its liberties. He answered laconically that he would see what he could do.

The wording of the charge against Van Dorp received by the city fathers, who were to act as his judges, was more detailed. He was accused of printing and divulging two anonymous pamphlets, one of which was entitled *Practiicke van den Spaenschen Raet.*[6] This was an expanded version of an earlier, also anonymous, pamphlet with the ambiguous title *Spaensche Raedt,*[7] which had appeared in 1617, in which the author had warned against a Spanish conspiracy to undermine the Republic from within. The title was a direct reference to the Inquisition, the symbol of the Spanish oppression in the Netherlands, which was generally known as the *Bloedraad,* the Council of Blood. The States of Friesland had used it as a political weapon in the struggle for power in the States General by having it reprinted because of its implicit accusation: the advice the Spanish king received from his council corresponded exactly with the activities of the Remonstrants. The more extensive pamphlet for which Van Dorp was responsible accused Van Oldenbarneveldt without mentioning his name, and pointed openly at the Remonstrants as willing instruments in Spanish hands: 'whether these cantankerous people [the Remonstrants] consider the *Spaensche Raedt* a matter for execution and whether they are ordered to do so by our enemy, they may know for themselves. We have always known that they actively practise what our enemy has advised and concluded'.[8] The author observed 'that they are such that they bring this counsel into practice; that their purses are always filled with money; that they travel and move daily from one town to the next; that they spend a lot of money and pay for the expenses of their friends'.[9]

This demagogic agitation against the Remonstrants was probably too unspecific to bring Van Dorp to justice before a Leiden court. The charge against the bookseller, that with the Remonstrants he accused the States of Holland of trying to bring the Netherlands back under Spanish rule, shows that the bailiff had read the implicit accusation correctly, but more substantial and specific evidence was needed for a conviction. The magistrates of Leiden were enraged because of two points mentioned in the pamphlet. Gael quoted them almost literally for the court when he wrote that the pamphlet stated 'that within this city the reformed ministers are forbidden to preach and that the Jesuits and the romish papists are allowed to practise their superstition and tempt people to popery; that also three citizens had been banished from this city because of the practice of the reformed religion'.[10]

For the Leiden administration these were flagrant lies, especially as far as the first accusation was concerned. In 1614 the Remonstrant and Contra-Remonstrant ministers had agreed to the principle of equality: each faction would have an equal number of elders, deacons and ministers to be appointed by the civic authorities and they would assist each other as brothers of the same church.[11] However, when towards the end of 1617 new elders and deacons had to be nominated, the Remonstrants were willing to follow the agreement of 1614, but the Contra-Remonstrants refused civic interference in ecclesiastical matters, even after the magistrates promised to appoint the proposed candidates. During the New Year's service in St Peter's Church on 1 January 1618 Festus Hommius, the minister who acted as the Contra-Remonstrant leader, read only the names of the Contra-Remonstrant candidates and invested them himself during the service of 7 January, in spite of an official ban. Hommius's fear of repercussions proved groundless: the civic authorities seemed to have accepted that the schism of the Leiden church was a fact.[12]

The second accusation, that three citizens had been banished for the sake of their religion, came closer to home but was at the moment of the trial no longer true. The presence of the *waardgelders* was to many Leiden burghers evidence of the rift between the authorities and the populace. Like every Dutch city Leiden had its own civic militia, the *schutters*, for the protection of the town. The *schutters*, however, being citizens, were mainly Contra-Remonstrant and could not therefore be trusted by their superiors. On 10 January 1618 a new company of *waardgelders* marched into the town for the reinforcement of the soldiers already present and a week later each individual *schutter* had to come to the town hall to renew his oath of allegiance to the authorities. This was an open demonstration of the distrust in which the magistrates held their own citizens and many members of the militia, among them Jan Claesz van Dorp,[13] refused to go. A delegation of four of their leaders, two of whom were the booksellers Jan Jansz. Orlers and Joost van Colster, were called to appear before the city fathers. Followed by 40 supporters they went to the town hall in protest and from there they proceeded to The Hague to ask for the Prince's support. In the course of the following two months Orlers and Van Colster and four others were condemned to a fine of £60, and two of the spokesmen (and later another *schutter* as well) were banished from the town.[14] In these months *De Practiicke van den Spaenschen Raedt*, in which the banished *schutters* were made into martyrs for the sake of religion, was written and published. The fines, however, were not collected and the exiles never had to leave the town, for an amnesty was announced on 22 April 1618,[15] two weeks before Van Dorp had been ordered to appear before his judges.

The whole affair of the renewal of the oath had clearly been misjudged and it is as though Van Dorp was being called to account because of the frustration felt by the magistrates. The first point of the official charge issued against Van Dorp was that, 'notwithstanding the fact that he had already meddled in evil affairs'[16] he had recently published another anonymous pamphlet entitled *Naeuwe overlegging van de Nootsaecke-lijcheden op 't aennemen der Waertgelders*. In this 'slanderous, irritating, seditious or libellous pamphlet'[17] the old accusation was repeated that the presence of the *waardgelders* ensured the protection of 'certain evil troubled consciences and restless spirits'[18] in order to enable them to bring their business to a godless end. Apparently Van Dorp had issued several editions of this pamphlet. The preface of what is probably the first edition says that the soldiers served 'to suppress the Contra-Remonstrant doctrine and its adherents',[19] a charge quoted literally by Gael. The bailiff continues, quoting another edition: 'or according to the changes of the defendant, *to suppress the honest and true reformed religion and its adherents*' (my italics).[20] By changing the wording of the preface and defining the Contra-Remonstrant religion as the true doctrine, Van Dorp was held personally responsible for rubbing some extra salt into the wounds of the Remonstrant city government, and the bailiff resented this. His threat of banishment and the official sentence he demanded of 200 gold reals are clear indications of his irritation.

Unfortunately, the file in the Leiden archives does not contain a report of the interrogation of Van Dorp, so that we do not know what he said in his defence. There is, however, a letter in the archives to [Dirck Gerritsz] Hogeveen, one of the four burgomasters of Leiden.[21] The identity of the author of this letter, who signs himself Th. Santen, I have not been able to ascertain without doubt, but he was somehow associated with the council of aldermen since he writes about this body as 'we'.[22] He must have held a fairly high social position, because he addressed Hogeveen as 'confrère' and 'friend'. This letter is at times obscure, but it contains interesting information about the reasons why the council of burgomasters and aldermen decided to convict Van Dorp. It shows that the self-assurance with which the Contra-Remonstrants seemed to proceed was more of a façade than the events suggest.

Hogeveen, in his capacity of burgomaster one of the judges, appears to have considered the evidence from the pamphlets against Van Dorp slight, and so seems to have been hesitant to bring him to justice. Santen writes to him that Van Dorp, when he appeared before the council, 'without creating difficulties mentioned the name known to you' as the author of the pamphlets, with the improbable defence that the Arminian minister of Leiden had acted as proof-reader; unfortunately, he does not reveal the author's identity at all in his letter. The reason why Santen wrote to Hogeveen was to express his indignation about the fact that a Leiden minister had threatened to reveal that Van Dorp had bribed him into an underhand arrangement of this affair, and he therefore writes

your Honour can see how this affects them and I beseech your Honour to take this matter seriously in hand, especially since he resorts to such gross lies. I never saw him nor spoke to him, and he never asked me anything.[23]

Santen reports that he had been visited by a Leiden minister, who, after expressing his care for Santen's reputation, had asked

how things were with the bookseller who had had these copies printed, since he [Van Dorp] had braggingly told him [the minister] that he had been to see me and had asked me to return his papers, at the same time offering me a handful of guilders.

Here the letter becomes obscured by Santen's assumption that Hogeveen knew the course of events; presumably this is the reason for the inexplicit nature of the entire letter. What probably happened after Van Dorp's initial confession and his defence that a Remonstrant preacher had been involved, was that representatives of both factions were asked to see the burgomasters. The confrontation between the disputing ministers apparently led to a situation which the Contra-Remonstrants felt could not pass unchallenged. Santen continues his letter by informing Hogeveen that the minister had also said

that [he] had been very amicable and had promised to talk to the aldermen, and that it [the pamphlet] was already being printed again, and that our [Contra-Remonstrant] ministers had not been very eager to talk to the burgomasters about this, since they were all Arminians and that they [the ministers] had drawn lots as to who would have to go, and that, in the preface of the edition that was now being printed, the two [Remonstrant] ministers who had been upstairs [to see the burgomasters] would receive a box on the ears. These were the words our minister felt he had a duty to relate to a man of the same faith, to which he [the undersigned, Santen] would be prepared to swear under oath that this was what had happened were the case inevitably to come to court.[24]

Santen concludes his letter, saying that he had informed the minister that he would report all this to Hogeveen with the confidence that he 'would have them retract the foul and false calumny and make them smart for it'.[25]

The implications of this letter make it possible to attribute all three of the known variants of this pamphlet[26] to Van Dorp. They are all three almost identical: A and B are almost exact copies, even the word division is practically the same. It would seem that A served as a copy for the compositor of B and that this compositor tried to follow A as closely as he could. Slips like the different spellings of *noo(d)tsaeckelijckheden* in the title are relatively rare. A was probably issued first. Edition C is a re-issue of B, apart from two changes; the title-page has been reset to add a meaningful quotation from Isaiah 33 : 1 and another addition is found on p.4 in which the Contra-Remonstrant doctrine is equated with the only true religion, an addition Van Dorp was accused by the bailiff of having made personally.

Van Dorp must have been brought to trial for the publication of C: in the bailiff's deposition the changes Van Dorp made to B were mentioned. The visit of the black-mailing minister to Santen took place on a Tuesday: this must have been Tuesday 1 May because during this visit the punitive changes Van Dorp was going to make were announced as a consequence of the confrontation between the ministers before the burgomasters. Van Dorp must have made his additions while B was being printed; this was the edition that the minister told Santen was being printed again because Van Dorp had thought that matters had quietened down. The bailiff must have carried out some preliminary research after the publication of A and have come to the conclusion that Van Dorp was responsible for it, hence the minister came to enquire 'how things were with the bookseller who had had these copies printed'. Gael had probably confiscated the manuscript while searching Van Dorp's premises: this would explain the minister's concern about Van Dorp, and Van Dorp's visit to Santen to try to get his papers back. It also explains why he used A as copy text for B. When Van Dorp published C he overplayed his hand. Van Dorp's textual emendation was a direct insult to the burgomasters and the basis of their policy and he was called to account for his actions.

The fine imposed on Van Dorp in the end was far less than the 200 guilders the bailiff had demanded. He had to pay 36 guilders within one day on penalty of banishment.[27] The relatively lenient verdict had no effect on the commotion of the following months. In the States General the Prince, who was now openly Contra-Remonstrant, was sent against the will of the States of Utrecht and Holland to the city of Utrecht to disband the *waardgelders*. Leiden's government tried to save the situation by giving in: the conscientious objectors were readmitted into the civic militia, the *waardgelders* were disbanded and on 4 September, almost a year after its erection, the 'Arminian bulwark' was dismantled. These measures came too late, however. On 20 October the Prince rode into the city with his army to purge the government. In the Authorized Version the quotation from Isaiah 33 : 1 which Van Dorp had added to the title-page of his pamphlet reads: 'Woe to thee that spoilest, and thou wast not spoiled; and dealest treacherously, and they dealt not treacherously with thee! when thou shalt cease to spoil, thou shalt be spoiled; and when thou shalt make an end to deal treacherously, they shall deal treacherously with thee'. It was a threatening and prophetic addition: only few of the old city fathers retained their office in the purge that followed the Prince's entry into the town. Among those who were allowed to stay was the burgomaster who had had hesitations about Van Dorp's trial: Van Hogeveen.[28]

A new name on the list of burgomasters was that of Jan Jansz. Orlers, the bookseller who had acted as spokesman for the incensed *schutters*. The old bailiff Loth Huygensz Gael was replaced in December 1619 by the eager, young professor of law Willem de Bondt, who became notorious for his persecution of the now illegal Remonstrants. In the years that followed this change of government the pressure on dissident booksellers was intensified by the new authorities: in 1619 the Remonstrant bookseller Govert Basson had to pay a fine of 200 guilders as demanded by the bailiff for the publication of a laudatory verse and a portrait of Hogerbeets, the arrested Pensionary of Leiden. Even as late as 1629 the bailiff confiscated the edition of the *Opera Omnia* by Arminius which Basson had published.[29]

Between 1615 and 1625 a remarkable increase can be seen in resolutions and decrees concerning prohibitions on publications by the States General and the States of Holland as compared to the previous years since Dutch independence; during the five years after 1620, until the Prince's death in 1625, the States General issued more of these decrees than at any other time during the 17th century:[30] an indication of the efforts by the new authorities in the Republic to establish a more centralised government. However, the application of these announced decrees depended completely on the local authorities. The degree to which censorship was applied at a local level and its effect cannot be determined at the present state of research. It may be true that the freedom of the press in the Dutch Republic, owing to its particularist structure,[31] was greater than elsewhere in Europe, but the story of Van Dorp[32] shows how, at the lowest governmental level, even under a city government that tried to achieve a certain measure of tolerance, a bookseller could inevitably become a scapegoat when personal convictions clashed with local policy.

## Notes

1. For an account of these events in Leiden, see P. J. Blok, *Geschiedenis eener Hollandsche Stad. Dl. III: Eene Hollandsche Stad onder de Republiek* ('s-Gravenhage, 1916), pp.106-16.

2. An extensive bibliography of literature on the theological and political aspects of this conflict can be found in H. G. van der Doel, *Daar moet veel strijds gestreden zijn* (Meppel, 1967), pp.197-98.

3. J. A. Gruys en C. de Wolf, *Typographi et bibliopolae Neerlandici usque ad annum MDCC thesaurus. Nederlandse boekdrukkers en boekverkopers tot 1700* (Nieuwkoop, 1980), p.140.

4. Gemeente Archief Leiden, Bonboeken Marendorp Rijnzijde f.506ᵛ. Van Dorp had bought the house in 1595 and sold it in 1623.

5. GAL Rechtelijk Archief, 30a, f.3. This file contains the official documents of Van Dorp's trial. Unless otherwise stated, quotations will be from this file.

6. PRACTIICKE / *VAN DEN* / SPAENSCHEN RAET, / Dat is: / Clare vertooninghe dat / den Raedt door I. Lipsium, Er. Puteanum, ende / Fr. Campanellam, ghegeven om de vereenighde / Nederlanden wederom te brengen onder 'tgebiet / van den Coning van Spangjen in alle hare dee= / len ofte alreede in 't werck gestelt is ofte / noch dagelijcks in 't werck ge = / steldt wordt. / Waer inne verscheyden swaricheden onder dese kercke- / lijcke ende Politijcke beroerten, voorgevallen, levendich / ende kortelijck worden voor ooghen gestelt. / Tot waerschouwinghe van alle Vrije, Vrome Nederlan = / ders, insonderheyt der gener die in de regieringe zijn / [ornament] / Ghedruckt uyt kracht vande Privilegien der / Vrije Nederlanders. Anno 1618. UB Amsterdam Pfl B.k.14 4°:AF⁴ ($3[-A1,-E1-3]), 52pp. All quotations from this pamphlet will be from this copy.

7. W. P. C. Knuttel, *Catalogus van de Pamflettenverzameling berustende in de Koninklijke*

*Bibliotheek* ('s-Gravenhage, 1889), Vol.I, part 1 1486-1620, no.2459. *Raet* means both 'council' and 'counsel'.

**8.** *Practiicke*, p.23

**9.** *Practiicke*, p.24

**10.** GAL, RA, 30a, f.2 (*Practiicke* p.31).

**11.** P. J. Wijminga, *Festus Hommius* (Leiden, 1899), pp.179-81.

**12** Wijminga, pp.257-60.

**13.** GAL, Burgem. Dagboeken 22-3-1618: Reprieffe van de Ed. Heeren van de Geregte van Leijden.

**14.** Blok, pp.107-12.

**15.** *ibidem.*

**16.** GAL, RA, 30a f.1.

**17.** GAL, RA, 30a, f1.

**18.** GAL, RA, 30a, f.1ᵛ.

**19.** GAL, RA, 30a, f.1ᵛ. This is a quotation from Knuttel 2569.

**20.** GAL, RA, 30, f.1ᵛ. This is a quotation from Knuttel 2571.

**21.** GAL, Rechtelijk Archief 32a.

**22.** He is not mentioned in the list of aldermen for 1618 in Orlers' *Beschrijvinge der Stad Leyden* (1641), which mentions Hogeveen as one of the burgomasters.

**23.** GAL, RA 32a, f.1ᵛ.

**24.** GAL, RA 32, fols 1-1ᵛ. I am indebted to Dr Arjan van Leuvensteijn of the Free University of Amsterdam for his valuable assistance in interpreting this passage.

**25.** GAL, RA 32a, f.1ᵛ.

**26.** These are the three variants:
(A) Knuttel 2570:
Nauwe Overlegging / *van de* / Nootsaeckelijckheden / / Op 't aennemen / der / WAERTGELDERS. / [ornament] / Gedruckt Anno 1618. 4° A⁴ ($3 [-a₁]) 8 pp.
(B) Knuttel 2571:
Nauwe Overlegging / *van de* / Noodtsaeckelijckheden / / Op 't aennemen / der / WAERTGELDERS. / [ornament] / gedruckt Anno 1618. 4° A⁴ ($3 [-a₁]) 8 pp.
(C) Knuttel 2572:
Nauwe Overlegging / *van de* / Noodtsaeckelijkheden / / Op 't aennemen / der / WAERTGELDERS. / Esaie 33.1. / Wee doch u, ghy verstoorder: meynt ghy, ghy en sult niet ver- / stoord worden? Ende ghy verachter, meynt ghy, men sal u niet verachten? Wanneer ghy het verstore geeyndight hebt, so sult ghy oock / verstoort worden: Wanneer ghy des verachtens een eynde ghemaect / hebt, so salmen u wederom verachten. / [ornament (see B)] / Gedruckt Anno 1618. 4° A⁴ ($3 [-a₁]) 8 pp.

**27.** GAL, RA 30a, f.3ᵛ.

**28.** Blok, p.117.

**29** See my *Govert Basson, Printer, Bookseller, Publisher at Leiden 1612-1630*, forthcoming.

**30.** S. Groenveld, 'Het Mekka der schrijvers? Statencolleges en censuur in de zeventiende-eeuwse Republiek', in *Eer is het Lof des Deuchts. Opstellen over renaissance en classicisme aangeboden aan dr. Fokke Veenstra* (Amsterdam, 1986), p.229.

**31.** G. C. Gibbs, 'The role of the Dutch Republic as the intellectual entrepôt of Europe in the seventeenth and eighteenth centuries', in *Bijdragen en mededelingen betreffende de geschiedenis der Nederlanden*, 86 (1971), p.327.

**32.** See also J. A. Jacobs, 'Jan Claesz. van Dorp en enkele door hem in 1618 gedrukte pamfletten', in *Uit Leidse bron geleverd*, edited by J. W. Marsilje *et al.* (Leiden, 1989), pp. 285-88.

Chris Coppens & Marcus de Schepper

# Printer to Town and University: Henrick van Hastens at Louvain

*With a check-list (1621-28)*

Henrick van Ha(e)stens *alias* Henricus Hastenius (*c*.1566-*c*.1629) may be termed one of the most intriguing characters on the Louvain printing scene of the first half of the 17th century. Although his activities there cover at most eight years, they show the characteristics of mature craftsmanship.

In singular contrast to the numerous printers and publishers of the Southern Netherlands who moved to the North for freedom of worship and clearer prospects of business success (in whatever order of priority), Van Hastens left Holland's University of Leiden in about 1621 to build up a new career in the Spanish Netherlands as a printer to the *Alma Mater Lovaniensis*.[1] What precisely influenced his decision to put an end to his activities at Leiden after a busy period of over 25 years, is not yet clear in great detail. Financial reasons seem to have played a prominent part in it, but religion, of course, formed the major dividing-line nearing the end of the Twelve Years' Truce (1609-21).

It might well have been the renowned Jesuit preacher Marc van den Tympel (1575-1636), originating from a prominent and influential Louvain dynasty, who converted Van Hastens to Catholicism and formed the Louvain connection. As a leading character of the Jesuit mission in Holland, especially at Leiden, he had to leave the North in precisely the same year: 1621. He and the Antwerp bishop Joannes Malderus (1563-1633), a former Louvain theology professor, attested to the printer's true faith.

At Louvain Van Hastens was protected by its leading university professor Erycius Puteanus (1574-1646), successor to the famous Justus Lipsius (1547-1606) who had also exchanged Leiden for Louvain exactly 30 years earlier (1591). Puteanus arranged for Van Hastens's settlement at Louvain. From the city the printer obtained a well-sited house, exemptions from guard duty, as well as from the billeting of soldiers and from excise duties. It also awarded him a subsidy towards the house-rent. The university granted him exemption from taxation and admitted him as university printer and bookseller by decision of the Senate on 28 January 1622.[2] Both decisions were clearly supported by Puteanus who was in need of a ready printer for his overwhelming literary production. During the year before the promised dwellings became available, Van Hastens stayed at Puteanus's castle on the Keizersberg (*Mons Caesaris*), acting like a professor's private press (*in arce* – see no.8). But this relationship was not to last long. After the printer moved into the house on the market-place, near the Town Hall, he hardly printed anything more for the complacent landlord. Early in 1624 Puteanus

# Waerachtighe Beschrijvinghe

Van d'Oude ende Nieuwe Stadt

# IERVSALEM.

Alsoo die geweest is ten tijden onses Salichmaeckers

# IESV CHRISTI,

ende daer nae ghedestrueert.

*Beschreven*

Van FL. IOSEPHVS ende HEGESIPPVS,

Alsoo oock teghenwoordich is /

*Bereyst ende beschreven*

Vanden Eerwveerdigen IACOB BOECKEN BERGE,
ende HIERONYMVS SCHEYT,
inden jaer 1600. ende 1612.

## TOT LOVEN,

Gedruckt by Henrick van Haestens /
In't Iaer 1628.

Fig.1    Title-page of *Waerachtighe Beschrijvinghe* (no.71). (Ghent University Library.)

t'Heyligh Landt

ende 'tNieu

# IERVSALEM;

Midtl-gaders

De voornaempfte plaetfen :

Bereyft ende Befchreben door de H.H.

Iacob Boekenberch, ende Ieronymus Scheyt

Int iaer 1600. ende 1612.

TOT LOVEN,

By Henrick van Haftens /

Int Iaer 1628.

Fig.2    Part-title of the *Waerachtighe Beschrijvinghe* (H4ʳ).

spat his venom on the ungrateful deserting printer in a letter to Fredericus Marselaer (1584-1670). Its fierceness, if anything, tells us more about its sender than about its victim.

Van Hastens apparently paved his way as a Louvain printer and bookseller. From 1622 onwards, starting with the basic 'Customs of the City of Louvain and its Purlieu' (no.3), he regularly printed for the town magistrates. In 1624 he was paid by the city for printing (and binding) a public letter written by Puteanus to Cardinal de la Cueva urging him to put an end to the billeting of Spanish troops (no.29). As usual, broadside ordinances formed the majority of city print orders. As they were ephemeral by nature, only a handful of them happened to survive in the city archives. They are easily recognisable by the presence of Van Hastens's characteristic decorative initial capital letters (nos.15, 58).

Even rarer are the university's printed ephemera, especially when considering the tragic fate of the Louvain university and college archives and libraries. But the connection with the university gave him even better opportunities. Starting with Puteanus, several professors entrusted him with the publication of their scholarly treatises and occasional writings. Best known today is Valerius Andreas, later to become the first librarian of the central university library established in 1636. In 1623 Van Hastens printed the first edition of his *Bibliotheca Belgica* (enlarged in 1643), the earliest major biographical and bibliographical sourcebook for the Low Countries. From none other of Van Hastens's Louvain publications do so many copies survive. Van Hastens printed first editions of original works by Louvain professors from all faculties: professors of theology like Jacobus Janssonius (1623), of history and letters like Valerius Andreas (1623, 1625) and Nicolaus Vernulaeus (1621, 1623), of medicine like Petrus Castellanus (1622) and Thomas Fienus (1624), as well as of law like Petrus Gudelinus (1624) and Joannes Wamesius (1625, 1628).

Equally important seem to have been the controversial and devotional texts associated with the Jesuit connection. Books by some 15 Jesuit authors were published by Van Hastens: Thomas Sailly (1622), Petrus Wadding (1622), Franciscus de La Croix (1623, 1624), Gregorius a Sancto Vincentio (1624), Pierre Bouille (1624), Giulio Negrone (1624), Franciscus Sacchini (1624), Hieremias Drexelius (1625), Martinus de Roa (1625), Laurentius Uwens (1625), Thomas Villacastin (1625), Antonius de Balinghem (1626), Herman Hugo (1627, 1628), Adrianus Crommius (1628) and Pedro Gomez (1628). Again next to nothing seems to have survived of their ephemeral publications (*Narratio*, 1623).

The treatise by Philippus Rovenius (1624, 1626) might be a fruit from Van Hastens's conversion to Catholicism while still in Holland. Rovenius, born at Deventer in 1573, studied at Louvain and, from 1614 onwards, conducted the Catholic mission in Holland. All this happened in conflict with members of the regular clergy such as the Jesuits. It is not unlikely that the printer and the *vicarius* met in Holland and that, in spite of the influence of van den Tympel, Van Hastens did appreciate Rovenius.

Van Hastens also printed numerous other religious writings: older ones like J. Beisselius's *Tria rosacea coronamenta* (1623) or more recent texts by W. Bosscharts O. Praem (1622, 1623), J. Paludanus (1623), Matthias Pauli OESA (1623, 1624), F. Conrius OFM (1624), J. Naevius OESA (1625), L. Landtmeter O. Praem. (1626), Thomas a Jesu

O. Carm. Disc. (1626), Michael de Dôle OFM Cap. (1627), David van Mauden (1627), Michael Paludanus OSA (1628). One famous name to be added is that of Luke Wadding (1624), Irish-born historian of the Franciscan order (no.45). Some other books of British interest are nos.14, 21, 34, 66, 68.

A number of Van Hastens's publications were printed for the city of Namur, which apparently at that time could not afford a regular printing business in town. In nearby Louvain Van Hastens was well qualified for the task, perhaps called upon by members of the University's *Collège de Namur*.[3]

Finally there are some publications occasioned by the death of Archduke Albert (especially the oblong folio volume *Pompa funebris*), a few scientific texts (Rietmakers 1622, and the *Theoremata mathematica*, 1624 – an intriguing oblong volume with oval emblematical engravings), and a number of literary texts in Dutch (De Jong 1625) and Neo-Latin (Vernulaeus 1623, Pignewart 1624, Lummenaeus a Marca 1625).

It is safe to assume that Van Hastens's output of some 75 books presents a nice cross-section of early 17th-century book production in an intellectual centre of the Southern Netherlands. After a good start protected by Puteanus, Van Hastens established himself as a printer-publisher in his own right.

## Notes

Together with Anna Simoni, the authors are currently at work on a reconstruction of Van Hastens's total production (both at Leiden and Louvain). They are happy to offer this fruit: 'To the onlie begetter (…) all happinesse and that eternitie promised by our ever-living poet'.

1. See Anna E. C. Simoni, 'Henrick van Haestens, from Leiden to Louvain via "Cologne" '. *Quaerendo*, 15, 1985, pp.187-94; Christian Coppens, 'Steadfast I hasten: the Louvain printer Henrick van Ha(e)stens', *Quaerendo*, 17, 1987, pp.185-204 and Id., 'La "Namur-connection" de l'imprimeur louvaniste Van Hastens'. *Archives et Bibliothèques de Belgique*, 60, 1989, pp.75-95.

2. Brussels, Algemeen Rijksarchief, Old University of Louvain, 64, f.321ᵛ. Puteanus's

first *supplicatio* is dated September 12, 1621. The authors gratefully acknowledge this information supplied by Pierre Delsaerdt, currently preparing a dissertation on Louvain University and the book trade 1425-1797.

3. See n.1 on the 'Namur-connection'. Information on St Anne's College (or Collège de Namur) in E. Reusens, *Documents relatifs à l'histoire de l'Université de Louvain (1425-1797)* vol.3 (Louvain, 1881-85), pp.243-57.

4. After this article had gone to press, we came across another work of Van Hastens's, printed in 1626 and connected with the Carmelites: the *Constitutiones* by Theresa de Jesus for the Carmelite nuns, but maybe published anonymously. See Grégoire Marie de S. Joseph, *Prologue historique sur les constitutions des religieuses déchaussées, etc.* (Ghent, 1859), p.xxxi. We have not yet been able to trace a copy.

# Check-list

The present list is a first attempt at an inventory of Van Hastens's Louvain output. Titles are listed chronologically, within one year alphabetically, anonymous works preceding authors' names. It gives the following information: (a) short-title, (b) imprint (original wording, occasionally abbreviating the formula 'town and university printer' by means of …), (c) collational formula (including pagination), (d) bibliographical references and occasional annotations, (e) copy described (usually one in The British Library), a cross ( + ) indicating the existence of more copies.

    At present our research has focused on collections in Belgium and The Netherlands, as well as on The British Library and the Bibliothèque Nationale (Paris). Information about missing editions or additional copies (especially in UK libraries) will be gratefully recorded for the complete bibliography, which will include copy-specific information (binding, provenance, etc).

## References

Allison & Rogers: *The Contemporary printed Literature of the English Counter-Reformation between 1558 and 1640: an annotated catalogue* by A. F. Allison and D. M. Rogers, Vol.I. (With the collaboration of W. Lottes). *Works in languages other than English* (Aldershot, 1989)

Allison & Rogers (1956): A. F. Allison & D. M. Rogers, *A Catalogue of Catholic Books in English printed abroad or secretly in England 1558-1640* (Bognor Regis, 1956) [ = Biographical Studies vol.3, no.3,4]

BCNI: *Bibliotheca catholica neerlandica impressa 1500-1727* (Hagae Comitis, 1954)

Bibl. Belg.: *Bibliotheca Belgica. Bibliographie générale des Pays-Bas.* Fondée par Ferdinand Van der Haeghen. Rééditée sous la direction de Marie-Thérèse Lenger, 7 vols (Bruxelles, 1964-75)

Doyen: *Bibliographie Namuroise. Indiquant les livres imprimés à Namur depuis le XVIIe siècle jusqu'à nos jours, les ouvrages publiés en Belgique ou à l'étranger, par des auteurs Namurois, ou concernant l'histoire du Comté ou de la province actuelle de Namur.* Tome I 1473-1799 (Namur 1887, repr. Nieuwkoop 1974)

Peeters-Fontainas: Jean Peeters-Fontainas, *Bibliographie des impressions espagnoles des Pays-Bas Méridionaux.* Mise au point avec la collaboration de Anne-Marie Frédéric, Centre National de l'Archéologie et de l'Histoire du Livre – Publication n° 1 (Nieuwkoop, 1965)

Rosier: P. Irenaeus Rosier O. Carm., *Biographisch & bibliographisch overzicht van de vroomheid in de Nederlandse Carmel van 1235 tot het midden der achttiende eeuw,* Studiën en Tekstuitgaven van Ons Geestelijk Erf X (Tielt, 1950)

Sommerv.: *Bibliothèque de la Compagnie de Jésus. Première partie: bibliographie,* par les Pères Augustin et Aloys De Backer. *Seconde partie: histoire,* par le Père Auguste Carayon, Nouvelle édition par Carlos Sommervogel SJ *Bibliographie,* 9 vols (Bruxelles-Paris, 1890-1900)

STC: *A short-title catalogue of books printed in England, Scotland, & Ireland and of English books printed abroad 1475-1640;* first compiled by A. W. Pollard & G. R. Redgrave; second edition, revised & enlarged, begun by W. A. Jackson & F. S. Ferguson, completed by Katharine F. Pantzer, 2 vols (London, 1976-86)

## Libraries

| | |
|---|---|
| A (RG) | Antwerp, Ruusbroec-Genootschap |
| B | Brussels, Koninklijke Bibliotheek Albert I |
| G | Ghent, Universiteitsbibliotheek |
| G (Carm.) | Ghent, Carmel |
| G (GS) | Ghent, Groot-Seminarie |
| G (KANTL) | Ghent, Koninklijke Academie voor Nederlandse Taal- en Letterkunde |
| H | The Hague, Koninklijke Bibliotheek |
| He | Heverlee (Louvain), Jezuïeten |
| L | London, The British Library |
| Le | Leeuwarden, Provinciale Bibliotheek van Friesland |
| Lv | Louvain, Universiteitsbibliotheek |
| Lv (SA) | Louvain, Stadsarchief |
| Lv (Theol) | Louvain, Bibliotheek Faculteit Godgeleerdheid |
| P | Paris, Bibliothèque Nationale |
| P (SG) | Paris, Bibliothèque Sainte-Geneviève |

**1621**

1 Libertus Fromondus, *Serenissimi Belgarum principis Alberti Pii laudatio funebris*
Lovanii, Typis Henrici Hastenii, 1621
8°: A-C⁸D⁴, 28 ff., *1-2* 3-50 *51-56*
L: 1193.l.6.(2.), +

2 Nicolaus Vernulaeus, *Oratio funebris in obitum Alberti Archiducis Austriae*
Lovanii, Typis Henrici Hastenii, 1621
8°: A-B⁸, 16 ff., *1-2* 3-27 *28-32*
B: V.H.26.778 A L.P., +

**1622**

3 [Louvain], *Costuymen der Stadt van Loven ende van haeren ressorte*
Tot Loven, By Henrick van Hastens (…), 1622
4°: *⁴A-X⁴, 88 ff., [8] 1-110 *III-112*, 1-39 *40-46*
B: II 14.532 A 7, +

3a Joannes Barth. vander Aa, *Grammatica Gallica*
Lovanii, Ex Officina Henrici Hastenii (…) Sumptibus ipsius Authoris, 1622
4°: A⁸ *B*⁴ 2B⁴ C-I⁴ ²I² ²D⁴ ²C⁴
³D⁴ K⁴ L², 64ff., 1-24 17-75 [=25-83]
*84* 25-40 [=*85*-100] *101-116* 77-87
[=117-127] *128*
P (SG): X8° 333 INV. 627 RÉS.

4 Willebrordus Bosscharts O. Praem., *Ordo Praemonstratensis clericalis seu canonicus assertus Tongerloensis coenobii in solemnitate P. N. S. Norberti die* [blank] *Iulii, 1622*
Lovanii, Apud Henricum Hastenium (…), 1622
4°: A-B⁴C⁶, 14 ff., *1-2* 3-26 *27-28*
BCNI 7027
H: 123 D 5, +

5 Petrus Castellanus, *Laudatio funebris Alberti Belgarum principis. Dicta Lovanii in Collegio Trilingui*
Lovanii, Excudebat Henricus Hastenius, 1522 [sic]
4°: A-H⁴, 32 ff., *1-2* 3-62 *63-64*
B: V.H.26.783 A, +

6 Erycius Puteanus, *Bibliotheca, sive operum omnium, quae scripsit hactenus, edidit, designavit, catalogus*
Lovanii, Ex Officinâ Henrici Hastenii, 1622
8°: *⁸, 8 ff., *1-3* 4-16
Lv: Rés.18 CA.A, +

7 Idem, *Bonae indolis iconismus. Adjuncta Methodus litterarum, et Institutio principis*
Lovanii, Typis Henrici Hastenii, 1622
12°: †⁶A-D¹², 54 ff., [12] 1-94 *95-96*

Bibl.Belg.IV 790-1 (P-228)
B: V.B.6983 A 3, +

8 Idem, *Diva Virgo Aspricollis: beneficia ejus & miracula novissima*
Lovanii, Apud Henr. Hastenium & Petr. Zangrium, 1622
(col.: Lovanii, Excudebat Henricus Hastenius in arce, 1622)
4°: *-**⁴A-V⁴, 88 ff., [16] 1-153 *154-160*
BCNI 7112; Bibl.Belg.III 1012-3 (L-396)
*Re-issued* 1623 with no. 26
L: 486.c.8.(2.), +

9 Idem, *Miracles derniers de Nostre Dame de Montaigu*, trsl. André Dauphin OSB
A Louvain, Chez Henri Hastens & Pierre Zangrius, 1622
8°: a⁸A-M⁸, 104 ff., [16] 1-184 *185-192*
BCNI 7113; Bibl.Belg.IV 791 (P-230)
B: III 93.707 A, +

10 Idem, *Musarum ferculum: carmina eius selecta*
Lovanii, Typis Henrici Hastenii, 1622
8°: A-F⁸G⁴, 52 ff., *1-3* 4-104
Bibl.Belg.IV 791-2 (P-231)
B: V.H.23.585. A L.P., +

11 Erycius Puteanus & Andreas Trevisius, *Phoenix principum: sive Alberti Pii morientis vita, Andrea Trevisi Epistolâ, & Eryci Puteani Paraphrasi explicata*
Lovanii, Apud Henr. Hastenium & Petr. Zangrium, 1622
4°: A-C⁴D², 14 ff., *1-2* 3-16 25-36[= 17-28]
Bibl.Belg.IV 790 (P-227)
B: V.H.26.298 B 4 L.P., +

12 Hubertus Arnoldus Rietmakers, *Tractatus de nephritico dolore*
Lovanii, Apud Henricum Hastenium, 1622
4°: A-K⁴, 40 ff., *1-2* 3-78 *79-80*
L: 781.d.1.(2.), +

13 Thomas Sailly SJ, *Mémorial testamentaire composé en faveur des Soldats combattans sous l'Estandart de la crainte de Dieu*
A Lovain, Chez Henri Hastens (…), 1622
8°: *⁸B-X⁸, 168 ff., [16] 1-315 *316-320*
BCNI 7131; Sommerv.VII col.408 (no.17)
Lv (Theol): Groot-Seminarie Mechelen E 531

14 Petrus Wadding SJ (Praes) / Joannes Baptista van den Cruyce
SJ (Def), *D.O.M. Theologia* (…) 26 July 1622
Lovanii, Typis Henrici Hastenii, 1622
4°: 13 pp. (unnumbered)
Allison & Rogers I 1342; Sommerv.VIII col.929 (no.3)
Not found

## 1623

15  [Louvain], *Alsoe diuersche Innegesetene deser Stadt* (…) 4 January 1623
1°: 1f.; initial of Van Hastens's decorative alphabet
Ordinance about night-watch
Lv (SA): Cuv.1605/H 56

16  *Narratio miraculorum anno M.DC.XXIII. aprili et maio, Munebregae Bilbilensium ad*
*imaginem S.P. Ignatii de Loyola*
Lovanii, Typis Henrici Hastenii, 1623
8°: A⁸B⁴, 12 ff., *1-2* 3-24
Sommerv.ix col.1193
Lv (Theol): SJ R 22 G 1577 H

17  Valerius Andreas, *Bibliotheca Belgica*
Lovanii, Apud Henricum Hastenium (…), 1623
(col: Lovanii, Typis Henrici Hastenii, 1623)
8°: a⁸b⁴ A-3C⁸3D², 406 ff., [24] 1-96 99-789[ = 97-787] *788*
L: 618.c.1, +

18  Judocus Beisselius, *Tria rosacea coronamenta pulcherrima atque devotissima Annae,*
*Mariae, Iesu*
Lovanii, Typis Henrici Hastenii, 1623
8°: A⁸, 8 ff., unnumbered
BCNI 7165
Lv (Theol): SJ R 22 G 1577 H

19  Willebrordus Bosscharts O.Praem, *Beatus Siardus Horti B. Mariae in Frisia Sextus*
*Abbas laudatus in annua congregatione Tongerloensis Coenobij*
Lovanii, Typis Henrici Hastenii, 1623
4°: A-B⁴C⁶, 14 ff., *1-2* 3-27 *28*
BCNI 7173
B: Cl. 12.834, +

20  Joannes Dillenus, *Panegyricus Serenissimae Isabellae Clarae Eugeniae. Et de origine*
*Francorum historicae dissertationes*
Lovanii, Typis Henrici Hastenii, 1623
4°: A-I⁴K⁶L-Z⁴, 94 ff., *1-2* 3-82 *83-87* 76-80 [ = 88-92] 93-188
*Re-issued c.1625 with a* Liber tertius *(*²A- G⁴, 28 ff., *1-2* 3-55 *56*; ²A1 *usually bound*
*between* A1 *and* A2 *of original issue)*
L: C.77.a.29, + (re-issue: B: II 62.445 A, + )

21  Marcus Antonius de Dominis, *Sui reditus ex Anglia consilium exponit*
Copy-imprint: Romae, Ex Typographia Reu. Camerae Apostolicae,
1623 (col: Lovanii, Typis Henrici Hastenii, 1623)
4°: A-C⁴D⁶, 18 ff., *I-III* IV-XXXV *XXXVI*
Allison & Rogers I 1552
L: 477.a.26.(10.), +

22  Jacobus Francquart & Erycius Puteanus, *Pompa funebris Alberti Pii veris
    imaginibus expressa a Iacobo Francquart. Eiusdem principis morientis vita, scriptore
    E. Puteano* (engraved)
    Bruxellae, 1623 (col: Lovanii, Typis Henrici Hastenii, 1623)
    2° obl.:π¹A-M¹, 13 ff., unnumbered + 64 engravings numbered
    I-LXIIII
    Peeters-Fontainas 1070
    B: V.H.26.770 C L.P., +

23  Jacobus Janssonius, *In propheticum librum Iob enarratio*
    Lovanii, Apud Henricum Hastenium & Petrum Zangrium, 1623
    2°: *⁴A-X⁶Y⁴, 134 ff., [8] 1-246 *247-260*
    BCNI 7216
    B: V.B.332 C, +

24  Franciscus de La Croix SJ, *Lust hofken Van de H. Maget Maria*, trsl. Joannes de
    Costere (engraved title)
    By Hendrick Hastens tot Loven, 1623
    16°: *-**⁸A-V⁸, 176 ff., [32] 1-310 *311-320*
    BCNI 7192; Sommerv.II col.1689-90 (no.1)
    A (RG): 3049 D. 18cf.⁷, +

25  *another edition* (identical engraved title)
    12°: A-P¹²Q⁶, 186 ff., [24] *1-3* 4-263 266-338 [ = 264-336] *337-348*
    *Another issue* dated 1624
    A (RG): 3049 D.18ᵅ, + (re-issue 1624: A (RG): 3049 D. 17⁷)

26  Justus Lipsius, *Diva Virgo Aspricollis: nova ejus beneficia & admiranda*
    Lovanii, Apud Henr. Hastenium & Petrum Zangrium, 1623
    (col: Lovanii, Apud Henricum Hastenium (…), 1623)
    4°: A-K⁴L², 42 ff., *1-8* 9-82 *83-84*
    BCNI 7088; Bibl.Belg.III 1012-3 (L-396)
    Combined with a re-issue of no.8 (A1ʳ: 'Diva Virgo Aspricollis: miracula eius
    praecipua a Iusto Lipsio et Erycio Puteano descripta')
    B: V.B.10.519 A 1, +

27  Joannes Paludanus, *Apologeticus Marianus* (engraved title)
    Lovanii, Typis Henr. Hastenii, 1623
    4°: A-2C⁴, 104 ff., [8] 1-200
    BCNI 7245
    L: 1217.c.13 (lacking half-title A1), +

28  Matthias Pauli OESA, *Den Goeden Vrijdach oft de Beclaginghe Christi over de
    ondanckbaerheyt der Ioden ende quade Christenen. Het I.deel* (engraved title)
    Tot Loven, By Henrick van Hastens (…), 1623
    8°: a⁸b⁴A-2O⁸, 308 ff., [24] *1-4* 1[ = 5] 6-586 *587-592*
    BCNI 7249
    See also no.41 (with combined re-issue)
    A (RG): 3028 i. 1¹, +

29  Erycius Puteanus, *Pro urbe et academia Lovaniensi dissertatio epistolica ad Cardinalem de la Cueva*
[Louvain, H. Hastens, October 1623]
4°: A⁴, 4 ff., *1-2* 3-8; initial of Van Hastens's decorative alphabet
Bibl.Belg.IV 792 (P-233)
B: II 11.145 A 5

30  Nicolaus Vernulaeus, *Theodoricus. Tragoedia*
Lovanii, Typis Henrici Hastenii, 1623
8°: A-E⁸, 40 ff., *1-3* 4-80
P: Yc.9502

### 1624

31  *Espejo espiritual o Relacion*
[Lovayna, H. Hastenio, 1624]
4°: ?
Peeters-Fontainas 397
Not found

32  *Instructio & Censura professorum in Academia Lovaniensi pro canonizatione B. Ioannae Valesiae Annuntiatarum fundatricis*
Lovanii, Typis Henrici Hastenii, 1624
4°: A-K⁴, 40 ff., 1-77 *78-80*
G (GS): (no press-mark)

33  Pierre Bouille SJ, *Den oorspronck ende mirakelen van Onse Lieve Vrouwe van Foye by Dinant*, trsl. Jacobus Susius SJ
Tot Loven, By Henrick van Hastens (…), 1624
8°: π¹H⁴B-G⁸, 53 ff., [10] *1* 2-96
BCNI 7328 and 7416 (as 'P. ROVILLE' !); Doyen 115; Sommerv.
I col.1920-1 (no.3) and VII col.1718 (no.1)
B: V.B.10.520¹ A 6 L.P., +

34  Florentius Conrius OFM, *Tractatus de statu parvulorum sine baptismo decedentium ex hac vita: iuxta sensum B. Augustini*
Lovanii, Ex Officina Henrici Hastenii (…), 1624
4°: *-**4****²B-2O⁴2P², 156 ff., [20] 1-289 *290-292*
Allison & Rogers I 267
L: 854.g.16, +

35  Thomas Fienus, *De formatrice foetus liber secundus*
Lovanii, Apud Henricum Hastenium (…), 1624
8°: *⁴A-L⁸ (H⁸⁻¹), 91 ff., [8] 1-170 *171-174*
Cancellandum H8 present in B: V.B. 4530 A
L: 1173.f.4, +

36  Gregorius a Sancto Vincentio SJ (Praes) / Gualterus van Aelst SJ (Def),
*Theoremata mathematica scientiae staticae de ductu ponderum per planitiem recta &*

*oblique horizontem decussantem. Die 29. Iulij* (engraved title)
(col: Lovanii, Typis Henrici Hastenii, 1624)
4° obl.: A-B⁶, 12 ff., 1-23 *24* + 20 oval emblematical engravings numbered 1-20
(on 10 unsigned ff.)
Sommerv.VII col.440-1 (no.3)
*Another issue*: Jo. Ciermans (Def.)
B: V.H.8181 B L.P. (other issue: Le: 327 Wk – not seen)

37. Petrus Gudelinus, *De iure feudorum commentarius*
Lovanii, Ex Officinâ Henrici Hastenii (…), 1624
4°: *-**⁴A-2N⁴2O², 154 ff., [16] 1-272 *273-292*
B: V.B.3160 B, +

38. Franciscus de La Croix SJ, *Lust hofken Vande H. Maget Maria*, trsl. Joannes de
Costere
By Henrick Hastens tot Louen, 1624
12°: A-P¹²Q⁶, 186 ff., [24] 1-264 267-338 [ = 265-336] *337-348*; title engraved
BCNI 7348: Sommerv.II col.1689-90 (no.1)
A (RG): 3049 D. 17*β*

39. *Another edition: Lust-hofken der heyliger Maghet Maria*, trsl. Joannes de Costere
Tot Loven, By Henrick van Hastens, 1624
12°: A-N¹²O⁶, 162 ff., *1-20* 21-314 *315-324*; title printed in red and black
A (RG): 3049 D.17*ᵅ*

40. Julius Nigronus SJ, *Dissertatio moralis de lectione librorum amatoriorum, iunioribus
maxime vitanda*
Lovanii, Ex Officinâ Henrici Hastenii, 1624
8°: A-C⁸D², 26 ff., *1-2* 3-51 *52*
BCNI 7386; Sommerv.V col.1617 (no.17)
L: 687.a.14.(2.), +

41. Matthias Pauli OESA, *De Beclagingen Christi over de ondanckbaerheyt der Joden ende
quade Christenen sermoon-wys wtgheleyt. Het II. Stuck* (engraved title)
Tot Loven, By Hen: van Hastens, 1624
8°: *8***⁴A-2Z⁸, 380 ff., [24] 1-703 *704-736*
BCNI 7398
Combined issue with no.28 (8°: *8***⁴a⁸⁽⁻¹⁾b⁴A-2O⁸, A-2Z⁸) in A (RG):
3028 i.3, +
A (RG): 3028 i. 1², +

42. Joannes Pignewart O.Cist, *Epigrammata in honorem sanctorum* [and] *Cato
Bernardinus*
Lovanii, Typis Henrici Hastenii, 1624
4°: *⁴A-C⁴D⁶⁽⁻¹⁾E- O⁴, 61 ff., [8] 1-26 25-49 [ = 27-51] *52*, [4] 1-57 *58*
BCNI 7402-3; Doyen 109-10
L: 11408.d.33, +

43 Philippus Rovenius, *Tractatus de missionibus*
Lovanii, Typis Henrici Hastenii, 1624
8°: ) : ($^8$A-G$^8$H$^4$, 68 ff., [16] 1-118 *119-120*
BCNI 7415
L: 867.f.22.(5.), +

44. Franciscus Sacchini SJ, *Epistola de lectione ad mensam data*
BCNI 7420; Sommerv.VII col.364-5 (no.5)
Not found

45. Lucas Wadding OFM, *ΠΡΕΣΒΕΙΑ sive legatio Philippi III. et IV. ad Paulum PP. V et Gregorium XV. De definiendâ controversiâ immaculatae conceptionis B. Virginis Mariae*
Lovanii, Ex Officinâ Henrici Hastenii (…), 1624
2°: *$^6$A-2Q$^6$, 240 ff., [12] 1-462 *463-468*
Allison & Rogers I 1313
L: 1229.g.16 and 490.i.17, +

### 1625

46 Valerius Andreas, *De toga et sago sive litterata armataque militia dissertatio*
[and Petrus Gudelinus, *Laudatio Divi Ivonis*]
Lovanii, Typis Henrici Hastenii (…), 1625
8°: A-F$^8$G$^4$, 52 ff., *1-2* 3-103 *104*
L: 11405.a.55.(2.), +

47 Joannes Dauvin, *Ordinata in congregatione synodali habita die 26. Martij 1625*
Namurci, Apud Franciscum Vivien (…), 1625
(col: Lovanii, Typis Henrici Hastenii (…), Sumptibus Franc. Vivien (…), 1625)
4°: A-D$^4$, 16 ff., *1-2* 3-29 *30-32*
Doyen 120
B: V.H.8101 A 1 L.P., +

48 Hieremias Drexelius SJ, *Schoone consideratien van de eewicheydt*, trsl. Guilielmus Deutels
Tot Loven, By Henrick van Hastens, 1625
8°: *$^8$A-V$^8$, 168 ff., [16] 1-315 *316-320*
BCNI 7489; Sommerv.III col.182-3 (no.3)
A (RG): 3072 B 1$^x$, +

49 Antonius Havetius, *Decreta et statuta synodi dioecesanae Namurcensis*
Namurci, Apud Franciscum Vivien (…), 1625
4°: A-F$^4$, 24 ff., *1-2* 3-47 *48*
Types, mark and initials of Van Hastens
Doyen 121
B: V.B.10.158 B, +

50 Joachim de Jong, *Een heerlijck Lof-toneel vande vermaerde oude Stadt ende Universiteyt van Loven*

Tot Loven, By Henrick van Hastens, 1625
4°: A-C⁴, 12 ff., unnumbered
B: II 26.013 A L.P.

51  Jacobus Cornelius Lummenaeus a Marca OSB, *Sampson. Tragoedia sacra*
Lovanii, Typis Henrici Hastenii (…), 1625
8°: A-B⁸, 16 ff., *1-6*7-31 *32*
Bibl.Belg.III 1162 (L-653)
G: G 7487, +

52  Joannes Neevius OESA, *Verclaeringe vande H. Sacramenten der biechten en des outaers*
Tot Loven, By H. van Hastens, 1625
8°: *8***⁴A-X⁸, 180 ff., [24] 1-335 *336*
BCNI 7533
G (KANTL): A.I D 4, +

53  Martinus de Roa SJ, *Den staet der sielen des Vageviers*
Tot Loven, By Henrick van Hastens, 1625
12°: †⁶A-P¹², 186 ff., [12] 1-359 *360*
BCNI 7558; Sommerv.VI col.1891-3 (no.14)
A (RG); 3047 i. 22, +

54  Franciscus Theophilus, *Instructio de sanctissimo sacramento eucharistiae*
Lovanii, Apud Henricum Hastenium (…), 1625
8°: A-D⁸, 32 ff., *1-2*3-51 *52-64*
H: 1118 H 39

55  Laurentius Uwens SJ, *Oratio in funere D. Petri Pecquii*
Lovanii, Ex Officinâ Henrici Hastenii (…), 1625
4°: A-E⁴, 20 ff., *1-2*3-37 *38-40*
Sommerv.VIII col.356-7 (no.1)
B: V.H.22.854 A, +

56  Thomas Villacastin SJ, *Onderwijs der godvruchtiger siele*, trsl. Jacobus Susius SJ
Tot Loven, By Henrick van Hastens, 1625
8°: A-2D⁸2E⁴, 220 ff., *1-2*3-432 *433-440*
BCNI 7596; Sommerv.VIII col.759-63 (no.2) and VII col.1718-9 (no.2)
A (RG): 3058 F.II, +

57  Joannes Wamesius, *Responsorum sive consiliorum ad ius forumque civile pertinentium, centuria prima*
Lovanii, Apud Henricum Hastenium & Petrum Zangrium, 1625
2°: *6(-1) A-2C⁶2D⁸, 169 ff., [10] 1-305 *306-328*
B: III 67.865 C I, +

**1626**

58  [Louvain], *Alsoe sekere Jaren herwaerts binnen deser Stadt* (…) 26 August 1626

1°: 1 f.; initial of Van Hastens's decorative alphabet.
Ordinance about mendicancy from outside the town
Lv (SA): Cuv.1604/B 54

59  Albert of Vercelli, patriarch of Jerusalem, *La première règle d'Albert confirmée et corrigée par nostre St. Père Innocent*
[Louvain, H. Hastens, 1626]
32°: [2] 1-254 *255-270*
Olim Lv (destroyed in 1940)

60.  Antonius de Balinghem SJ, *Lust-hofken der hemelscher wellusten*, trsl. Gerardus Zoes SJ
Tot Loven, By Henrick van Hastens, 1626
12°: A-I¹²K⁶, 114 ff., [24] 1-197 152[ = 198] 198 [ = 199] *200-204*
BCNI 7615; Sommerv.I col.839 (no.32) and VIII col.1517 (no.15)
A (RG): 3059 H.9, +

61  Joannes d'Espiennes du Fay, *Eximii viri Andreae de Wypion sacrae theosophiae laurea doctoralis XIII cal. novemb. M.DC.XXVI*
Lovanii, Typis Henrici Hastenii, 1626
8°: 14 pp.
Doyen 123 (copy in the collection of R. Chalon)
Not found

62  Joachim Junius, *Epitaphium symbolicum Ludovici ab Eynatten*
Lovanii, Typis Henrici Hastenii, 1626
4°: A-B⁴, 8 ff., *1-2* 3-16
G: 201 B 72

63  Laurentius Landtmeter O. Praem, *De clerici, monachi vetere institutio, Liber primus*
Lovanii, Ex officinâ Henrici Hastenii (…), 1626
4°: *-5*⁴A-2E⁴2F², 134 ff., *1-4* 5-34, [6] 1-227 *228*
BCNI 7682
L: 491.d.28.(5.), +

64  Philippus Rovenius, *Tractatus de missionibus*
Lovanii, Typis Henrici Hastenii, 1626
8°: A-L⁸M⁴, 92 ff., *1-2* 3-181 *182-184*
BCNI 7731
B: VI 5260 A 2, +

65  Thomas a Jesu O. Carm, *Instructio spiritualis eorum qui vitam eremiticam profitentur*⁴
8°: A-I⁸, 72ff., *1-2* 3-136 *137-144*
BCNI 7744; Rosier 852
G (Carm.): GPOCD MSFC.II

**1627**

66 John Barnewell (Praes) / F. Ferrall (Def), *Sententia divi Augustini de gratia*
Lovanii, Typis Henrici Hastenii, 1627
4°: 12 ff.
Allison & Rogers I 81
Olim Lv: Rec.4°, I 2 (destroyed in 1914)

67 Michael de Dôle OFM Cap, *Le miroir du pécheur poenitent* (engraved title)
A Lovain, Chez Henry Haestens (…), 1627
8°: *8**4A-T8, 164 ff., [24] *1*2-64 63-283 [=65-285] *286-304* + 24 engravings
numbered 1- 24
BCNI 7847
A (RG): 3034 E.3, +

68 Herman Hugo SJ, *The seige of Breda*, trsl. Gerrat Barry (engraved title)
Lovanii, Ex officina Hastenii, 1627
(col: Lovanii, Ex Officinâ Henrici Hastenii (…), 1628)
2°:π1*2A-V4, 83 ff., [6] 1-157 *158-160*
Allison & Rogers (1956) 408; Sommerv.IV 520-1 (no.7); STC 13926a
L: 591.f.21, +

69 David van Mauden, *Antidotum adversus calumniosos et venenosos libellos Ioannis Lillers*
Lovanii, Ex Officinâ Henrici Hastenii (…), 1627
4°: *4**2A-Y4, 94 ff., [12] *1*2-174 *175-176*
BCNI 7843
L: 713.f.2.(1.), +

70 David van Mauden, *Discursus morales in decem Decalogi praecepta, ad usum concionantium* (engraved title)
Lovanii, Apud Henricum Hastenium, 1627
(col: Lovanii, Ex Officinâ Henrici Hastenii (…), 1627).
2°:π1*4A-5O6, 641 ff., [10] *1*2-1248 *1249-1272*
BCNI 7528 ('1625'!) and 7844 ('Brussel, Vivien, 1627'!)
B: V.B.1882 C, +

**1628**

71 [Jerusalem], *Waerachtighe Beschrijvinghe van d'oude ende nieuwe Stadt Ierusalem. Beschreven van Fl. Iosephus ende Hegesippus. Bereyst ende beschreven vanden eerweerdigen Iacob Boeckenberch, ende Hieronymus Scheyt inden jaer 1600. ende 1612*
Tot Loven, Gedruckt by Henrick van Hastens, 1628
(part-title H4r: Tot Loven, By Henrick van Hastens, 1628)
4°: A-L4M2, 46 ff., unnumbered
BCNI 7904; Anna E. C. Simoni(art.n.1) p.191-2 n.13
G: Hi 8594

72  Adrianus Crommius SJ (Praes) / Otho Esquens SJ (Def), *Centum quinquaginta Psalmi Davidici compendiosa paraphrasi expositi, et sensu mystico illustrati*
Lovanii, Ex Officinâ Henrici Hastenii (…), 1628
4°: 36 pp.
BCNI 7925; Sommerv.II col.1692 (no.1)
Not found

73  Pedro Gomez SJ, *Briefve relation de la mort glorieuse de Paul Michi, Ian Goto et Iacques Ghisai Japonnois de la Compagnie de Jesus, Arrivée en Nangasachi le 5 Febvrier 1597*
A Louvain, Chez Henry Haestens, 1628
8°: A⁸, 8 ff., *1-2* 3-15 *16*
BCNI 7947; Sommerv.III col.1556 (no.3)
He: 78 N FABE 16180

74  Idem, *Cort verhael van de heerlijcke doodt van de salighen Paulus Micki, Joannes Goto ende Jacobus Ghisai, japonoisen der Soc. Jesu*
BCNI 7949; Sommerv.III col.1556 (no.3)
Not found

75  Herman Hugo SJ, *Pia desideria ed. 4a* (engraved title)
Vulgavit Boëtius à Bolswert, Typis Henr. Hastenii, Lovanii 1628
(col: Lovanii, Typis Henr. Hastenii, 1628)
24°: †⁸††⁺⁴A-M⁸χ¹, 109 ff., [24] *1-2* 3-190 *191-194*
BCNI 7956; Sommerv.IV col.513-20 (no.6)
*Another issue:* Antverpiae, Apud Henricum Aertssens, 1629
A (RG): 3043 F.5 (issue 1629: B: LP 3076 A (incomplete)

76  Michael Paludanus OSA, *Sacra et theologica chronologia*
Lovanii, Ex Officinâ Henrici Hastenii (…), 1628
4°: *⁴A-2O⁴, 152 ff., [8] *1* 2-296
H: 3191 F 24, +

77  Joannes Wamesius, *Responsorum sive consiliorum ad ius forumque civile pertinentium, centuria secunda*
Lovanii, Apud Henricum Hastenium (…), 1628
2°: π² A-2K⁶, 200 ff., [4] *1* 2- 373 *374-396*
B: III 67.865 C 2

## Index of Publishers/Printers

David Paisey

# Printed books in English and Dutch in early printed catalogues of German university libraries

... y mettre tous les vieux & nouveaux Autheurs dignes de considération, en leur propre langue & en l'idiome duquel ils se sont seruis ...

Gabriel Naudé, *Advis pour dresser une bibliothèque* (Paris, 1627)

When I selected this research topic to honour the special sympathies of Anna Simoni, whose friendship and help I have enjoyed throughout my working life – the history of learning, libraries and catalogues, and matters Anglo-Dutch – I should have reflected that surprises are liable to await those who first pick their topic and only then look at the evidence. The period before the Enlightenment, when Latin was still the prime medium of continental scholarship and of international scholarly communication, was unlikely, I thought, to produce great numbers of books in these particular foreign vernaculars at German universities (being languages of bourgeois trading; though French, and even Italian, as prestigious court languages would have been a different matter), and so assembling my evidence seemed a straightforward task. My intention was, and is, to document a small corner of linguistic internationalism in academic circles before vernacular-based nationalisms and the decline of Latin forced far-reaching educational and institutional changes, exemplified first of all at Halle, and then even more strikingly in the University Library at Göttingen, which, as is well known, was designed to serve the modern ideal of a university as a centre of original research, with a library to match.[1] The period I selected was therefore from the earliest printed catalogue as far as the mid-18th century.

But I had reckoned without the difficulty of locating copies of the early German university library catalogues usefully, if not exhaustively, recorded first by Erman/Horn,[2] and more recently by Paul Raabe.[3] Many of these are clearly very rare books indeed, and no one library seems to contain even a majority of them. What I first took for unaccountable gaps in the British Library's otherwise marvellous holdings in the history of institutional libraries proved to be a common failing, and even the Bayerische Staatsbibliothek at Munich lost several of the catalogues it once had through the bombs of the Second World War. One catalogue, that by Johannes Mensinga of the Bibliotheca Gooriana at Duisburg (1668), seems not to have survived at all. The varied locations of the copies I have been able to consult show how scattered they are, and my possibly still incomplete list involved considerable problems of supply.[4] The lesson to be drawn is that the catalogues were printed for largely local reasons, for instance as records for security purposes and to assist access to growing collections, or maybe to encourage patronage, and not widely marketed as useful bibliographies for scholars and collectors, still less as guides for potential remote users. Confessional differences within Germany made particularist state universities serve primarily their own 'national' student body, whose employment would most likely remain within the state concerned.

It is of course no use expecting early modern universities and their libraries to be anything like those of the modern period. Dedicated to the transmission of traditional learning and rhetorical skills in its presentation, they had as yet little need of current awareness. It was the Enlightenment that brought enhanced respect for new texts rather than republished old ones, and exploited journals to speed their transmission, for current rather than antiquarian books, for printed books rather than manuscripts, and for modern rather than ancient languages. In our period, library collections were still hardly ever systematically maintained, but were put together from private collections (which could have their own strengths and coherence), plus haphazard accessions from various sources. In the pre-cameralist age, public institutions like universities were not state-funded from the centre, and in their libraries funding was often quite inadequate, nearly always irregular, and mostly depended on student fees and fines of various kinds, bequests and gifts. The libraries were used far more by professors than by students – the professors, we must remember, still producing a high proportion of the thesis texts which the students merely defended;[5] and since professors maintained often substantial private libraries, to which many granted access to certain students[6] (often to the student lodgers most kept as a source of additional income), central library provision hardly seemed a priority. Often libraries were open only for a few hours each week, to enable borrowing and return of books, a practical restriction when one realises that most were unheated in winter. In Jena and Leipzig, some books were still chained in the early 17th century. And since the provision of regular librarians depended on regular funding, it was some time before the profession developed out of professorial rotas and part-timers.

The best succinct account of the history of German university libraries is by Ladislaus Buzás,[7] but there is a huge literature on the subject, and I shall only mention details which are directly relevant to those libraries whose catalogues I have investigated and which seem to require introduction. Each library catalogue is the product of different circumstances, and generalisations from particular holdings would be dangerous. However, taking all the surviving printed catalogues up to 1751 that I could get my hands on may legitimately give some idea of the spread of English and Dutch in German universities. The picture that emerges could, and probably should, be tested against a sample of private libraries,[8] and of libraries of other sorts, for example the usually better funded court libraries, or town libraries like Frankfurt am Main, whose marvellous printed catalogue of 1728[9] includes 110 books in Dutch and 19 in English.

In drawing up my list, I have cheated a little in including a modern catalogue of the Bibliotheca Palatina from Heidelberg, now in the Vatican, because it represents the Heidelberg holdings in 1623. But no apology is needed for citing the catalogues of the German Nations at the universities of Orléans and Padua, not German universities at all, but of particular interest in that they record collections assembled for German students by German students. My list, chronologically, is therefore as follows: Heidelberg (1623), Orléans (1664 & 1678), Frankfurt an der Oder (1676 & 1706), Wittenberg (1678), Duisburg (1685), Padua (1685 & 1691), Rinteln (1692, 1733 & 1751), Jena (1746). The absence of Catholic universities (with the exception of the anomalous Orléans and Padua) will be noted;[10] so will the strong representation of Calvinist institutions. It would be tempting to draw the conclusion that the publishing of library catalogues in these institutions of higher learning reflects the more open, less orthodox, attitude to access to information of the Protestant traditions. After all, the Netherlands had led the way in publishing university library catalogues (Leiden from 1595, Utrecht from 1608, and Franeker from 1656), as indeed it had also led in the production of auction catalogues, and the first Bodley catalogue appeared in 1605.

My concentration on books in Dutch or English really only allows conclusions about linguistic knowledge, not about the penetration of Dutch or English culture on a broader basis. It would be quite a different matter to consider the spread of literature by Dutch and English authors in Latin and in German translation, of which these German libraries contained a very great deal, though in fact I have not been able to refrain altogether from comment on that aspect of these catalogues. They would certainly repay consideration in that wider perspective. I shall first consider the collections one by one, then attempt a summing-up, and finally provide a list of the books I have found.

## [Heidelberg 1623]

Central library provision at Heidelberg University predated the invention of printing, and was in the form of faculty collections to which students were not given access. Then the Bibliotheca Palatina, originally a court library, passed to the University early in the 15th century, and was kept on the balconies of the Heiliggeistkirche. During the 16th century, printed books were regularly added from the Frankfurt Fairs,[11] and other accessions included the library of Ulrich Fugger, incorporated in 1584. The first permanent librarian was appointed in 1590, and from then on the library had regular opening hours (two days per week in summer, three in winter) and admitted students as well as professors. The Calvinist connection meant there were strong links with Holland, for instance the influential presence of Janus Gruter, Professor of History from 1592. In his period as University Librarian, he made the collections more accessible to visiting scholars from elsewhere. Manuscripts probably constituted the greatest strength of the library, for instance some important oriental manuscripts, which led to the study of Arabic at the University from 1612.[12]

There is no contemporary printed catalogue of the Palatina (though two copies of a manuscript catalogue of 1566 survive), but the circumstance of its being looted and removed to Rome in 1623 has allowed a modern cataloguer to present it, frozen at that date, as it still stands on the shelves in the Vatican:

Enrico Stevenson, *Inventario dei libri stampati Palatino-Vaticani*, 2 vols (Roma, 1886-91). (*Index*. Bearbeitet von Günter Richter, Nieuwkoop 1969.) These are not rare books, and therefore do not require locations.

When the books arrived in Rome, there were some 8,500 volumes (including manuscripts), but some were soon thereafter transferred to other collections. Stevenson's catalogue, which omits incunables, covers perhaps two-thirds of the original holdings, and has the great merit from my point of view of being arranged by language, even if the headings chosen for the English books show his grasp of that language to have been weak, despite his name. It was thus easy to see that there are five books in English and eight in Dutch, with in addition two polyglott editions containing English and two Dutch. In comparison, there are 19 books in Italian, 35 in French, and three in Spanish; Danish is represented in the Polyglott New Testament which also contains English. The numbers are, in relation to the whole, very small indeed, and do not permit conclusions about the reasons for the English and Dutch presence. The subjects represented are religion, recent history, philosophy, and art (two of Jacob Cats's emblem books), and the dates, with a few exceptions, after 1600: the majority of the books in the Palatina as a whole are of the 16th century, with apparently nothing later than 1619. It is interesting to note the presence of the London 1616 English edition of the works of King James I of England, in the town which housed his daughter, subsequently the luckless Winter Queen of Bohemia.

## Orléans 1664 & 1678

The University of Orléans, founded in 1235, became particularly famous for the quality of its faculty of laws, and attracted large numbers of foreign students, especially Germans. Part of its appeal lay in the reputation for purity of the French spoken in Orléans, and many German aristocrats visited it on their grand tour;[13] many Dutch students, too, stopped at Orléans on their *peregrinatio academica*,[14] amongst whom we meet Jacob Cats again, who took a law degree there. In addition, the fees were apparently thought to be relatively low, and degrees readily awarded.[15] One would naturally not expect to find English students studying Roman law abroad, but before 1538 there had been a Scottish Nation at Orléans (thereafter absorbed in the Norman Nation). The Nations were self-help and solidarity student organisations for aliens, probably deriving in structure from those at Bologna,[16] the German *Natio* at Orléans, which dated from the 14th century (there are statutes of 1378), being particularly large and well-organised. It had about 120 members by 1556 and included students from Brabant and Holland, Lorraine, Denmark and Norway. It had generous privileges, which in the 17th century applied to all members irrespective of rank: these included the right to carry arms, and also to five free seats at the theatre. The multinational composition of the German Nation seems to have led to the use of Latin as *lingua franca* by its members: 'Famuli Procuratoris & Quaestoris gratis inscribuntur, ex decreto senatus die 19. Novembr. anno 1631 modo latinae linguae non sint ignari'.[17] (We should not be surprised at the thought of servants knowing Latin, since poor students often acted as servants to rich aristocratic ones.) But the oath of membership of the *Natio* could be sworn in Latin, French, German or Dutch.[18] The 17th century, although reckoned a period of relative decline for the University as a whole, was at least one of considerable tolerance in religious affairs, between the Edict of Nantes (1598) and its revocation (1685), a matter of crucial importance for the many Protestant foreign students, and even non-Catholic theology could be studied. The Thirty Years' War brought numerous German Protestants to Orléans, but with the Franco-Dutch War of 1672-78 spelling the end of Dutch students too in the German Nation, by 1689 only the Beadle remained![19] The Nation led a shadowy existence in the 18th century, and the University itself failed to survive the Revolution.

The 'German' students themselves decided to found a library for their own use in 1565, which was run by librarians elected from their number, like the other officers of the Nation, and supported by funds from dedicated fees from members and by voluntary donations (obligatory in the case of officers), and as early as 1608 it could be described as 'belle et ample'.[20] No books seem to have been donated by professors, though they may have been allowed to use the library. After an early period when members of the Nation had to pay borrowing fees, the growing stock permitted borrowing without payment. Numbers of the books from this fascinating library survive in Orléans, and Charles Cuissard, who published an account of it in 1892,[21] planned to produce a catalogue of those he had found, but never did so, and left no manuscript amongst his papers when he died in 1912.[22]

Two catalogues of the library of the German Nation at Orléans were published during its heyday, each compiled by the current librarian, the first apparently a Dane, the second from Groningen:

[Emmichius Nedergordius], *Catalogus librorum qui Aureliae in bibliotheca Germanicae Nationis extant* (Aureliae: apud Antonium Rousselet, [1664]), pp.80. 4°.
Orléans, Bibliothèque publique.

Gisbert Edingh, *Catalogus librorum qui Aureliae in bibliotheca inclytae Nationis Germanicae extant* (Aureliae: apud Nicolaum Verjon: ex typographia Petri Rouzeau, 1678), pp.176. 8°.
British Library, 619. c.12.

According to Cuissard, a supplement to the latter was published in 1682 and is usually found with it, but it is not present in the British Library copy and I have not seen it. The Orléans printers have no Fraktur and no Roman w, and Rouzeau has no lower-case k.

These catalogues, arranged by faculty, are a marvellous source for German student reading in the 17th century and deserve a great deal of detailed study: I can characterise them only briefly here. The library covered all subjects, but is especially rich in law, history, and philosophy, with theology offering an extraordinarily liberal range of confessions; science and medicine are less well represented. Most surprising of all is a section of novels (over 100), mainly French, showing that the students also indulged in leisure reading, almost certainly partly as a linguistic exercise; there is also a strong section of grammars and multilingual dictionaries. Books in French are particularly numerous overall, maybe approaching in quantity those in Latin. German is the next favoured language, but Dutch and English (in that order) come very far behind, followed by even smaller representation of other languages. Cuissard and I differ in our estimates of the total number of books in the 1664 catalogue: he reckons over 4000, I reckon under 3000; but I have taken no account of multiple copies of certain works, of which there are many, for instance seven copies of Comenius's *Janua reserata*. The entries in the 1664 catalogue are extremely summary, only a few having dates and places of publication, and it is not always possible to determine which books are in

Dutch or English, or sometimes to identify works in question, let alone editions. The 1678 entries are of a higher standard, and usually have place and date. Again Cuissard and I differ in estimating the total number, he reckoning over 5000, I about 4000. He estimates the growth of the collection between the two catalogues as just over 900 items, or 64 per annum. By my count, in 1664 there are 22 books in Dutch, rising to 32 in 1678, and in English seven rising to nine, with the addition of several grammars and multilingual dictionaries. Given the large numbers of books in German in the library of the German Nation, it is noteworthy that the presence of an estimated one third overall of Dutch-speaking students in it failed to raise the proportion of books in Dutch much ahead of the tiny proportion of books in English.

## Frankfurt an der Oder 1676 & 1706

The University of Frankfurt an der Oder, founded in 1506, had become Calvinist with Brandenburg and its ruler Johann Sigismund in 1613. Its fine library, with the most extensive catalogues of those I am considering, grew from the bequest in 1516 of the books of the lawyer and Rector Siegfried Utensberger, mainly through the addition of other private collections. At the time we are considering it was open daily for an hour or two. It has the advantage of being presented in two marvellous catalogues by the same compiler:

Johann Christoph Becmann, *Catalogus Bibliothecae publicae Univ. Francofurtanae.* pp.488. In: *Memoranda Francofurtana*, edited by J. C. Becmann (Frankfurt an der Oder, 1676). 4°. British Library 126.i.23.

Johann Christoph Becmann, *Catalogus Bibliothecae publicae Universitat. Francofurtanae* (Frankfurt an der Oder, 1706), pp. 312. fol. British Library 731.1.10(2).

The librarian Becmann (1641-1717) was a Calvinist theologian, and author of several historical works on Brandenburg and Anhalt, as well as on the University of Frankfurt an der Oder. I should like to salute him, across the centuries, for the outstanding excellence of his catalogues, which are a pleasure to use. In the main, these are author catalogues, though there are some subject headings (for instance, *Anglicana*, or *Belgica anonyma*). Possibly their abandonment of arrangement by faculties makes them seem strikingly modern. Entries almost always provide place and date of publication, and there are several analytical entries. The second corrects mistakes and wrong attributions in the first, and sometimes recatalogues items (*Baconus* becomes *Verulamius*, for example).

I estimate the number of entries in the 1676 catalogue at some 15,000, though the number of books in the collection must have been considerably higher, as there are many tract volumes (occasional and academic publications, for instance). The humanities are more fully represented than science and medicine, and there are many books of the 15th and 16th centuries, with much Reformation theology and controversy. Again there is a liberal representation of the views of different confessions, including for instance catechisms of Catholics and Socinians, the *Canons and Constitutions* of the Church of England in Latin (London, 1604), and the *Malleus maleficarum* (Frankfurt am Main, 1588) as well as Spee's heroically progressive *Cautio criminalis*

(Rinteln, 1631). Books in the German language come a very poor second to those in Latin, and French is definitely the most numerous of the other foreign languages, of which there are several, with a good representation of grammars and linguistics. There are Bibles in many languages: polyglott, Hebrew, Greek, Latin, German, French, Italian, English, Hungarian, and Polish (but not Dutch), New Testaments in French, Spanish, Polish, and Danish (but not Dutch or English), and the Psalms in French, English, Italian, and Hungarian (but not Dutch). Dutch and English culture, and their authors, are strongly present in Latin, with many editions published in those countries, amongst which it is good to see Thomas James's Bodley catalogues of 1605 and 1620, but the proportion of books in Dutch and English is again minute: four books in Dutch,[23] and 22 in English. The numerous theological works of the early 17th century amongst the latter might suggest that they came to this library from a single source, were it not for the fact that the English additions in the 1706 catalogue also contain works in the same category. Becmann tells us that this second catalogue contains more than 2000 additions, which would average out at a rate of 66 accessions per annum, and these include both recent and earlier literature, as we have seen. There are nine more books in Dutch, making 13 in all, and five more in English, making 27 in all. The exact percentages are not significant (0.08% and 0.16% respectively), but it is clear how extremely low they are.

Before leaving Frankfurt's excellent librarian Becmann, I should like to record that he seems to have had a personal interest in English matters. He edited the *Basilikon doron* of James I (1679), and in the section on English history in his *Historia orbis terrarum* (2nd ed., Frankfurt an der Oder 1680, pp.553-605), which concentrates on the 17th century, he introduces English quotations in prose and verse, suggesting that he knew the language well; in the geography section he lists the financial contributions of each British county to the cost of the Anglo-Dutch war of 1665 (pp.113-19).

## Wittenberg 1678

The university library in this stronghold of Lutheranism was a poor thing in the 17th century. In 1536 the Bibliotheca Electoralis had been made accessible to professors and students (the university having been founded in 1502), but in 1547, when it comprised some 3000 volumes, it was removed first to Weimar, then in 1549 to Jena. Thus bereft of books, Wittenberg slowly built up its own collection with regular but not over-generous funding, and its catalogue of 1678 runs to less than 1500 entries:

Andreas Sennertus, *Bibliotheca Academiae Wittebergensis publicae librorum quà* (1) *theologicorum* (2) *Juridicorum* (3) *medicorum* (4) *philosophicorum* (5) *historicorum* (6) *orientalium* (7) & *qui noviter huic de anno LXXII. accesserunt… usui academico eidemque privato publicoque exhibiti* (Wittebergae: impensis editoris, 1678), pp. 54. 4°.   Wolfenbüttel Bb.2238.

Friedrich K. G. Hirsching, the Bernhard Fabian of his day, in his marvellous but alas! not exhaustive survey of German libraries in the late 18th century,[24] remarks that this catalogue by Sennertus was even then very rare: 'die gelehrte Welt verliehrt aber auch nichts daran, da es viele Fehler hat und nur bloss die Titel der Bücher enthält, fast wie sie auf dem Einband erscheinen, ohne den Druckort oder das Jahr der Herausgabe anzuzeigen'. I can only echo his judgement on the cataloguing standards, though even a poor catalogue is better than none at all. Arrangement is first by faculty classes, then by format, and the books are overwhelmingly in Latin. Even German is not well represented, and other modern languages are mostly restricted to editions of the Bible. There are no books in Dutch, and two in English: a Bible and a catechism. Sennertus's own interest was in Middle Eastern languages, and he lists the 'libri in orientalibus linguis; ex legato maximè meo'. The accessions from 1672 to 1678, under his librarianship, are not all contemporary, but amount to only about 60 works, or less than ten per annum.

### Duisburg 1685

The Calvinist university at Duisburg was founded in 1655, and from 1657 professors and rectors took turns as librarian. The most important of early accessions to the library was the collection formed by Heinrich von Goor, who had been mayor of Moers, and who bequeathed his books for public use, though not to a specific institution: his heirs gave them to the university in 1666 on condition they be inventoried and kept together, and made available on two days per week. A catalogue was therefore produced by Johannes Mensinga and printed in 1668:

Johannes Mensinga, *Catalogus librorum Bibliothecae Goorianae usui Academiae Electoralis Duisburgo-Clivensis dicatae* (Duisburg, 1668). Copy formerly in Bonn University Library (to which the Duisburg books were transferred in 1818) but destroyed in the Second World War. No other copy known.

Karlheinz Goldmann, who described the catalogue before its destruction,[25] tells us that it was arranged in faculties, and listed over 1400 volumes, being richest in theology, but rather meagre in Goor's own subject of law because many of his law books were excluded from the bequest. As a result of the wars with France, the 1670s saw much disorder in Duisburg and this library, which seems to have lost several books to occupying troops. Nevertheless, a salaried post of librarian was created in 1677, and Professor Gerhard von Mastricht appointed. He produced a new catalogue in 1685:

Gerhard von Mastricht, *Bibliothecae Publicae Electoralis Academiae Duisburgensis ut et Bibliothecae Goorianae, ejusdem Academiae usibus dedicatae, catalogus* (Duisburg, 1685), pp.94. fol. UB Heidelberg (F 8633); incomplete copy in UB Düsseldorf (B.W.41)

This is an author catalogue, no longer by faculties, and entries are very short, mostly without imprint or date. There are some analytical entries, and a few 'dumps', for instance for anonymous anti-Jesuit books in German, Giessen theses, or Leiden theological theses. Goldmann estimated some 1600 entries in this catalogue, but I think there are considerably more, representing perhaps over 3000 works in all. The books are overwhelmingly in Latin, with small and decreasing representation for other languages in the order: German, French, Italian, Dutch, Greek, English, others. There are 22 books in Dutch, mainly theology, with a few in history; and five in English, of which four are theological, and all of the late 16th or earlier 17th century. A catalogue of the Bodleian Library makes another appearance, but it is not possible to say which, as the entry is undated. The theological books are dominated by Calvinism, and there is much Calvin (in French) and the popular early 17th-century theologian Matthias Martini who taught in Emden and Bremen (in Latin), but little Luther apart from the Jena *Works* in Latin of 1556. The library never flourished properly after its promising beginnings, and when recatalogued in 1717 is aid to have run to just over 2000 entries.

## Padua 1685 & 1691

The German Nation at Padua (which included Dutch students) split into two parts in 1553, the law students ('legisti') and the rest, *ie* the students of theology, philosophy and medicine ('artisti'), and both sections had libraries. Antonio Favaro, *Saggio di bibliografia dello studio di Padova*, pt. 1 (Venice, 1922), lists one printed catalogue for each (nos. 445 & 529), though it is clear from the title of the second that it must have had a predecessor which Favaro does not mention:

*Bibliotheca medico-philosophico-philologica Inclytae Nationis Germanae Artistarum quae Patavij degit* (Patavij: typis Petri Mariae Frambotti, 1685), pp.133[-?]. 4°.   Padua University, Sez.Ven.A.II.1 bis 3.[26]

*Catalogus librorum altero se correctior comptiorque qui Patavii in Bibliotheca I.N.G.J.* [ = Inclytae Nationis Germanae Juristarum] *inveniuntur* (Patavii: ex typographia Pasquati, 1691), pp.[8?], 56. 4°.   Padua University, Sez.Ven.A.II.1.3.

I can provide only brief notes on these catalogues, having obtained xerox copies only at the last moment. The first contains nearly 5300 volumes, and the second some 2800, but in each case the number of works is considerably smaller, as multiple copies and separate volumes of multi-volume sets are separately entered.

Entries in the first catalogue are very brief, but most include the date and place of publication. The majority are of the 17th and later 16th centuries, though earlier items are present too. The catalogue is divided into two main parts of comparable size, for medical books and the rest, and within each part by format. The language representation is interesting: in medicine nearly all is in Latin, with a mere 40 works in German, 30 in Italian, 9 in French, 2 in Greek, and one each in Spanish and Dutch; amongst the 'libri philosophici et mixti', however, while again Latin rules, there are over 450 books in Italian, compared with about 70 each in German and French and much lower numbers in other languages, including six in Dutch and two in English. Clearly much leisure reading was done in Italian, no doubt partly to improve fluency in the language, as we saw with the French books at Orléans.

The names of two librarians of the INGJ appear on the title-page of the 1691 catalogue, but it is not clear whether they compiled it. The severely abbreviated entries have no date or place of publication, and authors are listed in a very old-fashioned arrangement by the initial of their first name. The catalogue is divided into three sections: 'Libri juridici' (all in Latin); 'Libri historici latini' (humanities, plus a little science and mathematics); and 'Libri italici, germanici, hispanici, & gallici' (ditto). The last group, in which all titles are listed in Italian, whatever the language of the edition in question, is overwhelmingly in Italian, with under 50 items in French, just over 30 in German, and less than 20 in Spanish; the one book in English (a breviary) seems to have got there by mistake, and there is no Dutch.

### Rinteln 1692, 1733 & 1751

Rinteln, a Lutheran university, had no library for more than 20 years after its foundation, which underlines how far university libraries could be subordinated in importance to scholars' private libraries in this period. It began rather modestly in 1644 with gifts of books and money from professors and the University printer Peter Lucius I., and was also to receive gifts from the Swedish commander Oxenstierna. It had regular funding from 1666, plus prescribed fees from new professors and from graduands. Professors were expected to deposit copies of their own publications, and the University printer copies of his products. There was no permanent librarian until 1705, and in the same year regular opening hours on Wednesday and Saturday afternoons were instituted. But the early 18th century was a period of neglect for the library, in terms both of financial support and physical conditions.

There are three Rinteln catalogues to consider:

(Johannes Kahler), *Catalogus librorum qui in Bibliotheca Academica Rinthelii asservantur* (Rinteln, 1692), pp.171. 4°.  Copy in Göttingen University Library (H.lit.libr.VIII.3051); another in Augsburg University Library (02/I.1/4.28) lacks all after p.152.

Johann Nicolaus Funck, *Publica illustris Ernestinae Rintelensium Academiae Bibliotheca* (Rinteln, 1733), 5 pt.: pp.52, 207, 131, 86, 156. 4°.  Copy in Munich University Library (4°H.lit. 472); this copy was originally in Landshut. The copy now in Marburg University Library (VIII B 1300 f) was formerly in the Ernestinum at Rinteln

Johann Nicolaus Funck, *Publicae in illustri Ernestina Rintelensium Bibliothecae accessio* (Rinteln, 1751), pp.312. 4°.  Copy in Wolfenbüttel (Bb.1850)

The layout of the earliest of these catalogues is particularly interesting, presenting a great deal of blank space and wide margins, as if for manuscript additions. That it was so used is proved by the incomplete copy now in Augsburg, which has large numbers of books (especially law books) and their shelf-numbers added in manuscript and must have been an 'in-house' catalogue at Rinteln. So the rarity of printed German university library catalogues is seen in at least this one case to be due to production for purely local use. (I am reminded of the British Museum, which for so long even in the 20th century printed its accessions of printed books solely for incorporation in its own loose-leaf catalogues.)

The 1692 catalogue, according to Schormann,[27] represents a collection of some 2000 books. I would have thought there were more, but estimation is difficult, particularly since large sets like the *Bibliotheca magna patrum* and the German works of Luther are set-out. The catalogue is arranged in faculties, and within each by author. Entries are very abbreviated, though many give place and date of publication, and must have been copied from a manuscript listing, as some books are noted as missing. The books are overwhelmingly in Latin, with a low proportion of German; other languages are very sparsely represented. There are runs of the *Diarium Europaeum* and *Acta eruditorum*, and the most famous book ever printed at Rinteln, Spee's *Cautio criminalis* of 1631 (already noted at Frankfurt an der Oder), still anonymous here, together with the Rinteln professor of law's traditional views on the same subject: Hermann Goehausen, *Processus juris contra sagas* (Rinteln, 1630), which the *Cautio* quotes and refutes. There are a few books by English authors in Latin, including Harvey's *De motu cordis* (Rotterdam, 1671) and works by Bacon and Hobbes, and in German in the case of some Quaker texts printed in the Netherlands. But there are no books in the English language. What I take to be the only two books in Dutch, geographical works by Blaeu and de Laet, are catalogued as if they were in German, which suggests that the cataloguer knew no Dutch.

Schormann tells us that the catalogues of 1733 and 1751 by Funck were much admired at the time (and indeed they are excellent), but that the collections had risen to only some 2500 works by 1733. The former catalogue (which incidentally reveals the authorship of the *Cautio*) now includes two English Bibles and the Psalms, but still only the two Dutch works already mentioned. In a table based on the dates of publication of the books in this 1733 catalogue, Schormann[28] demonstrates that during the 17th century Rinteln gradually came to acquire more and more recently published literature, but declined again in this respect in the early 18th century. Funck was not appointed librarian until 1730 and does seem to have done his best for the library. In his 1751 *Accessio*, really an account of his stewardship, he ascribed the improvement in the library's fortunes ('Quam tristis nostrae fuerit ante hos viginti annos bibliothecae facies') mainly to the generosity of Friedrich, Landgrave of Hesse, and of a number of other named individuals, though funds still came *inter alia* from student fees. He tells us that graduands in theology, law and medicine had to pay more than graduands in philosophy, suggesting a lower prestige for the latter faculty. The entries seem to me to amount to several thousand, but it is hard to estimate how many books they represent because of the set-out entries and tract volumes. I counted six books in English (none contemporary) and only one more in Dutch (a theological work of 1657). During the later 18th century, Rinteln failed to transform itself on the Göttingen model, and when it was dissolved in 1810, the library had only grown to some 8000 volumes.

## Jena 1746

In 1557, the Gymnasium at Jena was translated into a university, which opened its doors in the following year. The Bibliotheca Electoralis from Wittenberg, as we have already seen, had been moved here in 1549, and formed the basis of the new (Lutheran) university's library. It was supported by the ducal house and had regular funding, but the majority of its accessions came from gifts and bequests. It had the right to claim copies of books printed by Jena printers since 1557. Lending to professors only was permitted in the early years, when the library was open for at most a couple of hours per day, but from 1627 students were admitted and could borrow books for eight days at a time. Though there is very little documentation of the use of university libraries in general, it is recorded that in Jena in 1721 up to 60 students could be found waiting for the library to open. From 1650 to 1750 it was called 'Bibliotheca Publica'. In 1678 it had 6000 volumes, rising to 10,000 in 1700 and no less than 50,000 in 1769.[29]

So when the first catalogue appeared in 1746, Jena University Library was a vigorously growing institution:

Johan Christoph Mylius, *Memorabilia Bibliothecae Academiae Jenensis* (Jena & Weissenfels, 1746), pp.640. 8°.  British Library 271.b.9

But this is only the first of a projected series of Jena catalogues, later volumes of which did not appear. It covers only part of the library therefore, and in a very selective way at that. Omitting 'minor works', it covers principally books from the 'Bibliotheca Electoralis', including accessions to the beginning of the Thirty Years' War, the 'Bibliotheca recens adjecta' (acessions since the Thirty Years' War), and the collection of Dominicus Arumaeus, strong in law books, bequeathed in 1639. The future catalogues projected by Mylius would have been three in number, and would have covered more recent accessions of scholars' libraries. We may particularly regret his failure to produce volume four, which was planned to include the 'Bibliotheca Birckneriana', a collection largely devoted to history and including '(numerus) librorum rarissimorum, prohibitorum et historicorum, quos Memoires uocant, lingua anglica, italica et gallica conscriptorum'.

If it is possible to make deductions about a cataloguer's psychology from his or her catalogues – and most people who have trained cataloguers will say that it is – then we may be permitted to have some doubts about Mylius's from the generally less than competently managed structure and somewhat erratic entries of his 1746 catalogue. It is divided first by collection, then by format, and then by faculties, and there is a partial date and place index of books 1459-1521, as there are many early imprints; the majority of books are of the 15th to the 17th centuries, with a much lower proportion from the 18th, no doubt because recent books would have been more in evidence in the future volumes. But it is not altogether a surprise to learn that Mylius's work got on top of him, and the poor man committed suicide in 1756. Perhaps he couldn't bear the thought of organising his remaining cataloguing task, though Kunoff[30] blames financial difficulties. In the catalogue he did produce there may be some 4000 entries for printed books, but many are tract volumes. Latin is again overwhelmingly the first language, followed by German, with French yet again in third place. Other languages, of which there is little, follow in the probable order: Italian, Spanish, English, Dutch, and others. As usual, there are plenty of books by English and Dutch authors in Latin, but in the vernacular only three in English, plus a polyglott New Testament, and two in Dutch.

Summing up what my evidence shows is a rather hazardous operation, not only because of the special circumstances of each of the libraries concerned, but also because the acquisition of every book mentioned involves factors not accessible via simple catalogue entries. Nevertheless, I feel it is worth trying a few deductions, and also worth presenting details of the works concerned, despite the difficulty of identifying texts and editions from frequently barbarously abbreviated and inadequate data. In the concluding list, I have been immensely aided by *STC* and *Wing* in identifying English books, and I have felt the acute need for *STCN*: though I have resorted to *NUC* and the BL catalogue, as well as various other sources, in the case of many Dutch books I have been obliged to leave entries as I found them. But naming all the books, even in uncorrected form, will allow readers to make their own deductions too.

A major caveat must apply to the fact that many universities are not represented amongst those which happened to produce printed catalogues in this period. Many have surviving manuscript catalogues and records which must contain masses of further evidence. One of my catalogues (Jena) covers only a part of the relevant holding, certainly omitting numbers of books in English.

It is clear that books in Dutch and English comprise an insignificant, not to say minute, proportion of the holdings investigated. Latin remains the first language of learning in Germany, with German second and French third, the other languages coming a long way behind. Though vernacular publishing for scholarly works was well established in Holland and Britain, particularly the latter, texts by Dutch and British authors are most frequently met with in Latin, with German or French translations as occasional alternatives. Of course, the Dutch and English languages were not taught systematically at German universities during this period, nor indeed for a long time to come. That is one reason why Gabriel Naudé's words which I have taken as my epigraph[31] seem to have been ignored by this group of libraries for the intellectual elite, for all the immense contemporary prestige of his views on library-building. Naudé was a fine professional librarian, and possibly part of the trouble in Germany stems from the slow emergence of the profession. Perhaps librarians really do influence what people read after all: what is read is certainly a function of what can be read.

Whether my books in Dutch and English were read, and by whom, is an un-answerable question. We have already seen students at Jena queueing for the library in 1721, but by contrast J. N. Funck in his Rinteln catalogue of 1733 complained that many students there lacked the motivation to use the library. I am encouraged by the example of the two German Nations, however, particularly that at Orléans, where students built up a splendid library for themselves, but the situation clearly varied from place to place, from one time to another, and of course from student to student. Surviving records of loans at Rostock University Library (which did not publish a catalogue) during the 40 years 1650-90 reveal that there were only 138 borrowers in all, including 52 students and 40 professors, and that only 707 works were lent; of the professors, two borrowed 35 times each, the remainder on average only six times.[32] That professors read a great deal (no doubt mostly in their own libraries, so they did not yet need university libraries), and that they tried to inculcate at least the appearance of book-learning in their students, is attested by the copious references in academic dissertations. I have always resisted the idea of citation indexes as a modern librarian's guide to what he or she ought to be buying, because they would make us all buy the same canonical texts, but there would be much to be gained from a citation index to texts of the past. By such means we might hope to reconstruct the literary canon of our period, and gauge its breadth or narrowness.

Other pointers to the canon could be found in contemporary general bibli-ographies, but it would take a whole research programme to reconstruct it. Leaving aside law (where Latin codes were the subject of university study and in any case England practised the wrong variety) and medicine (where imperfectly understood foreign instructions could have had fatal consequences), a couple of random exam-ples produced no texts in Dutch or English.[33] That books in Dutch or English were far from canonical is, I think, clearly demonstrated by my detailed list below of the relevant holdings of university libraries, in which no books in Dutch and only two at least partly in English prove to have been held by more than one library, George Downame's *Treatise concerning Antichrist* (1603) at Frankfurt an der Oder and Duisburg, and the 1599 polyglott *Bible* at Heidelberg and Jena.

Which is not to say that books in Dutch and English were not available in Germany. The *Bibliotheca exotica* of Georg Draudius (Frankfurt am Main, 1625) is a catalogue of foreign-language books (*ie* books not in German or Latin!) ostensibly available for purchase, and possibly largely compiled from the Fair Catalogues. It lists four times more books in French than in the next most numerous language, Italian, a long way behind which come English (309 items) and Dutch (142), then Spanish, and, last and least, Hungarian. Despite Draudius's claim to list books since 1500, nearly all those in Dutch and English are of the period 1600-24. That the Thirty Years' War adversely affected the trade in foreign books, and particularly English books, is well known, and attested in the Fair Catalogues. Not until the later 18th century did English books at the Fairs attain again the numbers they had managed in the early years of the 17th century. Dutch books, always more numerous, recovered their position by the mid 17th century, but then suffered another decline, with a low point in the first decade of the 18th century, rising again as the century progressed.[34] These curves are in fact reflected in the dates of the tiny numbers of books I record below (though there are no books at all in Dutch of the 18th century, and only three in English), and it would be interesting to discover what proportion of them appeared in the Fair Catalogues. However, the extremely small figures involved hardly constitute a significant sample.

It would also be a mistake to imagine that they reached the libraries by way of the trade in new publications. I suspect that many, possibly even most, of the books listed were not new when they entered these institutional collections, and that they came willy-nilly as part of private collections given or bequeathed, rather than as antiquarian purchases. This could only be proved by access to possibly non-existent acquisitions records, but it is suggested by the evidence of some of the catalogues above. Dated and datable books with imprint dates subsequent to the founding of each institution and prior to the publication of its first catalogue could theoretically have been acquired new; this applies to all Dutch or English items in the Heidelberg catalogue (1623), where we know that current purchases were in fact made from the Fairs. It also applies to all Dutch or English items in the first Orléans catalogue (1664), the first Frankfurt an der Oder catalogue (1676), to the single relevant item in the Wittenberg catalogue (1678), to the dated items in the first Padua catalogue (1685), and to the six relevant items in the Jena catalogue (1746). However, the second Orléans catalogue (1678) has only four out of 33 items with dates subsequent to its first catalogue, and the second Frankfurt an der Oder catalogue (1706) only one out of 17 in the same category: if acquisitions followed a consistent pattern in both institutions (admittedly a big if), new books in Dutch or English were much less likely to be acquired than old. At Duisburg, only one out of 14 items could theoretically have been acquired as a new book, and at Rinteln in all three catalogues the Dutch and English books (fourteen in all) could only have been acquired second-hand.

The subject breakdown of the books listed is interesting, though probably not very significant, as it leaves out of account translations from our two languages, of which these catalogues show large numbers. Theology leads the field by a long way (45

English items, 33 Dutch), which fits well with the known influence of heterodox theology from abroad on developments in Germany, though there is very little from the later 17th century, when English thought probably exerted its important influence on emergent Pietism through the medium of translation. Next in total numbers comes language (12 English, 14 Dutch), appropriately enough in a country where the two languages were so unfamiliar academically, followed by three areas in which Dutch is notably better represented than English; history and politics (6 English, 22 Dutch), geography (2 English, 14 Dutch), and belles-lettres (2 English, 10 Dutch). Other subjects trail lamely; law (1 English, 6 Dutch), medicine (3 Dutch, 2 English), science (2 English, 4 Dutch) and art (1 Dutch).

These Dutch and English holdings (179 in total, 107 in Dutch and 72 in English), when measured against the possible sum of maybe 45,000 books/entries in the catalogues I have considered, however great the margin of error in my calculations, produce a joint proportion of only 0.4%, separately 0.24% for Dutch and 0.16% for English. There can be do doubt that the dawn of interest and competence in these languages in Germany was still to come, whatever exceptions may exist (and they certainly do). Large academic libraries have since then moved some way in the direction of Naudé's ideal, adding some vernaculars which would have astonished him, but losing Latin as the international language of learning. Its replacement would probably have astonished him too.

## *Summary list of the books in English and Dutch in the catalogues considered*

Wherever identification was possible, entries have been updated. At a given university, only the first appearance of a book is recorded. Abbreviations: D = Duisburg, F/O = Frankfurt an der Oder, H = Heidelberg, J = Jena, O = Orléans, P = Padua, R = Rinteln, W = Wittenberg

### 1. English

Abernethy, John, *Physick for the soule* (London, 1622), 4°. (*STC* 74) F/O 1676
Adams, Thomas, [*Conciones variae*, Angl.] (London, 1615), 4°. (*STC* 107, 114 or 133)
   F/O 1706
— *The souldiers honour* (London, 1617), 4°. (*STC* 127) F/O 1706
Andrewes, Lancelot, *Sermons* (London, 1641), fol. (Wing 3142) R 1751
Attersoll, William, *The new covenant* [London, 1614] (*STC* 889.5) D 1685

Bacon, Francis, *The life of king Henry the seventh* (London, n.d.), fol. (various editions,
   *STC* 1159-1161) F/O 1676
Baxter, Richard, *Practical theologie and cases of conscience* (London, 1678), fol. R 1751
Bible, vol.1. (London, n.d.), 8°. F/O 1676
— *The holy Bible* (Edinburgh, 1633), 8°. (*STC* 2311 or 2311a) W 1678
— *The holy Bible.* (London, 1642), 12°. (Wing 2201a) R 1733
— *The whole booke of Psalmes* (Sternhold & Hopkins.) (London, 1602), 4° (*STC* 2506
   or 2506.5) F/O 1676
— *Davids Psalmes* (London, 1617), 12°. (?*STC* 2558.5) R 1751
— *The whole book of psalmes* (London, 1642), 12°. (Wing 2389, 2390, or 2391) R 1733

— *The whole book of psalmes* (Amsterdam, 1645), 12°. (Wing 2410A) R 1733

— *The New Testament*, Tr. L. Tomson. (Dort, 1603), 8°. (*STC* 2903) H 1623

— *The New Testament* (London, 1613), 12°. (no 12° in *STC*) R 1751

Blackwell, Elizabeth, *A curious herbal* (London, 1739), fol. J 1746

[Breviary] P 1691

Brinsley, John, *the Elder, The third part of the true Watch* (London, 1623), 4°. (*STC* 3787) F/O 1676

Broughton, Hugh, *A concent of scripture* (London, [1590]), 4°. (*STC* 3850 or 3851) R 1733

Bruce, Robert, *Sermons upon the Lords Supper* (Edinburgh, 1590), 8°. (*STC* 3924) F/O 1676

Buenting, Heinrich, *Itinerarium S. Scripturae*. Angl. (London, 1623), 4°. (*STC* 4018) F/O 1676

Catechism, [no title, place or date] W 1678

Caussin, Nicolas, *The holy court*. Tr. Thom. Hauwkins (London, 1650), fol. (Wing 1547) O 1664

Chaloner, Edward, *Six sermons* (London, 1623), 8°. (*STC* 4936) F/O 1676

Cowper, William, Μυστομια *reformata* (London, 1724), fol. J 1746

Delamothe, G., *The French alphabeth* (London, 1615). (*STC* 6548), P 1685

Dod, John, *Exposition of the Ten Commandements* (London, 1612), 4°. (*STC* 6971.5) F/O 1676

Donne, John, *Letters* (London, 1651), 4°. (Wing 1864) O 1664

— *Poems* (London, 1639), 8°. (*STC* 7047) O 1664

Downame, John, *The conflict between the flesh and the spirit* (London, 1618), 4°. (*STC* 7139) F/O 1676

— *A treatise concerning Antichrist* (London, 1603), 4°. (*STC* 7120) D 1685; F/O 1676

Dyke, Daniel, *the Elder, Two treatises, of repentance, & of Christs temptations* (London, 1616), 4°. (*STC* 7408) F/O 1676

Dyke, Jeremiah, *the Elder, Good conscience* (London, 1626), 8°. (*STC* 7415.5) F/O 1676

Elton, Edward, *The complaint of a sanctified sinner answered* (London, 1618), 4°. (*STC* 7610) F/O 1676

Feltham, Owen, *Resolves divine, morall, politicall* (London, 1636), 4°. (*STC* 10761) O 1664

Field, Richard, *Of the church, five bookes* (London, 1606). (*STC* 10857 or 10857.5) D 1685

Fortescue, Sir John, *A learned commendation of the politique lawes of England*. Tr. Robert Mulcaster (London, 1599), 8°. (*STC* 11196) H 1623

Gough, John, *The academy of complements* (London, 1656), 12°. (this ed. not in Wing) O 1664

Gunter, Edmund, *The description & use of the sector, cross-staffe and other instruments* (London, 1624), 4°. (*STC* 12522) F/O 1676

Hall, Joseph, *Epistles* (London, 1608). (*STC* 12662?) P 1685

Heldoren, J. G. van, *A new and easy English grammar* (Amsterdam, 1675), 12°. (Alston II 513) O 1678

Hieron, Samuel, *Sermons* (London, 1614), fol. (*STC* 13378) F/O 1676

*The images of the Old Testament* (London, 1549), 4°. (*STC* 3045: Lyons) F/O 1676

James I, King of England, *The workes* (London, 1616), fol. (*STC* 14344) H 1623

Le Mayre, Marten, *The Dutch schoolemaster* (London, 1652), 12°. (Not in Wing. *STC* 15453.7 is a 1606 8° edition) O 1664

Lever, Thomas, *Sermon preached at S. Pauls Crosse* (London, 1550), 8°. (*STC* 15546 or 15546.3) F/O 1706

Lily, William, *An English grammar* (London, 1641), 8°. (Wing 2262) F/O 1706
— *Lilies grammar in English by R. R.* (London, 1641), 4°. (Wing has no 4° edition of this date) F/O 1676

Lucanus, Marcus Annaeus, *Pharsalia* (London, 1631), 8°. (*STC* 16888) O 1664

Lyly, John, *Euphues and his England* (London, 1586), 4°. (*STC* 17073) F/O 1706

Mauger, Claude, *French grammar* (London, 1670), 8°. (Wing 1339) O 1678

Norris, Sir John, *A complete sett of new charts, containing the North Sea, Cattegat and Baltick* (London, 1723), fol. R 1751

Perkins, William, *Workes*, vol.I. (London, 1612), fol. (*STC* 19650) R 1751
— *Lectures upon the three chapters of the Revelation* (London, 1604), 4°. (*STC* 19731) H 1623

Philips, Edward *Certaine godly and learned sermons* (London, 1605), 8°. (*STC* 19853) H 1623

Playfere, Thomas, *The whole sermons* (London, 1623), 8°. (*STC* 20003) F/O 1676
— *Hearts delight* (London, 1623). (*STC* has 1603 & 1633 editions, respectively 20010 & 20013) F/O 1676

Prideaux, John, *Eight sermons* (London, 1621), 4°. (*STC* 20351) F/O 1706

Ravius, Christianus, *A general grammar for Ebreu, Chalde, Syriac, Arabic, Samaritan* (London, 1648), 8°. (?part of Wing 310) F/O 1676
— *Some notes upon Martinii Ebreu grammar in English* (Amsterdam, 1646), 8°. (not in Wing) F/O 1676

Ray, John, *The wisdom of God manifested in the works of the creation.* 2nd ed. (London, 1692), 8°. (Wing 411) J 1746

Reynolds, Edward, *Meditations on the holy sacrament* (London, 1639), 4° (*STC* 20930) O 1664

Sancroft, William, *Modern policies* (London, 1657), 12°. (Wing 559) O 1678

Sibbes, Richard, *Divine meditations and holy contemplations* (London, 1638), 12°. (*STC* 22490) O 1678

Smith, Sir Thomas, *De regimine Angliae.* Anglicè. [no place, no date] (*STC* has various editions, starting in 1583, 22857ff.) D 1685

Williams, Griffith, *Seven golden candlestickes* (London, [1624 or 1627]). (*STC* 25719 or 25720/25720.5 respectively) D 1685

## 2. English in polyglott works

*Bible, Novum Testamentum,* ed. Elias Hutter (Nürnberg, 1599), fol. (*STC* 2795.5) H 1623; J 1746

Gesner, Conrad, *Nomenclator aquatilium animantium* (Zürich, 1560), fol. H 1623
*Grammaire angloise & françoise* (Rouen, 1652), 8°. (Alston II, 168) O 1678

Habrecht, Isaac, *Janua linguarum silinguis* (Strasbourg, 1629), D 1685
Howell, James, *Lexicon tetraglotton* (London, 1660), fol. (Wing 3087) O 1678

## 3. Dutch

Ackersdyck, T. d' & G. van Zyll, [Grammar] (Utrecht, 1650), O 1664
Adrians, Cornelis, *Sermonen*, D 1685
Aitzema, Lieuwe van, *Verhael van de Nederlantsche Vrede Handelung* (The Hague, 1650),
    4°. F/O 1706
— *[Derde] Vervolg van Saken van Staat en Oorlogen van A.1692 tot A.1697* (Amsterdam, 1699),
    fol. F/O 1706
*Anabaptista quidam van dat Huys der Levendigen, van dat verstand des Nachtmaels.* D 1685
*Anabaptistae van de Evangelische Ceremonien, en leeren der Geloovigen in Christo, ende van het
    Nachtmael.* D 1685
*Antidotarium.* Belgicè, 4°. [Perhaps an edition of the Antidotarium Gandaviense?]
    P 1685

Baker, Sir Richard, [Translation of *Meditations and disquisitions upon the Lord's Prayer*]
    D 1685
Baudart, William, *Memoryen der gedenckweerdichste so kerkelike als werltlike Geschiedenissen
    van 1603 tot 1614* (Arnhem, 1624), fol. F/O 1706
Bandello, Matteo, *Histoires tragiques.* Belgicè (Rotterdam, 1608), 8°. O 1678
Bartholinus, Thomas, *Anatomia.* Tr. Th. Staffard (Dordrecht, 1656), 8°. O 1678
*Beschrijvinge der Nederlanden.* 2 tom. (Amsterdam, 1660), 12°. O 1664
*Beschrijvinge van den Geschiedenissen in der Religions-Sacken toegedragen in den Nederlanden,
    1500-1566* (1569), 8°. F/O 1706
*Beschrijvinge van Vranckrijck*, 5 vol. (Amsterdam, 1662), 12°. O 1678
Bible, *Biblia sacra.* 4°. P 1685
— pt.2. (Leiden, 1542), 12°. O 1678
— *Oude Hollandsche Bibel nae de Copye van Biesken tot Harlingen 1585.* [This is the
    Mennonite Bible, used by Lutherans until 1648.] D 1685
— [Bible] (Dordrecht, 1596), fol. O 1664
— *Biblia* (Amsterdam, 1624), 8°. O 1664
— *Davidis Psalmi belgice* (Hoorn, 1643), 12°. [Possibly the missing part of Gruys & Wolf
    108] P 1685
— *Petri Datheni Psalterium Belgicè.* D 1685
— *Psalmenbuch in Niederländischer Sprach.* D 1685
— [New Testament] (Dordrecht, 1603), 8°. O 1664
— [New Testament & Psalms] (Amsterdam, 1629), 12°. O 1664
Blaeu, Willem, *Zeespiegel* (Amsterdam, 1627, 23), fol. R 1692
Brachelius, Adolphus, *Geschiedenissen onses tijdts* (Nijmegen, 1659), 8°. O 1664

Casas, Bartolomé de las, *Spiegel der Spaense tyrannie in West-Indien* (Amsterdam, 1620),
    O 1664

Cock, David, *De Cyfer-Konst.* [There was an Amsterdam ed. of 1652] O 1664
Cornelis, Broeder, *Historie en Sermons* (Amsterdam, 1607), 8°. F/O 1676
Craufurd, James, *Historie van het Huys Est.* D 1685

*Daventriensis Petri computum liber belgicè,* 1596. 8°. P 1685
*Ein deuoot boecxkē vā Marien seuē bedroeffnissē.* (Antwerp, [ca. 1532?]), 8°. H 1623
Dyke, Daniel, *the Elder, Michael ende de Draecke* (Amsterdam, 1626), 4°. F/O 1706
— [Translation of *The Mystery of self deceiving*] (Delft, 1619), 4°. F/O 1706

*Englesche boetpredicatien.* (Bolsward, 1657), 4°. R 1751
Everaert, Merten, tr. *Tragische Historien.* 8°. O 1664

*Fama Fraternitatis* ([Amsterdam?], 1615), 8°. J 1746
Fokkens, Melchior, *Beschryvinge van Amsterdam* (Amsterdam, 1662), 12°. F/O 1706

Goodwin, Thomas, *De Yde[sic] theil der Gedachten* (Rotterdam, 1646). 12° F/O 1706
Grim, Egbert, *Pauselijcke Heyligheit* [Wesel, 1635?] D 1685
Grotius, Hugo, *Inleiding tot de Hollandsche rechtsgeleertheyd* (The Hague, 1631), 4°. O 1664

*Heidelberg Catechism,* ed. Gellius de Bouma (Amsterdam, 1645), 12°. O 1678
Heidfeldius, Johannes, *Sphinx theologica-philosophica,* Tr. P. Iacobi (Amsterdam, 1623), 4°. H 1623
Herentals, Thomas, *Den speghel des kerstē leuēs* (Antwerp, 1532), 8°. H 1623
*Historica descriptio vitae Johannis van OldenBarnevelt.* Belgicè. D 1685
Hooft, Pieter, *Gedichten* (Amsterdam, 1649), 8°. O 1664
— *Van't Huys de Medicis.* D 1685

Inga, Athanasius, *West-Indische Spieghel* (Amsterdam, 1624), 4°. D 1685
*D'Instructie van de Hove van Hollandt.* 1603. 4°. O 1664
— 1639. 4°. O 1664

James I, King of England, *Apologie voor den eedt* (Amsterdam, 1609), 8°. O 1678

*Kort bericht om te komen tot het gehoor des Woorts Godes.* D 1685
Krul, Jan, *Minne popiens* (Amsterdam, [n.d.]), 12° or 16°. P 1685
Ksnekenius[sic], Jasp., *Brief memorial van t'Apostolisch comptoir* (Amsterdam, 1670) 12°. O 1678

La Court, Pieter de, *Historie der gravelike regieringe in Hollandt.* 8°. O 1678
Laet, Johannes de, *Beschrijvinghe van West Indien* (Leiden, 1630), fol. R 1733
— *Nieuwe Wereldt* (Leiden, 1625), fol. R 1692
La Grue, Thomas *Grammatica* (Amsterdam), 8°. O 1678
Lansbergen, Philippus van, *Quadrans ende astrolabium* (Middleburg, 1633), 4°. O 1664
Lauterbeck, Georg, *Regenten-boeck.* D 1685
Lipsius, Justus, *Politica.* 1594. O 1664
— *Politica* (Delft, 1628), 8°. O 1678

Mander, Karel van, *Het leven der moderne Italiaensche schilders,* bk. 2. (Amsterdam, 1616), 4°. H 1623
*Het leven van Marcus Aurelius* (Amsterdam, 1595), 12°. O 1664

Meteren, Emanuel van, *Commentarien vanden Nederlandtschen Staet.* ('Schotland buyten Danswijck' [ = Amsterdam 1610]) (Simoni M 85) H 1623
— *Historia Belgica*, Belgicè. D 1685
Meusevoet, Vincentius, *T'Hemelschat* (Amsterdam, 1620), 4°. O 1664
Munting, Abraham, *Naauwkeurige Beschryving der aardgewassen* (Leiden, 1696), fol. J 1746

Napier, John, *Over de Openbaringe Johannis.* D 1685
*Navigatie gedaan in Turckyen* (Antwerp, 1576), 4°. O 1664
Nispen, Adriaen van, ed. *Verscheyde voyagien* (Dordrecht, 1652), 12°. O 1664
*Dat nye Land Recht*, 1618. 4°. O 1664

*Olde Ambster Landtrecht* (Groningen, 1618), 4°. O 1678
*t'Ommelander Landtrecht* (Groningen, 1647 & 1618), 4°. O 1678
Ovid, *Opera* (Antwerp, 1615), 8°. O 1678

*Persianische Reijs* (1635), 4°. [Perhaps a version of Georg Tectander's German *Iter persicum*] P 1685

*Roomse mintriumphen* (The Hague, 1651), 4°. O 1664

Sande, Johan van den, *Nederlandtsche historica* (Amsterdam, 1650), 12°. O 1664
Schrieck, Adriaen van, *Van t'begin der eerster volcken van Evropen* (Ypres, 1614), fol. (Simoni S 83) H 1623
Sibelius, Caspar, *Christelicke gebeden* (Campen, 1637), 12°. O 1678
Sidney, Sir Philip, *Arcadia*, 3 vol. (Delft, 1639), 12°. O 1664
Smith, Thomas, *The arte of gunnerie*, Belgicè. 4°. P 1685
Stevin, Simon, *Wisconstige gedachtenissen* (Leiden, 1608), fol. H 1623

Tauler, Johann, *Sermonen.* D 1685

Udemans, Godfried, *Korte verklaring van het Hooglied van Salomo.* D 1685
Ursinus, Zacharias, *Schat-boeck der verklaringen over den Nederlandtschen Catechismus,* D 1685
Utenbogaert, Jan, *Kerkelyke Historie* (Rotterdam, 1647), fol. F/O 1706

*Vita Caroli V.,* Belgicè. O 1664
Vondel, Joost van den, *De Helden Godes.* D 1685
— *Poëzy* (Amsterdam, 1650), 8°. O 1664
*Vreemdicheden van Vranckrijck* (Amsterdam, 1619), 8°. O 1678

Wagenaer, Lucas, *Groote dobbelde Spiegel der Zeevaert van de Navigatie der Westersen zee* (Amsterdam, 1600), fol. F/O 1676
— *Thresoor de Zeevaert* (Amsterdam, 1606), 4°. F/O 1676
*Weghwijser door Italien* (Amsterdam, 1655), 12°. O 1678
*Weghwijser door Vranckrijck* (Amsterdam, 1657), 12°. O 1678
Weyer, Matthaeus, *Cort bericht om tot Godsalicheyt te comen, uyt syne Brieven getrocken,* D 1685

## 3. Dutch in polyglott works

Arsy, Jean Louis d', *Grammaire Flamende et Françoise* (Rouen, 1647), 8°. O 1678

— *Le grand dictionnaire françois-flamen* (Rotterdam, 1663 & 1643), O 1678

Bible, [Psalms, in French & Dutch] (Amsterdam, 1594), 12°. O 1678
— [Liturgical Epistles & Gospels, in French & Dutch] (Antwerp, 1579), 8°. F/O 1676

Cats, Jacob, *Silenus Alcibiadis*, 2nd ed. (Amsterdam, 1619). (Simoni C 65) H 1623
— *Monita amoris virginei* (Amsterdam, 1619), H 1623

Dictionaries, [Latin, Greek & Dutch] (Amsterdam, 1600), 8°. O 1678
— [Latin, Greek, French & Dutch] (Amsterdam, 1612), 8°. O 1678
— [French & Dutch] (Rotterdam, 1599), 8°. O 1678
— [Dutch & Spanish] (Antwerp, 1659), 4°. O 1678

Mellema, Elcie Édouard Leon, [Dutch & French dictionary] (Antwerp, 1589), 4°. O 1678

Sasbout, Mathias, [Dutch & French dictionary] '1567' [should this read 1576?] 4°. O 1664

## Notes

1. Hugo Kunoff, *The foundations of the German academic library* (Chicago, 1982). This deals specifically with Göttingen, Leipzig, Halle and Jena.

2. Wilhelm Erman & Ewald Horn, *Bibliographie der deutschen Universitäten*. Teil 2. (Leipzig & Berlin, 1904).

3. Paul Raabe, 'Bibliothekskataloge als buchgeschichtliche Quellen. Bermerkungen über gedruckte Kataloge öffentlicher Bibliotheken in der frühen Neuzeit', in *Bücherkataloge als buchgeschichtliche Quellen in der früben Neuzeit*, edited by Reinhard Wittmann, Wolfenbütteler Schriften zur Geschichte des Buchwesens, 10 (Wiesbaden, 1985).

4. For help in gaining access to my evidence I am indebted to the generosity of Reinhard Feldmann (Cologne), Hans Dieter Gebauer (Bonn), Manfred Komorowski (Duisburg), Ulrich Kopp (Wolfenbüttel), Heino Krüger (Marburg), Margret Laue (Rinteln), Paul Berthold Rupp (Augsburg).

5. Gertrud Schubart-Fikentscher, *Untersuchungen zur Autorschaft von Dissertationen im Zeitalter der Aufklärung* (Berlin, 1970).

6. Caspar Coerber, in the dedication to his *Historia Goslariensis* (Goslar, 1679), a German translation of his Jena thesis of 1675, describes his intention as a student to research the history of his native town: 'Dieses auszuführen, gab mir das Glück eine bequeme Gelegenheit an die Hand, dass ich mit Herrn D. Sagittario Historiarum Professore Publico bekannt wurde, welcher mir, nach dem ich ihm mein fürhaben eröffnet, seine stattliche bibliothec und Anleitung hiezu williglich und geneigt anboht'.

7. Ladislaus Buzás, *Deutsche Bibliotheksgeschichte der Neuzeit, 1500-1800*, Elemente des Buch- und Bibliothekswesens, 2 (Wiesbaden, 1976).

8. Some of these will be exceptional, for example that described by Frans Blom, *Christoph and Andreas Arnold and England: the travels and book-collections of two seventeenth-century Nurembergers*, Schriftenreihe des Stadtachivs Nürnberg, 34 (Nürnberg, 1982), which was extraordinarily rich in English books.

9. Johann Jakob Lucius, *Catalogus Bibliothecae publicae Moeno-Francofurtensis* (Frankfurt am Main, 1728).

10. If much of the literature of Protestant countries was considered harmful and undesirable by Catholic censors, how far more suspicious books in their vernaculars much have seemed. But we should beware of stereotypes; in the 18th century, the library of

the Schottenkloster at Regensburg had a notably large and eclectic collection of books in English.

11. Elmar Mittler, 'Bibliothek and Universität: Skizzen zu ihrer Wechselbeziehung', in *Semper apertus: Sechshundert Jahre Ruprecht-Karls-Universität Heidelberg 1386-1986*. Bd.4. (Berlin, etc, 1985).

12. Ibid p.8.

13. R.J. Brunt, *The influence of the French language on the German vocabulary, 1649-1735* (Berlin, New York, 1983), p.69.

14. Paul Dibon, *Le voyage en France des étudiants néerlandais au XVIIème siècle* (The Hague, 1963).

15. Louis Rigaud, 'La Nation germanique de l'ancienne Université d'Orléans', in *Revue d'histoire de l'église de France,* année 32, tom. 27 (1941), pp.46-71, here p.68.

16. Friedrich Schulze & Paul Ssymank, *Das deutsche Studententum von den ältesten Zeiten bis zur Gegenwart*. 4.Aufl. (Munich, 1932), p.50.

17. F. C. von Buri, 'Synopsis statutorum, privilegiorum ac novellarum constitutionum inclytae et Imperialis Nationis Germanicae in Academia Aurelianensi', in *Johann George Estors kleiner Schrifften dritter Band* (Giessen, 1739), pp.185-237, here p.199.

18. Abraham Goelnitz, *Ulysses Belgico-Gallus* (Leiden, 1631), p.240.

19. Dibon, op cit, p.12.

20. Rigaud, op cit, p.63.

21. Charles Cuissard, 'La Bibliothèque de la Nation germanique à l'Université d'Orléans', in *Centralblatt für Bibliothekswesen* 9 (1892), pp.8–21.

22. Information kindly supplied by Anne Monginoux, Bibliothèque municipale, Orléans.

23. Becmann mistakenly thought a Lübeck *Postilla* of 1492 was in Dutch, whereas it can only be the Poppy Printer's *Plenarium* in Low German (Goff E 90).

24. Friedrich Karl Gottlob Hirsching, *Versuch einer Beschreibung sehenswürdiger Bibliotheken Teutschlands*, 4 Bd. (Erlangen, 1786-91).

25. Karlheinz Goldmann, 'Geschichte der Universitätsbibliothek Duisburg', in *Zentralblatt für Bibliothekswesen* 59 (1942), pp.85-135, here p.88f.

26. The copy lacks pp.73/4, and the xerox supplied lacks all after p.133, a recto, though I doubt if much more than the minimum one page is wanting.

27. Gerhard Schormann, *Academia Ernestina. Die schaumburgische Universität zu Rinteln an der Weser, 1610/21-1810*, Academia Marburgensis. 4 (Marburg, 1982) p.144.

28. ibid p.150.

29. Konrad Marwinski, *425 Jahre Universitätsbibliothek Jena. Kurzgefasste Bibliotheksgeschichte* (Jena, 1983).

30. Kunoff, op cit, p.146.

31. There were times when I felt I should have chosen a different text, perhaps 'As I was going down the stair/ I met a man who wasn't there'.

32. Fritz Milkau et al, *Handbuch der Bibliothekswissenschaft*, 2.Aufl. Bd.3. Hälfte 1 (Wiesbaden, 1955), p.656.

33. Paulus Bolduanus cites none in a series of bibliographies: *Bibliotheca theologica* (Jena 1614) and its *Complementum* (1622) have only works in Latin or German, as has the *Bibliotheca historica* (Leipzig 1620), even in the sections *Belgica* and *Britannica*; his *Bibliotheca philosophica* (Jena 1616) has a section devoted to grammars, but although Italian, French, Polish, Hungarian, and Turkish are represented, there is no English Grammar, and only one for Dutch (in Latin). Johann Heinrich Boecler's *Bibliographia historico-politico-philologica curiosa* (Germanopoli [=Frankfurt am Main], 1677, also unchanged reprint 1696) lists large numbers of works under the headings *Belgica* and *Britannica*, all in Latin.

34. Johann Goldfriedrich, *Geschichte des deutschen Buchhandels vom Westfälischen Frieden bis zum Beginn der klassischen Literaturperiode, 1648-1740*, Geschichte des deutschen Buchhandels, 2 (Leipzig, 1908), p.77 & p.80f.

Cis van Heertum

# *Willem Christiaens van der Boxe's translation of* The Parlament of Women *(1640)*

Seven years before the appearance of the anti-Royalist *The Parliament of Ladies*[1] the printer John Okes brought out a quite different *Parlament of Women* in 1640.[2] This *Parlament of Women*, which was printed in 1646, 1647, 1656 and 1685,[3] is a satire against women very much in the spirit of the various gossips' greetings, meetings and other female conclaves, in which women were 'overheard' reviling, ridiculing and condemning their husbands.[4] *The Parlament of Women*, too, has its fair share of complaining and bickering women, but, as the title indicates, is set within the framework of an all-female parliament, with a list of their laws annexed.

    *The Parlament of Women* is embedded in the story of Papirius Praetextatus, a favourite historical anecdote used in satires against women to illustrate their garrulity.[5] The actual Parliament takes off at the moment when Papirius's mother rallies the Matrons of Rome to convene on what she believes is the making of a scandalous new law. The earlier sources only mention the Roman Matrons, but in the more democratic atmosphere of *The Parlament of Women* the artisans' wives and other commoners, hearing of the imminent opening of a female parliament, demand to have their voices heard also. A Lower and an Upper House is set up accordingly:

and a great Parlour serving for a Parlament House, every one tooke their place according to their degrees, and which was a wonder amongst women, they suffered one to speake at once (A2ᵛ)

That person is Papirius's mother. Embarking on a measured (and potentially long-winded) speech, she is deftly cut short by another eager speaker. A third speaker then continues with stirring references to the viragos and amazons of old. The assembled women, duly inflamed by her militancy, hurry to air their grievances against men in general and their husbands in particular. The assembled Parliament then proceeds to discuss ways to redress the balance ('how to wrest the power in men from wronging their wives', A4ʳ). After laws to that effect have been drawn up, the women march in a body to the Senate house, at which point the anecdote of Papirius Praetextatus is again picked up and concluded.[6]

    *The Parlament of Women* is a lively satire against women, on the whole successfully sustaining the tone of an occasionally rowdy Parliament, as in the following passage, in which a speaker aims to propose relief for the temporarily bereaved wives of sailors to an obviously clamorous audience:

suppose a handsome Lasse marries a Sea-faring man, perchance his occasions cals him to goe a long Voyage to Sea, as to the East or West *Indies*, or to the Straights of *Magellan*, the Reed or Red sea; or to the *Persian* Gulfe: hee is bound to stay a yeare, two, or three, before he can returne: do you (nay, prithee good sister) let me not be interrupted in my speech; pray silence, or I will say no more; for I now speake to the purpose (A5$^r$)

With five editions in the 17th century, *The Parlament of Women* may be classed as one of the more 'popular' satires against women.

Three out of the five editions still extant were printed in the 1640s. Although one of the two editions printed in 1646 and 1647 would seem to be a more obvious candidate for the copy-text, Van der Boxe used a copy of the 1640 edition for his own translation, which came out in 1649 or 1650. Concerning the Senate's response to the women of Rome, Van der Boxe translated what he found in the text, which in the 1640 edition reads: 'but in conclusion they greatly covered their wives levity and inconstancy' (B4$^r$). Van der Boxe translates: 'maer in 't besluyt/ deckten sy de pot toe: soeckende te bemantelen de ongehestadige wispeltuyricheden van haer Vrouwen' (C1$^r$) [but in conclusion, they covered it up: seeking to cloak the fickle inconstancies of their Wives]. In the 1646 and 1647 editions, the senators more traditionally condemn their wives' actions.[7]

Willem Christiaens van der Boxe, active as printer and bookseller in Leiden from 1631-58,[8] is perhaps mostly known in England for his involvement in the translation and/or publication of a number of Puritan tracts in the 1630s and early 1640s, amongst which is William Prynne's *Histrio-mastix*.[9] His interest in English books, however, was not confined to the Puritan cause. Out of the 117 books printed by Van der Boxe which are held by the Royal Library in The Hague, there is one book printed in the original English language, while another 16 are translated from the English. Van der Boxe translated six of them himself. Of these 17 books, only five can be classed as Puritan or anti-Papist books, while a further three books report on events during the English Civil War. The other nine books range from ephemera to sermons.[10]

In 1652, six years before the end of his career as a printer, Van der Boxe referred to his activities as a translator in the Epilogue to his translation of Anthony Maxey's *Certain sermons preached before the Kings maiestie*,[11] but he was already applauded for his efforts in translating English works in 1641. Admittedly, the praise occurs in a commendatory poem prefixed to his translation of Joseph Swetnam's *The Araignment of Lewd, Idle, Froward and Unconstant Women*, which came out in 1641. The poem is nevertheless interesting because the author, Isaac Burchoorn, a printer and bookseller active in The Hague, provided a list of publications by Van der Boxe:

> al doet 'et u wat spijts,
> Hij heeft ons wel vertaelt de *Deeg'lijckheyt des Tijts, Den politijcken Dief*;
> Daer bij *Den Witten Duyvel*,

---

> Daer naer *Het Goud' Trompet*,

---

Oock heeft hij ons verthoont, *Practijcke van Bekeeringh*

---

> Oock *t Nieuws van Over-Al*,

---

Jae, dit 's deselve Man, die dese *Recht-bancks* Letters
Uyt *Brittens* Tael herstelt.[12]

Three of the five identified translations in this poem are religious or devotional in nature.[13] Yet Van der Boxe also translated and published with great gusto two English satires against women. Joseph Swetnam's *The Araignment of Women*, mentioned above, was originally published in London in 1615, and came out as *Recht-banck tegen de Luye, Korzelighe en Wispeltuyrighe Vrouwen* in 1641. His translation of *The Parlament of Women* came out in 1650, or possibly in 1649,[14] under the title *Der (Engelsche) Vrouwen Parlament*. Van der Boxe presented these two satires as companion pieces, declaring on the title-page of *Der Engelsche Vrouwen Parlament* (1650) that it was 'bequaem om te worden gevoecht by de vertaelde *Recht-banck*' [a suitable addition to the translated *Recht-banck*]. This was a timely reminder, as in 1649 Van der Boxe had reprinted the *Recht-banck* in an enlarged edition. Copies of this edition might still have been for sale in his bookshop in 1650. In his Preface to *Der Engelsche Vrouwen Parlament*, Van der Boxe reinforced the link between these two satires against women,[15] while a brief note following the third part of the 1649 edition of the *Recht-banck* had already announced the publication of *Der (Engelsche) Vrouwen Parlament*: 'Ick ben oock van meeinghe U.L. mede te deelen/ Het Parlament van Vrouwen' (D4[v]) [I also intend to present to you, The Parliament of Women].

There are two known editions of *Der (Engelsche) Vrouwen parlament*, one dated 1650, one undated, while in 1651 *Der Engelsche Vrouwen Parlament* was re-issued with some additions as *Der Vrouwen Advocaet*.[16] The undated edition is advertised on the title-page as the second, enlarged and improved edition, and includes one of Erasmus's *Colloquia* (in Dutch) which is announced by Van der Boxe in his Preface to the Reader as follows: 'Alsoo my bekent was, dat onder andere geleerde ende gheneughlijcke t'Samen-sprekhingen van den vermaerden D. Erasmus van Rotterdam, mede eenen was, de welcke hy 't Vroutjens Vroedtschapje noemt; soo hebbe ick niet kunnen na-laten het selve U. L. mede te deelen, ende te voeghen voor het Parlement der Vrouwen' (A2[r]) [As it was known to me, that amongst other learned and pleasant colloquia of the renowned D. Erasmus of Rotterdam there was also one, which he called 't Vroutjens Vroedtschapje, I could not refrain from presenting it to you, and to prefix it to the Parlement der Vrouwen].[17] Although *'t Vroutjens Vroedtschapje* cannot be found in the 1650 edition, this is not an argument for establishing the precedence of the 1650 edition, as it in turn has two 'Placcaeten' [Proclamations] and three poems which are not found in the undated edition. The 'Placcaeten' are written in the spirit of *The Parlament of Women*, while *'t Vroutjens Vroedtschapje*, for all Van der Boxe's protestations, does not really compare. The choice of omission for a new edition would therefore probably have fallen on Erasmus's colloquy, which would mean that the undated edition precedes the 1650 edition.[18] As there are hardly any significant textual differences between the texts of *Der (Engelsche) Vrouwen Parlament* proper, and as it is likely that Van der Boxe would have considered the 1650 edition, with its additions and a new wood-cut, as the real 'improved' edition, the dated edition has been chosen as the basis for discussion.

Van der Boxe may have expected *Der Engelsche Vrouwen Parlament* to be popular

Fig.1    Title-page of the 1640 edition of *The Parlament of Women.* (H.E. Huntington Library, San Marino.)

DER

Engelſche Vrouwen

# PARLAMENT,

Midtſgaders de

WETTEN, PRIVILEGIEN, ende PLACCATEN
by hun-luyden (in hare Vergaderinge) ingeſtelt ; de ſelfde
door hare Macht / Gebiet / ende Authoriteyt / den Mannen
wel ſcherpelick belaſt ende bevolen te onderhouden / ende
in alles na te komen : op pene ende ſtraffe / omme teene-
mael te verlieſen hun Liefde / Affectie / en goede
genegentheyt tot de Mannen.

Vertaelt uyt het Engels.

Zijnde bequaem om te worden gevoecht by de vertaelde
RECHT-BANCK.

Gedruckt / ende uptgegeven tot LEYDEN, by Willem
Chriſtiaens. In 't Jubel-Jaer 1650.

Fig.2    Title-page of the 1650 edition of *Der Vrouwen Parlament.* (Royal Library, The Hague.)

with its readers, although the evidence of *Der Vrouwen Advocaet* proves this was not the case. The undated edition still features a wood-cut unrelated to the subject of *Der Engelsche Vrouwen Parlament*, but for the dated edition Van der Boxe commissioned a wood-cut based on that of the title-page of *The Parlament of Women*. This suggests that Van der Boxe may have anticipated printing further editions of *Der Engelsche Vrouwen Parlament*, and so wanted a 'matching' wood-cut.

The English wood-cut (fig.1) is rather static and presents what seems to be a court-room, with a woman arraigned at the bar, rather than the setting of the female parliament (it may therefore not have been especially made for *The Parlament of Women*). The Dutch wood-cut (fig.2), on the other hand, does show 'a great Parlour', with the Speaker seated at a table in front of what looks like a massive fireplace. The women are seated in distinctly cosy chairs, while the defendant in the foreground of the English wood-cut has been replaced by two women obviously in the midst of a heated argument: one of the two with mouth wide open in angry protest, her right hand raised, the other tight-lipped but otherwise expressively pointing her index finger at her forehead in a gesture we can still recognise today.

The Dutch wood-cut suggests that Van der Boxe put more effort into the presentation of *Der Engelsche Vrouwen Parlament* than had been the case for the English original. The addition of a poem of 38 lines on the occasion of this satire against women, again by Isaac Burchoorn, printer and self-styled poet, confirms that impression. Van der Boxe also edited his text more carefully, indenting far more liberally than had been the case in the English original, thus making for greater readability. But his editorial efforts did not end there. He also expanded the English passage on the institution of the Parliament, which in the original reads:

though the Matrons were noble, and they but Mechanicks, and poore Trades-mens Wives, yet no Parlament could bee held, but there must be a lower House as well as a higher, and Speakers for both: and further, that nothing could be concluded in the higher, but it must first bee debated in the lower (A2$^{rv}$).

Van der Boxe translates and adds:

hoe-wel dat die *Matroonen* edel waren/ ende syluyden maer Handt-werckers Vrouwen/ evenwel en konder gheen Parlament worden gehouden/ ofte daer moste oock een Lager-huys mede gestelt zijn/ om te spreecken voor de generale goede Gemeente/ soo wel als het Hooger-huys was voor den Adel ende de Edelen/ om voor-spraecken te wesen tot haer beyden: ende verder/ datter niets konde worden besloten in 't *Hooger-huys*, (al-hoewel het tot voordeel soude strecken van haer allen) ofte het moste eerst in 't *Lager-huys* oock overlegt ende gedebateert wesen (A3$^{v}$).[19]

Van der Boxe's gloss on the institution of the female Parliament is thus almost more cautious than the matter-of-factness of the original English. Towards the end of *Der Engelsche Vrouwen Parlament* he adds another comment which illustrates a certain reverence towards the nobility. Where the English text reads: 'And now (with no common pace) trudge these Parlementers' (B4$^{r}$), Van der Boxe translates: 'Aldus/met meer als een gemeenen gangh/ drongen dese *Parlementeersters*, metter haest voort: de geringer soorte/ waren aen-sienlijcker gemaeckt door de Edele Matroonen' (C1$^{r}$) ['the meaner sort, were made more respectable by the Noble Matrons'].

Van der Boxe also understood that Papirius's mother's speech was meant to sound a rather high-flown note. Where the English text introduces her speech merely with: 'who said as followeth' (A2ᵛ), Van der Boxe translates: 'die (als volght) begon dese wel-spreeckende Oratie' (A3ᵛ) [who (as followeth) began this eloquent Oration].

These might be regarded as incidental editorial decisions, but Van der Boxe's translation shows the signs of a sustained editorial practice. There are a number of additions and omissions in the Dutch text, all of which are based on careful consideration rather than careless procedure. The largest single omission is that of the 'cure for old and new cuckolds', advertised on the title-page of *The Parlament of Women* and taking up three pages (B2ᵛ-B4ʳ). As the text is clearly an interruption of the narrative of *The Parlament of Women,* and in itself different in tone from the rest of the text, Van der Boxe was not being fastidious when he decided to cut out this lengthy passage. Two other fairly large omissions (both 9 lines) are repetitive phrases which do not really add to the effect of the arguments presented. Another more or less major omission (13 lines) is in itself not repetitive, but does present a change of tone in the speaker's argument. Up to the point of the passage omitted by Van der Boxe the speaker ('Mistris *Dorothy Doelittle*', dubbed '*Angenietje Soetemondt*' by Van der Boxe) comes across as rather precious:

I hold it requisite also, that every woman of sence, should take delight to please her eye with the most curious objects (...): Her eare rather with curious and choyse Musick (…): Her smell rather with sweet and redolent flowers at home (…): her touch… with the Plush and Taffaetas of her owne gay garments (…). Her taste, with all dainty and deare fare' (A7ʳᵛ).

But she soon changes her tune and, true to her name, bellows forth:

And for our more ease, let us lye a bed till ten of clock, and then have a Caudle brought to our bed side for our breakfast (…) and if they aske the reason thereof, tell them it must be so; because it must be so (A7ᵛ).

Perhaps such gross laziness would have offended house-proud Dutch housewives; in any case Van der Boxe's omission brings greater coherence to the character of Mistris Doe-little, while the name chosen for her, Angenietje Soetemondt ('Sweetmouth') shows once again Van der Boxe was sensitive to the tone of the text.

The additions to the Dutch text include another brief portrait of a wife with a grudge (not included in the undated edition), an enlarged description of 'Mistriss Tabitha Tearesheet', dubbed 'Juffrou Lijntjen Scheurlaecken' by Van der Boxe,[20] and a number of rhyming couplets, some of them introduced as 'old proverbs'. The addition of the rhyming couplets may have been intended to pad out the text, but even here Van der Boxe tried to blend his additions in with the original text, as in:

Wie licht betrouwt, wert licht bedot,
En oock van alle-man bespot

Dit wierde heel redelijck gehouden/ ende oock gekeurt waerdig te wesen om gestelt te worden in 't Register-boeck (B4ʳ)

*Who easily trusts, gets easily done,*
*And is also mocked by everyone*

*This was considered to be very reasonable, and also judged worthy of inclusion in the Register.*

The bulk of the added material to *Der Engelsche Vrouwen Parlament*, however, can be found in the ten women's laws annexed to the text of *The Parlament of Women*. Van der Boxe omitted two laws, and added twelve others. He also added new material: two 'Placcaeten' and three poems.

The 'Placcaeten' are written in the spirit of *Der Engelsche Vrouwen Parlament*, although occasionally they seem to be embedded in a distinctly Dutch context. Item no. 3 of the second 'Placcaet' probably refers to a controversy which had raged in the middle years of the 1640s. Its subject was that which had earlier occupied William Prynne in *The Unlovelinesse of Lovelockes*, and in the Dutch republic, too, sentiments ran high over the length of men's and women's hair. The Synod of Holland had condemned the 'wildt hair' of men and women in 1640, after which a pamphlet war broke out, some earnest expositions of the Synod's point of view, others amused or sophisticated contributions to the general upheaval. But it was a sermon by the popular Dordrecht preacher Jakob Borstius, avidly copied and published without his permission, which really fuelled the controversy. Early in 1644 he had exclaimed to his congregation:

En is zij niet bevreest dat het haar reputatie zal verminderen, dat zij den peerden en leeuwen niet geheel ongelijk is, als zij door haar lokken en blessen de hangende manen van die beesten schijnt na te bootzen?

*And is she not afraid that it will lower her reputation, to be not unlike the horses and lions, when by her locks and tresses, she would seem to imitate the drooping manes of those animals?*[21]

Rather surprisingly perhaps, Borstius's sermon appears to have ruffled not a few feathers in his day, and Van der Boxe seems to remind his audience in 1650:

Niemandt sal haer/ om heur gefriseerde en gepoperde lockjes/ met de naam van Leeuwtjes/ gelijck onlangs in openbare druck is geschied/ mogen noemen (D1$^r$).

*No one shall be allowed to call them by the name of Lions, as has been publicly printed recently, on account of their curled and rustling locks.*

Van der Boxe was not only an adequate editor. He was also on the whole a careful and inventive translator. Apart from the common occurrence of doubling of words, which is a feature of Dutch translation in the 17th century,[22] Van der Boxe's translation in general remains quite close to the original. He tries to preserve the stylistic features of the text as much as possible, for instance in the case of the many alliterative phrases in *The Parlament of Women*:

If our husbands be peevish, we may pout; when they are harsh wee may be humorous; they curst, we crabbed (A6$^v$).

which Van der Boxe translates as:

*als onse mannen pauteren/ wy dan mogen pruylen: indien sy ons boos ende hardt zijn/ wij mogen oock humeureus ende jaloers wesen: sy quaedt zijnde/ wy mogen korselig wesen* (B2$^r$).

Where he cannot match the alliteration, he nevertheless tries to create a 'special effect', as in:

keeping one for her delight, the other for her drudgery (A3ʳ)

which has assonance in the translated version:

*houdende den eenen/ om ons te behagen/ ende den anderen/ om voor ons te slaven* (A4ʳ)

The translations of the satirical names in *The Parlament of Women* are well matched, too, as in 'Juffrouw *Magdalena Mans-verdriet*' (B1ᵛ) for 'mistris *Tabitha Tireman*' (A6ʳ); '*Dirckje Altoos-dweers*' (B2ʳ) for 'Mistris *Eleanor Ever-crosse*' (A6ᵛ); '*Stijntje Stouts*' (B2ᵛ) for '*Mary Malepart*' (A7ʳ); '*Heyltje sonder schaemt*' (B2ᵛ) for 'Mistris *Bridget Bold-face*' (A7ᵛ) and '*Grietje noyt te vreen*' (B3ʳ) for '*Anne Ever-crosse*' (A8ʳ) – whether or not Van der Boxe translated the last name differently because he wanted to avoid repetition, it is very apt to translate 'ever cross' as 'never pleased'.

It cannot be determined with exactness whether Van der Boxe was absolutely *au fait* with colloquial English. Sampling of colloquialisms in *The Parlament of Women* against *Der Engelsche Vrouwen Parlament* would however suggest that Van der Boxe had some grasp of colloquial English, and that he always tried to provide an 'intuitively correct' translation when he appeared not to know the English. For the phrase 'Pea-goose' (A3ᵛ) (*simpleton*) Van der Boxe offers 'prongelaer' (A4ᵛ) (*bungler*); for 'curtain-hearted' (A3ʳ) (*hen-pecked*) he offers 'bloot-hertich' (A4ʳ) (*cowardly*). The meaning of these words he may have been able to derive from the context. But for 'Patch-pannell' (A3ᵛ), an abusive Elizabethan term for a 'botching carpenter', the meaning of which he could not easily grasp from its context, he has 'Lapslenter' (A4ᵛ) (*rag*), which must have come to him because of the 'patch' in 'Patch-pannell': not a close translation perhaps, but one abusive word is as good or bad as another. When there was a literal translation available, Van der Boxe would use the opportunity: 'making Cuckolds' (A6ʳ) thus becomes 'Koeckoecken maken' (B1ᵛ); 'mettle' (A3ʳ) becomes 'metael' (A4ᵛ); and 'the whole businesse' (A2ʳ) becomes 'den gantschen handel' (A3ᵛ). The same applies for the many proverbs which are used in *The Parlament of Women*. A proverb like 'have … two strings to their bow' (A2ᵛ) could be translated literally as 'twee snaren aen haren Boogh … hebben' (A4ʳ). But the proverb 'put finger in the eye and cry' (A3ᵛ), on the other hand, which Van der Boxe translated literally as 'stack de Vinger in haer ooge' (A4ᵛ) has a quite different proverbial meaning in Dutch. He also translated 'I intreat that I may have a finger in the pye' (A4ᵛ) literally as 'ick versoeck mede een Vinger in de Pastey te hebben'(B3ʳ) – a proverb which does not seem to have existed in Dutch at that time. But on the whole Van der Boxe appears to have attempted to provide adequate contextual translations in those cases in which he seems not to have been quite sure of the meaning of the English.

One of the very few instances where Van der Boxe has provided an indifferent gloss is in his translation of 'Juniper Lecture' (B1ᵛ) as 'een andere lesse' (B4ʳ). The first quoted instance of 'Juniper lecture' in *OED* dates to 1706. When *The Parlament of Women* came out in 1640, the phrase 'Juniper lecture' may not have been too current, either, but may rather have reflected the policy of John Okes, for whom *The Parlament of Women* was printed, to promote an item in his own stock. *A Juniper Lecture*, ascribed to John Taylor the Water-Poet, came out in 1639, and was also printed for John Okes. Its title-page promised a 'description of all sorts of women, good and bad'. *A Juniper Lecture* is another satire against women, and mentioning its title in the equally satirical *The Parlament of Women* was both politic and appropriate.[23] Van der Boxe, understandably, was not aware of the existence of *A Juniper Lecture* or of a possible sales campaign discreetly plotted by John Okes.

Both the English *The Parlament of Women* and the Dutch *Der (Engelsche) Vrouwen Parlament* were clearly cheap and 'popular' products, intended to provide light reading. Yet a comparison of both texts in terms of presentation will certainly award higher marks to Van der Boxe's *Der (Engelsche) Vrouwen Parlament*, while his careful editing and translating of *The Parlament of Women* – even though it is a *'parvum opus'* – underscores the expertise of this sympathetic and industrious translator of English works.

## Notes

1. [H. Neville], *The Parliament of Ladies, or divers remarkable passages of Ladies in Spring-garden, in Parliament assembled* ([London], 1647), *Wing* N 511.
—[second edition] ([London], 1647), *Wing* N 512.
—*The Ladies, a second time assembled in Parliament* ([London], 1647), *Wing* P 507.
—*The Ladies Parliament*, [London], 1647], *Wing* N 508.

2. *The Parlament of Women. With the merry Lawes by them newly enacted* (London, 1640), *STC* 19306. Entered to John Okes on 18 June 1640 (Arber, *A Transcript of the Stationers' Registers*, iv.513).
Collation: 8° ($4) A-B4. Pp. [1] 2-24. A1r title, A1v-B4v text. The only copy of the 1640 edition is in the Huntington Library, San Marino, California.

3. *Wing* P 505, *Wing* N 512A, *Wing* P 506, *Wing* P 506A. The 1647 edition, with variant title: *The Parliament of Ladies*, is attributed to Henry Neville in *Wing. GK* notes that it is another edition of *The Parlament of Women*.

4. *Eg* Samuel Rowlands, *A whole crew of gossips all met to be merry* (London, 1609), *STC* 21413; W. P., *The gossips greeting* (London, 1620). *STC* 19080.5.

5. The anecdote occurs for instance in Macrobius's *Saturnalia*, book one, chapter 6. It was available to English readers amongst others in the translation of Pedro Mexia's 16th-century compendium of (classical)

anecdotes *The Foreste or a Collection of Histories* (London, 1571), *STC* 17849. It was clearly a popular anecdote, as it had also become jestbook material, *cf* W. C. Hazlitt, *Shakespeare's Jest-Books* (London, 1864), vol.1: *Mery Tales, Wittie Questions, and Quicke Answeres*, [London, 1576], pp.31-33: 'Of Papirius Praetextatus'.

6. Sigs B2v-B4r are devoted to a 'cure for any old or new cuckolds', announced on the title-page of *The Parlament of Women*, but quite obviously inserted to pad out the text. In the 1640 edition, this part of the text is printed in italic.

7. The 1646 (B3v) and 1647 (B4v) editions read: 'but in conclusion, they greatly condemned their wives levity and inconstancy'. This is the orthodox conclusion to the story of Papirius Praetextatus.
    The 1640 edition also reads: 'a tenement with one Landlord' (A2v), while the 1646 and 1647 editions read: 'a tenant with one landlord' (A2v). Van der Boxe translated according to the 1640 edition: 'een Lant-heer met eene Heerlijckheyt' (A3v).

8. J. A. Gruys and C. de Wolf, *Thesaurus 1473-1800. Dutch Printers and Booksellers*, (Nieuwkoop, 1989) p.22.

9. See Harry Carter, 'Archbishop Laud and scandalous books from Holland', in *Studia Bibliographica in Honorem Herman de la Fontaine Verwey.* (Amsterdam, 1968), pp.43-55; A. F. Johnson, 'Willem Christiaens, Leyden, and his English books', in *The Library*, fifth series, vol.10 (1955), pp.121-23.

**10.** The five Puritan or anti-Papist books are:
**a.** John Bastwick, *The beast is wounded* [Leiden?, 1638], *STC* 22031.5.
**b.** William Prynne, *Histrio-mastix ofte Schouw-spels trevr-spel* (Leiden, 1639), *cf STC* 20464.
**c.** *De ratte-val, ontdeckt in dit hoogh-loffelijck jubel-jaer* (Leiden, [1641]).
**d.** James Cranford, *Yrelandtsche traenen* (Leiden, 1642), *cf Wing* C 6824.
**e.** *Een vermaeckelicke, doch eenvoudige en bondighe predicatie [...] over het onder-teyckenen van 't kerkelijcke verbondt, tegens de papistische ceremonien* (Leiden, [1642]).
    The three Civil War items are:
**f.** *Verscheyden handelingen en propositien, voor-gevallen ende gehouden door zijn hooghst-ghedachte majesteyt van Groot-Brittanien, in beyde [...] huysen des parlements* (Leiden, 1641).
**g.** *Copye wt een ghedruckten brief, door een edelman van Warwijck* (Leiden, 1642).
**h.** *Lijck-sermoen van Willem Laud, aerdtz- bisschop van Cantelberg* (Leiden, 1645), *cf Wing* L 599.
    The other nine items are:
**i.** Reinald Scot, *Ontdecking van tovery* (Leiden, 1637), *cf STC* 21864.
**j.** *Gods wonder-werken nu onlangs voor-gevallen in Enghelandt [...] op eenen sondagh, in de parochie-kercke van Withycombe, onder de predicatie* (Leiden, 1639), *cf STC* 25607.
**k.** Anthoni Maxey, *Des menschens heerliickheyt* (Leiden, 1641), *cf STC* 17693.
**l.** [Pierre de la Primaudaye], *Houwelycschen staet ende houwelycsche voorwaerden* (Leiden, 1644), *cf STC* 15233.
**m.** *Der vrouwen schildt* (Leiden, 1645), *cf STC* 15233.
**n.** Joseph Swetnam, *Recht-banck teghen de ydele, korzelighe, en wispeltuyrighe vrouwen* [three parts, third corrected edition] (Leiden, 1649), *cf STC* 23533.
**o.** *Der Engelsche vrouwen parlament* (Leiden, 1650), *cf STC* 19306.
**p.** *Der vrouwen advocaet* (Leiden, 1651), *cf STC* 19306.
**q.** Antonius Maxeyus, *Seven godzalige en christelijcke tractaten, over verscheyden texten der Heyliger Schriftuer* (Leiden, 1652), *cf STC* 17693. Van der Boxe translated e, j, l, n, o, (p) and q himself.

**11.** 'Ick twijffel niet, of U:E: hebt al over vele jaren (soo t'eeniger als t'ander tijden) mijn Naem gelesen op gedruckte Boeken die door mijn (nevens mijn swaer en moeyelijck Beroep) uyt het Engels vertaelt en in 't Nederduyts gebracht sijn)', Epilogue to *Seven godzalige en Christelijcke tractaten ... door Antonius Maxeyus* (Leiden, 1652), X4$^r$ [I do not doubt but that for many years now [you] have been reading my Name at one or another time in printed books which (next to my hard and difficult profession) I have translated from English into Dutch]. The works he translated were either devotional or entertaining, he says, and some of them were anonymous.

**12.** Although you may be sorry for it,
He aptly translated for us the *Deeg'lijckheyt des Tijts*,
*Den politijcken Dief*; Furthermore *Den Witten Duyvel,*

--------------------------------------------------

    After that *Het Goud' Trompet,*

--------------------------------------------------

He also showed us *Practijcke van Bekeeringh,*

--------------------------------------------------

    Also *t Nieuws van Over-Al,*

--------------------------------------------------

Yes, it is the same man, who translated
This *Recht-banck's* Sentence
Out of the English language (aa4$^v$).
    C. W. Schoneveld, *Intertraffic of the Mind* (Leiden, 1983), identified four translations: *Deeg'lijckheyt des Tijts* [512]; *Den Witten Duyvel* [48]; *Het Goud' Trompet* [56] and *Practijcke van Bekeeringh* [212]. See also M. Buisman, *Populaire prozaschrijvers van 1600 tot 1815* (Amsterdam, 1960), no.464, for *Den politijcken Dief*, which Buisman lists as translated from the French.

**13.** Nos.48, 56 and 212 are devotional works. 512 is a translation of a moralistic pamphlet (*STC* 20986), *Den politijcken Dief* is a translation of a 'vagabond' pamphlet. *'t Nieuws van Over-Al* has not been identified.

**14.** The preface to the 1650 edition suggests that this is not the first edition. Van der Boxe refers to *Der Engelsche Vrouwen Parlament* as 'voor desen by my in Druck uytgegeven/ ende oock uyt het Engels vertaelt' (A2$^r$) [previously printed and published by me, and likewise translated from the English].

**15.** 'De Drukker, aen de Lezer: Also ick nu onlanghs (voor de vierde mael) hebbe herdruckt mijn vertaelde RECHT-BANCK ... soo hebbe ick niet konnen nalaeten omme het Vrouwen PARLAMENT, (...) wederom te herdrucken' (A2ʳ). [The Printer, to the Reader: As I have recently reprinted (for the fourth time) my translated RECHT - BANCK ... I have not been able to resist once again to reprint het Vrouwen PARLAMENT.]

16. In spite of Van der Boxe's efforts to sell *Der Engelsche Vrouwen Parlament* in an enlarged edition, the public was clearly not too interested, since in 1651 he issued *Der Vrouwen Advocaet*, using sheets A-C of *Der Engelsche Vrouwen Parlament*, adding a new title-page and a new sheet to complete the text of *Der Engelsche Vrouwen Parlament* and to add the 16 articles that make up *Der Vrouwen Advocaet*.

17. The last Dutch language edition of Erasmus's *Colloquia Familiara* prior to 1650 is the *Colloquia familiaria of gemeensame t'Samen = sprake[n]*, printed in Kampen in 1644. *Senatulus, of Der Vroukens Vroetschappen* is featured on sigs DD4ᵛ-EE2ᵛ.

18.(a) *Der Vrouwen Parlament, ofte Vergaderingh ende Raedt-houdinge* (...) Den tweeden Druck/ vermeerdert ende verbetert. [wood-cut] Gedruckt met toe-latinge van de spitsvinnige Wijven, in 't Jaer als de Mannen de Broeck verloren.
Collation: 4° ($3) A-D4 [4]5-29[3].
A1 title and blank; A2ʳ 'Beminde Leser', signed 'W.C.'; A2ᵛ 'Aen de Vis-Teven en Veer-Wijven', signed 'I. Burchoorn'; A3ʳ-B3ʳ (pp.5-13) text *'t Vroutjens Vroedtschapje*; B3ᵛ-D3ᵛ (pp.14-29) text 'Het Parlement der Vrouwen', D3ᵛ-D4ᵛ 'Hier volgen de voornaamste Hooftstucken van de Wetten der Vrouwen, besloten in dit haer gehouden Parlement'.
(b)*Der Engelsche Vrouwen Parlament* (...) Vertaelt uyt het Engels. Zijnde bequaem om te worden gevoecht by de vertaelde Recht-banck. [wood-cut] Gedruckt/ ende uytgegeven tot Leyden, by Willem Christiaens. In 't Jubel-Jaer 1650.
Collation: 4° ($3) A-D2 [4]5-28.
A1 title and blank; A2ʳ 'De Drukker, aen de Lezer', signed U.L. genegen Vriendt Willem Christiaens'; A2ᵛ 'Aen alle Vrouw-Personen', signed 'I. Burchoorn' [this is the same poem as in the undated edition but with an altered title]; A3ʳ-C1ʳ (pp.5-17) text *Der Engelsche Vrouwen Parlament*, C1ʳ-C2ᵛ (pp.17-20) 'Hier volghen de voor-naemste Hooft-stucken van de Wetten, Placcaten ende Vryheden der

Vrouwen/ besloten in dit haer gehouden Parlament', C2ᵛ-C4ʳ (pp.20-23) 'Placcaet, besloten in ons Parlament, tot voordeel vande Getrouwde Vrouwen', running title: 'Placcaet tot voordeel vande Vrouwen'; C4ᵛ-D2ʳ (pp.24-27) 'Placcaet tot voordeel en behouf va[n]de Vrijsters ende alle huwbare Maaghden', D2ʳᵛ (pp.27-28) 'Toegift op dit Werck. Een heel Rijcke en Schoone Vrijster'; D2ᵛ (p.28) 'Tegen de Vrouwen' and 'Voor de Vrouwen'; running title 'Toegift' (D2ᵛ); all three unsigned.

19. [although the *Matrons* were noble, and they but Artisans' wives, yet no Parliament could be held, but a Lower House must be instituted also, to speak for the general commonwealth, even as the Higher House was for the Nobility and Nobles, to speak for both: and further, that nothing could be concluded in the *Higher House* (although it would be to the advantage of all) but it must first be presented and debated in the *Lower-House* also].

20. The addition to Mistriss Tabitha Tearesheet's portrayal runs to nine lines. It may be that 'Lijntjen Scheurlaecken', the name Van der Boxe chose, was a known character in a popular play. She is described as an extremely tall woman, loud-mouthed, a Roaring Girl who fights fencing-masters, intimidates inn-keepers, and is highly regarded by the Roaring Boys of Rome. These seem rather individual strokes, and might therefore have referred to an existing fictional character.

21. The 1640 Act of the Synod of Holland is referred to in one of the contributions to the controversy, Irenaeus Poimenander [pseud], *Absaloms-hayr* (Dordrecht, 1643). Borstius revised his sermon, which was published in 1645, with the approval of Voetius, De Maets and Hoornbeeck. See M. M. Toth-Ubbens, 'Kaalkop of Ruyg-hoofd. Historisch verzet tegen het lange haar', in *Antiek*, 1977, no.6, pp.371-85, for an account of the controversy and Borstius's sermon.

22. Schoneveld, *Intertraffic of the Mind*, p.47. Examples of these word pairs are: 'hulpe ende bystandt' for 'assistance'; 'voor-te-koomen ende te verhoeden' for 'to prevent'; 'aboleeren ende te niet maecken' for 'to abrogate';

'vergaderinghe ofte by-eenkomste' for 'meeting'; 'gnorren ofte morren' for 'grumbling'.

23. In the Epistle to the Reader of *A Juniper Lecture* the author is at some pains to explain the title: 'Here's a strange lecture towards (...) I know you have heard of a Curtain Lecture [*STC* 13312, published 1637] before now, and shall shortly heare of a Crab-tree Lecture [*STC* 23747, printed 1639] also' (A3ʳ, 1652 edition).

*A Juniper Lecture* was entered to Okes on 4 August 1638 (Arber, *Transcript*, iv.401). Taylor refers to the imminent publication of his *Divers crabtree lectures*, which was also entered to Okes, on 4 April 1639 (Arber, *Transcript*, iv.438).

# LEVIATHAN:

## OF VAN DE

## STOFFE, GEDAENTE,

### ende MAGT van de

### KERCKELYCKE

### ENDE

### WERELTLYCKE

### REGEERINGE.

*Befchreven door*

## THOMAS HOBBES

### van MALMESBURY.

### TOT AMSTERDAM,

By JACOBUS WAGENAAR, Boeck-verkooper,
op de hoeck van de Mol-fteegh, in *Des-Cartes*.

### ANNO 1667.

Fig.1   Letterpress title-page of Thomas Hobbes's *Leviathan*, translated into Dutch by
Abraham van Berkel and published in Amsterdam by Jacobus Wagenaar, 1667. (Utrecht
University Library, 100 C 31).

Arie-Jan Gelderblom

# *The Publisher of Hobbes's Dutch* Leviathan

As we know, the Anglo-Dutch wars of the mid-17th century hardly hampered the cultural connections between the two nations. The year 1667 may serve as an example. In the same year in which the Dutch fleet under Michiel de Ruyter broke the big chain across the Thames and captured the *Royal Charles*, a momentous specimen of English thought penetrated into the Netherlands, as the first Dutch translation of Thomas Hobbes's *Leviathan* was published in Amsterdam.

The reception of Hobbes's work in Holland during the 17th century has been carefully explored and mapped by C. W. Schoneveld. In his Leiden dissertation *Intertraffic of the Mind*, Schoneveld discusses the Dutch translation of *Leviathan* and discloses the identity of its translator, which had hitherto been unknown.[1] In the introduction that precedes the actual text of *Leviathan*, the translator reveals himself as an ardent supporter of Grand Pensionary Johan de Witt and the ruling States party; fully aware, on the other hand, that by translating Hobbes he is handling political, philosophical and religious gunpowder, he is so cautious as to sign his initials only at the end of the preface: A.T.A.B. As Schoneveld shows, this stands for Abrahamus Theodori à Berkel, a theologian and doctor of medicine.[2] Some years earlier he had anonymously translated Sir Thomas Browne's *Religio Medici*, and for some time he found his friends among the followers of Spinoza.[3]

The publisher of the 1667 Dutch *Leviathan* took fewer precautions where his identity was concerned. His name, Jacobus Wagenaar, appears in a cartouche on the engraved emblematic frontispiece (itself a copy of the 1651 London original). The letterpress title-page moreover features his printer's device and his full address: 'JACOBUS WAGENAAR, Boeck-verkooper, op de hoeck van de Mol-steegh, in *Des-Cartes*' (fig. 1). Who was this courageous bookseller? Moreover, the question arises why he was the right person to publish the Dutch *Leviathan*. Until now, his role in this enterprise has not been dealt with. For answers we first have to return to Abraham van Berkel and the spinozists.

Van Berkel was born in 1639.[4] In the late 1660s he lived in the free town of Culemborg in Gelderland, not far from the centre of the Republic, but out of reach of its authorities. Schoneveld suggests his exile in Culemborg might have something to do with his translation of *Leviathan*.[5] In these same years he was in touch with several spinozists. 'One of them, to whom he was particularly close, was Adriaan Koerbagh.'[6]

This Adriaan Koerbagh, doctor of medicine and doctor of law, was a free-thinker and a personal friend of Spinoza's. The heartrending story of his life has been told by K. O. Meinsma and, in Meinsma's footsteps, by P. H. van Moerkerken.[7] The following is based on their information.

In 1668 Koerbagh published *Een Bloemhof van Allerley Lieflijkheyd* ('a flower-garden full of sweetnesses of all kinds'), 'a small dictionary of words of foreign origin with explanations and commentaries, which contained a great many freethinkers' heresies'.[8] A follow-up volume, *Een Ligt Schijnende in Duystere Plaatsen* ('a light shining in dark places') was just being printed in Utrecht, when the printer there, Everard van Eede, grew suspicious of the contents and handed over the manuscript and some of the already printed sheets to the local bailiff. This officer duly informed his colleague in Amsterdam, where copies of the *Bloemhof* were just then stirring alarm among the Calvinist clergy and the city magistrates. Hearing this and fearing extradition, Koerbagh quickly left Culemborg.

A traitor told the Amsterdam judiciary where Koerbagh could be found, and was richly paid for his denunciation. Consequently, Koerbagh was taken prisoner, brought to court, judged and sentenced to ten years' imprisonment, after that a banishment from the city for ten years, and 4000 guilders fine on top of it all. The sentence was delivered on 27 July 1668. Adriaan Koerbagh died in the 'Willige Rasphuis' in October 1669.

On some occasions Van Berkel comes into this story. Together with Adriaan's brother Johannes he negotiates with the printer Van Eede. The traitor, calling Van Berkel a quick wit ('een gaeuw man'),[9] tries to accuse him of the co-authorship of the *Bloemhof*. In the courtroom his name was frequently mentioned. Schoneveld sums it up and we will follow his account here.

When captured and summoned to appear before the Amsterdam magistrates Koerbagh had to admit among other things that his friend Van Berkel had at least seen the proofs, but although the person who had betrayed Koerbagh had said that Van Berkel was probably the main instigator of his writings, Koerbagh refused to admit anything more. So Van Berkel went scot free and returned to Leiden in 1669.[10]

We will leave Van Berkel there and turn our attention to the Koerbagh family. Adriaan was the second of three children.[11] His father came from outside Amsterdam and the parents probably settled there after the children were born: Lucia (born in 1629), Adriaan (born in 1632 or 1633) and Johannes (born in 1634 or 1635). They belonged to the official church. Johannes was to become a free-thinker in his own right and seems to have always been very close to his brother. The girl, Lucia, married Jacob Blauwenhelm, a draper, in 1647.

Her husband had a sister, Aeltie Blauwenhelm, who married the bookseller Johannes van Ravesteijn in 1649. The two Blauwenhelms were not to live long. Jacob died in 1658, Aeltie in 1660.[12] Apparently the bereaved widow and widower, sister-in-law and brother-in-law, got along nicely for they became husband and wife in 1662. On 10 February of that year Johannes van Ravesteijn and Lucia Koerbagh registered for marriage. They had three children. Lucia died in 1672 and was buried in the Nieuwe Kerk on 29 October. Johannes was buried there on 3 January 1681.[13] Van Ravesteijn had his will made on 3 November 1676. The three children from his marriage with Lucia were each to receive one quarter of his assets; the remaining quarter was for a child from Lucia's first marriage, Catharina Blauwenhelm. Kleerkooper and Van Stockum, who mention this will, add a specification between brackets: Catharina Blauwenhelm was married to Jacobus Wagenaar.[14]

The connection we were looking for has now been established. By marrying Lucia's daughter Catharina, Jacobus Wagenaar became associated with the Koerbagh family. As we will see further on, Adriaan Koerbagh knew him well as early as 1666. It is safe to assume that Abraham van Berkel, while translating *Leviathan*, discussed the text and possibilities for its publication with his close friend Koerbagh. It must not have taken too long before they decided to ask Jacobus Wagenaar, a bookseller by profession and the husband of Adriaan Koerbagh's niece Catharina.

The Gemeentearchief (Municipal Archives) in Amsterdam, consulted via its indexes, yields further particulars. Jacobus Wagenaar from Leiden, bookseller, takes his oath as a burgher of Amsterdam on 15 July 1666. Less than two months before, his marriage to Catharina Blauwenhelm had been officially announced. On 29 May 1666 the couple had appeared for registration in the Nieuwe Kerk. Jacobus, 22 years old, carried a written consent from his parents. Catharina, sweet seventeen, was accompanied by her mother Lucia.

The teenage bride must have been pregnant at the time. On 12 September 1666 she and Jacob bring their son Matheus into the Nieuwe Kerk to have him christened by *dominee* Coop à Groen. They are accompanied by two witnesses who also sign their names: Judith Wagenaar and 'Mr. Adrian Coerbag'. This may prove that Adriaan had become a close friend of the young couple. A fortnight later Jacobus carried his baby son into the Nieuwe Kerk again, a short walking distance to the other side of the Nieuwe Zijds Voorburgwal. This time it was to have him buried. To quote the register of burials for 25 September 1666: 'Jacobus Wagenaer opt hoeckje vande Molsteegh sijn kint'.

Almost exactly two years later, 26 September 1668, a daughter Lucia is christened in the Nieuwe Kerk by *dominee* La Plancq. Johannes van Ravesteijn and grandmother Lucia Koerbagh sign their names as witnesses. The two years between Matheus' death and young Lucia's birth must have been eventful. They saw the production and publishing of the translated *Leviathan*, and Adriaan Koerbagh's persecution and imprisonment. It is too far fetched to suppose that his fate cast a shadow over the festivities for the new baby?

After 1668, our image of the family begins to fade; just a little more is known about Jacob's professional activities. He is known to have taken part in an illegal booksale in February 1671.[15] In that same year he brought out Jan Luyken's first volume of poetry *Duytse Lier* ('Dutch hurdy-gurdy'), in collaboration with his colleague and neighbour in the Molsteeg, Adriaan Veenendaal.[16] In 1672 he published a second edition of the Dutch *Leviathan*. Two years later, on the surging tide of Orangeism and conservatism, the book was banned.[17]

The end of Jacobus Wagenaar's activities as a bookseller and publisher has not yet been established. Neither has the date of his death. Catharina died in 1678 and was buried in the Nieuwe Kerk on 9 November. According to the register of burials she was a widow by then and lived on the Singel. There were probably few assets left. In

1681 the heirs of Jacobus Wagenaar (who were they?) are mentioned as debtors in the inventory of the late Daniel Elsevier's estate: 'dogh soo als iets sal schuldigh blijven soo sal bij de erffgenamen wijnigh te halen wesen'.[18] If any debts remain, there will be little chance to recover them from the heirs.

His appearing in the Nieuwe Kerk for official functions proves that Jacobus Wagenaar was a member of the official Reformed Church. But his other activities show him as a fervent supporter of modern thought. He calls his shop 'Des-Cartes'. He is publishing Hobbes. He publishes Jan Luyken, who was a young man with a background of religious non-conformism.[19] He is close to Adriaan Koerbagh, who himself was a friend of Spinoza's. But perhaps the most telling evidence in this respect is his printer's mark. Punning on his name (wagenaar = charioteer), it depicts a shining sun-god Apollo on his chariot.[20] The motto ILLUSTRANDO seems to refer directly to the goals of the modern philosophers of the time: to bring light into the darkness of traditional religious and political thought. Is it sheer coincidence that this motif, 'een ligt schijnende in duystere plaatsen', also turns up as the title of Adriaan Koerbagh's ill-fated last book?

## Notes

1. C. W. Schoneveld, *Intertraffic of the Mind: Studies in Seventeenth-Century Anglo-Dutch Translation with a Checklist of Books Translated from English into Dutch, 1600-1700*, Publications of the Sir Thomas Browne Institute, Leiden, New Series, 3 (Leiden, 1983).

2. Schoneveld, p.8 and pp.46-47.

3. Schoneveld, p.9

4. Schoneveld, pp.130-31, provides a biographical note on Van Berkel.

5. Schoneveld, pp.9 and 130.

6. Schoneveld, p.9.

7. K. O. Meinsma, *Spinoza en zijn kring: historisch-kritische studiën over Hollandsche vrijgeesten* (The Hague, 1896), pp.151-53 and pp.273-324; P. H. van Moerkerken, 'Adriaan Koerbagh 1663-1669', *De Vrije Bladen*, 19:2 (1948). See also *Nieuw Nederlandsch Biografisch Woordenboek*, VII, col.719-21.

8. Schoneveld, p.9.

9. Meinsma, p.307.

10. Schoneveld, p.10.

11. Meinsma, pp.151-52.

12. Meinsma, p.152; M. M. Kleerkooper and W. P. van Stockum, *De boekhandel te Amsterdam voornamelijk in de 17e eeuw* (The Hague, 1914-16), 2 vols. I, 578.

13. Meinsma, p.152; Meinsma, p.324; Kleerkooper and Van Stockum I, 579 and 581; *NNBW* II, col. 1169-71.

14. Kleerkooper and Van Stockum I, 581.

15. Kleerkooper and Van Stockum II, 1480.

16. A. J. Gelderblom and J. W. Steenbeek, 'De illustraties in de *Duytse Lier* van Jan Luyken (1671)', *De Nieuwe Taalgids* 73 (1980), 394-95.

17. Schoneveld, p.59.

18. I. H. van Eeghen, *De Amsterdamse boekhandel 1680-1725*, 5 vols. (Amsterdam, 1960-1978), III, 113.

19. K. Meeuwesse, *Jan Luyken als dichter van de Duytse Lier*, second edition (Groningen, etc, 1977), pp. 1-42. A. J. Gelderblom, 'Jonge zieltjes, vlucht tot trouwen! Een nieuwe interpretatie van Jan Luykens *Duytse Lier*', *De Nieuwe Taalgids* 75(1982), 483-504. Also in A. J. Gelderblom, *Mannen en maagden in Hollands tuin* (Amsterdam, 1991), pp.94-119.

20. Gelderblom and Steenbeek, p.395.

Jonathan I. Israel

# Propaganda in the making of the Glorious Revolution

One of the most sensational publications in 17th-century Dutch and English history, and indeed one of the greatest propaganda coups of early modern times, was William III's *Declaration* to the English people issued simultaneously in Britain and on the continent in November 1688.[1] The text is dated The Hague '10 October 1688' but its release was delayed by over a month so as to coincide with the landing of William III and his army of invasion at Torbay on 15 November (new style). In an age in which normally even the most noticed controversial tracts were rarely printed in more than two or three editions, or more than 2000 or 3000 copies,[2] William III's *Declaration* stands out as altogether exceptional given the very large quantity of copies printed, the large number of editions, and the variety of languages into which it was translated. In an era when propaganda tracts generally circulated only in a fairly restricted geographical area, William III's *Declaration* became well-known all over Europe and on both sides of the Atlantic. Finally, in an era in which it was unusual to report the impact of a piece of printed propaganda, in this case there is a range of contemporary evidence testifying to the crucial impact of this text on the course of the Glorious Revolution, one of the great events of world history.

Indeed, it is remarkable that William III's 'manifesto', as it was frequently referred to in England at the time, was recognised as a publication of exceptional importance even before its contents were known to more than a small circle of the Prince's confidants. As soon as he heard of its existence, the English ambassador at The Hague at the time, the Marquis d'Albeville, made energetic efforts to obtain a copy, but without success. 'It would be of the greatest importance imaginable to His Majestie', wrote James II's secretary of state, the Earl of Middleton to D'Albeville, from London, on 28 September, 'to see the *Declaration* they intend to sett out, as soon as is possible, and this I am well assur'd, that you have us'd your best endeavours to gett it, yet the better to enable you, you are to spare for no money, nor stick at any summe, that may procure it'.[3] Normally, not sticking 'at any summe' was more than enough to procure vital documents from the secret corridors of The Hague. But not on this occasion. 'You may imagine I have taken all possible care to come by the *Declaration* which I hear is on the press', D'Albeville replied, but 'the States printer is not to be corrupted; I have employ'd some to see if any of his servants can be; they are all sworn, and their places so lucrative they will not endanger them; I will leave no stone unmoved.'[4]

Fig.1   *The declaration of his Highnes William Henry…* (The Hague: Arnout Leers, 1688).
BL 8132.h.8.

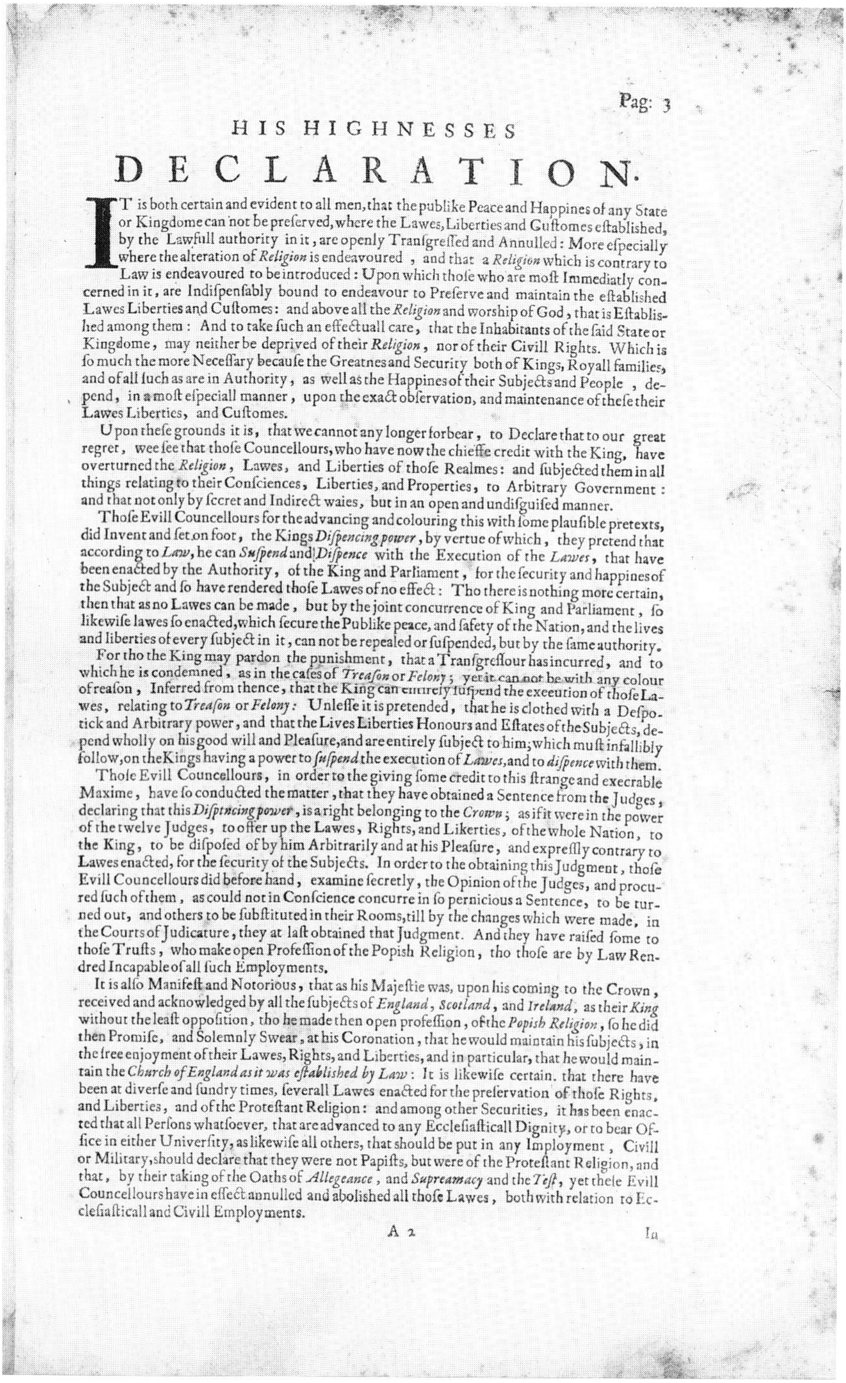

## HIS HIGHNESSES
# DECLARATION.

IT is both certain and evident to all men, that the publike Peace and Happines of any State
or Kingdome can not be preserved, where the Lawes, Liberties and Gustomes established,
by the Lawfull authority in it, are openly Transgressed and Annulled: More especially
where the alteration of *Religion* is endeavoured , and that a *Religion* which is contrary to
Law is endeavoured to be introduced : Upon which those who are most Immediately concerned in it, are Indispensably bound to endeavour to Preserve and maintain the established
Lawes Liberties and Customes: and above all the *Religion* and worship of God , that is Established among them : And to take such an effectuall care, that the Inhabitants of the said State or
Kingdome, may neither be deprived of their *Religion*, nor of their Civill Rights. Which is
so much the more Necessary because the Greatnes and Security both of Kings, Royall families,
and of all such as are in Authority, as well as the Happines of their Subjects and People , de-
pend, in a most especiall manner, upon the exact observation, and maintenance of these their
Lawes Liberties, and Customes.

Upon these grounds it is, that we cannot any longer forbear, to Declare that to our great
regret, wee see that those Councellours, who have now the chieffe credit with the King, have
overturned the *Religion*, Lawes, and Liberties of those Realmes: and subjected them in all
things relating to their Consciences, Liberties, and Properties, to Arbitrary Government :
and that not only by secret and Indirect waies, but in an open and undisguised manner.

Those Evill Councellours for the advancing and colouring this with some plausible pretexts,
did Invent and set on foot, the Kings *Dispencing power*, by vertue of which, they pretend that
according to *Law*, he can *Suspend* and *Dispence* with the Execution of the *Lawes*, that have
been enacted by the Authority, of the King and Parliament , for the security and happines of
the Subject and so have rendered those Lawes of no effect : Tho there is nothing more certain,
then that as no Lawes can be made , but by the joint concurrence of King and Parliament , so
likewise lawes so enacted, which secure the Publike peace, and safety of the Nation, and the lives
and liberties of every subject in it, can not be repealed or suspended, but by the same authority.

For tho the King may pardon the punishment, that a Transgressour has incurred, and to
which he is condemned , as in the cases of *Treason* or *Felony*; yet it can not be with any colour
of reason , Inferred from thence, that the King can entirely suspend the execution of those Lawes, relating to *Treason* or *Felony:* Unlesse it is pretended, that he is clothed with a Despo-
tick and Arbitrary power, and that the Lives Liberties Honours and Estates of the Subjects, de-
pend wholly on his good will and Pleasure, and are entirely subject to him; which must infallibly
follow, on the Kings having a power to *suspend* the execution of *Lawes*, and to *dispence* with them.

Those Evill Councellours, in order to the giving some credit to this strange and execrable
Maxime, have so conducted the matter , that they have obtained a Sentence from the Judges ,
declaring that this *Dispencing power*, is a right belonging to the *Crown*; as if it were in the power
of the twelve Judges, to offer up the Lawes, Rights, and Likerties, of the whole Nation , to
the King, to be disposed of by him Arbitrarily and at his Pleasure, and expressly contrary to
Lawes enacted, for the security of the Subjects. In order to the obtaining this Judgment, those
Evill Councellours did before hand, examine secretly , the Opinion of the Judges, and procu-
red such of them , as could not in Conscience concurre in so pernicious a Sentence, to be turned out, and others to be substituted in their Rooms, till by the changes which were made, in
the Courts of Judicature, they at last obtained that Judgment. And they have raised some to
those Trusts, who make open Profession of the Popish Religion, tho those are by Law Ren-
dred Incapable of all such Employments.

It is also Manifest and Notorious, that as his Majestie was, upon his coming to the Crown ,
received and acknowledged by all the subjects of *England*, *Scotland*, and *Ireland*, as their *King*
without the least opposition, tho he made then open profession , of the *Popish Religion*, so he did
then Promise, and Solemnly Swear, at his Coronation, that he would maintain his subjects , in
the free enjoyment of their Lawes, Rights, and Liberties, and in particular, that he would maintain the *Church of England as it was established by Law :* It is likewise certain. that there have
been at diverse and sundry times, severall Lawes enacted for the preservation of those Rights,
and Liberties, and of the Protestant Religion : and among other Securities, it has been enacted that all Persons whatsoever, that are advanced to any Ecclesiasticall Dignity, or to bear Office in either Univerfity, as likewise all others, that should be put in any Imployment , Civill
or Military, should declare that they were not Papists, but were of the Protestant Religion, and
that, by their taking of the Oaths of *Allegeance*, and *Supreamacy* and the *Test*, yet these Evill
Councellours have in effect annulled and abolished all those Lawes, both with relation to Ecclesiasticall and Civill Employments.

A 2

In

Three days later, on 15 October, D'Albeville further reported that the

manifesto or *Declaration* can not be yett had at any rate for I have offer'd considerably for it, and you will, I believe, see it there sooner than we here. They give out they will insert in it a copy of a capitulation between both kings [*ie* James II and Louis XIV] notwithstanding all assurances given to the contrary, engaging to suppress the Protestant religion and destroy these States for that end.[5]

On the same day, the English consul at Amsterdam, Daniel Petit, reported to Middleton that 'order is come hither from The Hague for the printing of 20,000 copies of the Prince's manifest', adding that 'a proportionable number is printing at Rotterdam and att The Hague, and are to be distributed at the same time that the Fleet putts to sea'.[6]

Security at the printers employed by the Prince and the States at Amsterdam and Rotterdam was evidently as tight as at The Hague, for on 21 October, D'Albeville wrote to Middleton that the 'manifest can not be had for any money that I offer'd, giving as a main reason that several of William's English accomplices 'are so des-crib'd, tho not nam'd, that they may be easily discover'd'. He then added the following information: 'all the manifests printed were brought to the Prince himselfe, and seal'd up by him, except two that were given to the author, before they were brought to Benting's quarters'.[7] This reveals not only the scrupulous care which William took to guard the secrecy of his *Declaration* until what he judged was the right moment but also that Bentinck, the Stadtholder's closest associate in the work of planning the invasion of Britain, and who we know from other evidence master-minded the distribution of the *Declaration* in England, was from the outset put in charge of the entire stock of copies and made responsible for ensuring that there were no leaks.

Actually D'Albeville had finally obtained several copies 'with the arms of England upon it' by 20 October (new style) which, given the long delay in the sailing of the fleet, due to the contrary winds and stormy weather, should have given James much more time to react to William's propaganda coup than he was actually to have.[8] D'Albeville sent a copy 'by an express' and then another copy to Lord Middleton in London but his messengers were 'detained as well as the couriers of Spayne and France at Maerdyk, nobody being suffer'd to pass that way or by any other till the Prince set sayle'.[9] On 28 October new style, two and a half weeks before the landings at Torbay, and several days after sending off the couriers with the copies of the manifesto, D'Albeville wrote: 'I doubt not but this memorial has allready come into your Lordship's hands, some thousands having been sent into England to be dispers'd at the Prince his landing; they are not to be had here as yett'.[10] But in fact the security measures taken in the Republic, and Bentinck's careful undercover methods in Britain, worked so well that, despite the long delay in the sailing of the fleet, the Prince's *Declaration*, though now present on a massive scale in both Britain and the Netherlands, remained concealed from the eyes of the government in London almost to the last moment. Bentinck had instructed his agents to begin distribution only after hearing of the landing; but, in fact, the first copies seem to have started circulating in London after the fleet made its first attempt to set out, at the end of October.

According to the contemporary Huguenot historian Abel Boyer, 'just as the Prince was about to leave, Captain Langham who belonged to one of the English regiments in Holland was seized [in London] upon suspicion, and in his portmantle were found a parcel of the Prince of Orange's *Declaration* which were the first that were brought over'.[11] However, according to what James II himself told the Archbishop of Canterbury and other bishops whom he summoned to the palace on 2 November (old style) 'he had seized a person who had brought into the city a great number of the Prince of Orange's declarations, and had begun to disperse them; for His Majesty had received five or six copies from several persons, to whom they have been sent in penny-post letters, which he had thrown into the fire; but that he had still one copy'.[12] James's purpose in discussing the Prince's *Declaration* with the bishops, on 2 November, was to challenge them, as he had the Bishop of London, Henry Compton, the day before, on the passage in the text where the Prince claimed that he had been 'invited' to appear in arms in England by numerous 'lords temporal and spiritual'. James assured the bishops that he did not believe a word of what was in the *Declaration* concerning them – Compton brazenly lied to the King in denying any involvement – but asked them to issue a public statement denying that they had 'invited' William to invade. The bishops agreed to discuss the matter among themselves; but, subsequently, on various pretexts, refused to issue any statement. In the interview on 2 November the King did not actually permit the bishops to see the copy which he held up as he spoke and had already refused the previous day to put it into Compton's hands. James had a secretary read the relevant passage concerning the bishops 'pointing to the place where he would have him begin and end'.[13] The bishops were thus sent off without having actually perused a copy and without having a copy to discuss amongst themselves. On 3 November, Lord Clarendon 'being at the King's levee, His Majesty took me into his closet, and showed me the Prince's *Declaration,* as he had done yesterday to the bishops', but again James avoided parting with the copy he showed Clarendon. Later that day – two days before William III landed at Torbay – Clarendon waited on Princess Anne: 'she lent me the Prince of Orange's declaration', saying 'the King had lent it her, and she must restore it to him tomorrow'.[14] No doubt James expected that she would be as shocked as he was by the contents of the *Declaration* and not least the doubt it cast on the legitimacy of her five-month old brother, the heir to the throne, James, Prince of Wales.

James's initial response, then, was to endeavour to suppress the text at court and 'keep the Prince's *Declaration* from the knowledge of the people'.[15] He issued a royal proclamation from Whitehall, on 2 November, denouncing the treasonable declaration designed to 'seduce our people and (if it were possible) to corrupt our army, a very great number whereof being printed, several persons are sent and employed to disperse the same throughout our kingdoms'. The proclamation warned

all our subjects, of what degree or quality soever, that they do not publish, disperse, repeat or hand about the said treasonable papers or declarations, or any of them, or any other paper or papers of such like nature, nor presume to read, receive, conceal or keep the said treasonable papers or declarations … without discovering and revealing the same as speedily as may be … to the justices of the peace or other magistrates, upon peril of being prosecuted according to the utmost severity of the law.[16]

With the landing of the Prince's invading army, at Torbay, on 5 November, however, Bentinck's distribution machine suddenly sprang into action and his agents began distributing copies everywhere. In London, evidently, one of the main suppliers of the *Declaration* was the Spanish embassy.[17] Simultaneously, the *Declaration*, which the States General's printers had prepared in Dutch, French and German, as well as English, editions, was released in the Republic, D'Albeville writing to Sunderland on 6 November from The Hague that the 'manifesto is now sold publickly, and in all languages'.[18]

So great was the impact of the *Declaration* in the days immediately following the landing that James's ministers were quickly brought to the realisation that the King's initial policy of suppression was not just ineffectual but positively dangerous. The manifesto had to be resolutely and effectively confronted. Not only was London inundated with copies but the *Declaration* was now circulating in abundance all over England. Also both the main *Declaration*, and the separate Declaration of the Prince for Scotland, were circulating north of the border.

James thus switched to a very different tack. Using the *London Gazette*, then the only licensed, regular newspaper in England, the King now deliberately drew attention to the 'late [*Declaration*] published by him', announcing to the public that its seemingly high-sounding principles and phrases were, in reality, just 'specious and plausible pretences', the Prince of Orange's real aim being

an absolute usurping of our crown and royal authority, as may fully appear by his assuming to himselfe in the said *Declaration* the regal style, requiring the peers of the realm, both spiritual and temporal and all other persons of all degrees, to obey and assist him in the execution of his designs, a prerogative inseparable from the imperial crown of this realm.[19]

During the next month, as the struggle unfolded and William's army advanced slowly towards London, the government tried to press home its counter-attack by having the *Declaration* reprinted in London – and also Edinburgh – along with, as Boyer expressed it, 'a preface and some frivolous animadversions upon it'.[20]

These government-inspired versions of the *Declaration*, complete with hostile commentary, concentrated on denouncing the tone of the *Declaration*, with its obvious resonances of regal authority, the lack of any attempt in it to demonstrate a conspiracy between James II and Louis XIV against the United Provinces, and the slur contained in the *Declaration* regarding the legitimacy of James II's five-month old son, the heir to the throne, James, Prince of Wales.

The style of the *Declaration*, attacked by James already in the *London Gazette*, was made much of. 'To use in England the style of We and Us, commanding, having of Parliaments and settling the nations, and last of all that he will then send back his Army which sheweth he intends to stay behind himself, can declare nothing else to us but that his design is to be King.'[21] As for the alleged Anglo-French conspiracy, D'Albeville had already pointed out that William, in his propaganda in the Netherlands, had made much of the alleged plot of the two kings, James and Louis, against the Protestant religion and, as part of this, against the United Provinces, in order to sway Dutch opinion in favour of intervention in Britain at a time when James was experiencing difficulties with his domestic opposition. The absence of any reference to this alleged conspiracy in the *Declaration* was pounced upon by James's propagandists as clear evidence of William's cynical manipulation of public opinion in both the Republic and Britain: 'the first thing I looked for', wrote one of James's commentators on the *Declaration*, 'was the exposing of our clandestine League with France, so much talk'd of, to excuse the Dutch preparations and invasion; but I find after all, not one word said of France, or any such secret league, the main thing pretended and expected'.[22] Another of James's commentators told how the rumours of a 'secret league between His Majesty of Great Britain and the French king to extirpate all Protestants' had been 'with so much art and cunning spread, as to startle the most considering Protestants of all persuasions, whence nothing could be more eagerly desired, than a sight of the Prince of Orange's *Declaration*'; however, 'there not being one word of any such treaty, we cannot see why it is that the Prince comes over'.[23] In addition to his 'usurping a regal style, and commanding obedience from the King's subjects', misleading the public about James's relations with the French king, and outrageously insulting the birth of the Prince of Wales whom William, allegedly, well knew to be the legitimate heir to the throne, there was some sarcastic comment about the methods William customarily used to get his way with the Dutch provincial assemblies and States General, one of the Jacobite commentators on the *Declaration* calling him a 'Prince who having well nigh enslaved his own States, is come to fight us into Liberty'.[24]

The points made by James II's publicists were both pertinent and hard-hitting. Yet the enormous impact which the *Declaration* made in Britain was wholly advantageous to William. The government's 'animadversions on it' appear to have had little effect. Later Jacobite and French propaganda unswervingly pointed to the Prince's *Declaration* as having played a key role in 'debauching' the English public, making them forget their true allegiance and turn against their legitimate monarch.[25] But discerning pro-Revolution writers, especially those who had no reason to stress the contribution of William's Whig allies to the actual invasion, were just as emphatic in seeing the *Declaration* as crucial. 'Though there was not all that men had fondly expected in this *Declaration*', recalled Edmund Bohun, a moderate Tory pro-Revolution writer,

yet there was enough to satisfie any rational man that the expelling this Prince and his Army before our Religion, Liberties, Properties and Government were effectually settled in Parliament, and those who had so outrageously attempted the ruine of them were call'd to account, would certainly end in the ruine of them, and was a kind of cutting up our Laws and Religion with our swords. This and nothing else was the cause that wherever the Prince's *Declaration* was read, it conquered all that saw or heard it, and it was to no purpose to excite men to fight against their own Interest, and to destroy what was more dear to them than their lives.[26]

During the early weeks of the Glorious Revolution, both William himself in southern England, and his Whig and Tory accomplices in other regions of the country, used the *Declaration* as the main justification for the Prince's 'appearing in arms' in England, as the invasion was euphemistically termed, and for Englishmen supporting the invasion.[27] On entering Exeter, the first important town occupied by the Dutch army, William summoned those of the Anglican clergy who remained – the bishop and dean had fled – to the cathedral where Gilbert Burnet 'read aloud the Prince's *Declaration* and reasons for this his expedition'.[28] In the first fortnight, hardly anyone among the English dared come out in support of William. When the nobility did begin to desert James, they used the *Declaration* to justify their doing so. In early December, on seizing Durham, Lord Lumley read out the *Declaration* to the gentry of the county at Durham Castle.[29] In the north-west, the Williamite rebels, having disarmed James's troops at Chester, 'read the Prince's *Declaration* and declared for him'.[30] Lord Delamere, who seized Manchester the next day, also had the manifesto publicly read there.[31] At Oxford the Glorious Revolution culminated in the blowing of a trumpet at Carfax and the Prince's *Declaration* 'being read openly to the multitude by Lord Lovelace'.[32] Much the same scene was re-enacted all over England, from Leeds to Portsmouth and from Bristol to King's Lynn.

In her discussion of the significance of William III's *Declaration*, Lois Schwoerer has assumed that it was essentially a Whig document and that, by making use of it, William provided the basis for the limiting of his own power, in the shape of the Declaration of Rights, when he replaced James as king: 'in a certain sense William really was hoisted on the petard of his own propaganda'.[33] The fact that the *Declaration*, which was designed to 'persuade the public of his selfless purposes' was published in his name was, she has argued, 'a central consideration in persuading the Prince to agree to a statement which he otherwise might well have refused'.[34] But the view that the *Declaration* was basically a Whig initiative which had the effect of boxing the Prince in is, arguably, greatly to exaggerate the role of Parliament and parliamentarians in the making of the Revolution. It is also to misrepresent what was in fact the basic purpose of the *Declaration*.

An exact assessment of the political significance of the *Declaration* has to begin with the undoubted fact that it was not a Whig, or in any sense an English parliamentary, document. It was actually written, under William's close supervision, by his right-hand-man in the States of Holland, the Pensionary Gaspar Fagel, and then translated into English by Gilbert Burnet.[35] Its basic purpose was two-fold: firstly, it was intended to justify William's armed intervention in Britain as self-proclaimed guardian of the English and Scots constitutions; secondly, it was designed as a legitimation of the Prince's seizure and exercise of *de facto* power in the interim period that would necessarily intervene before the Prince, as he promised to do in his *Declaration*, could convene a Convention Parliament. Although the drafting of the *Declaration* by Fagel was preceded by the submission of various proposed drafts for the *Declaration* by William's Whig accomplices, the actual text concocted by William and Fagel was concealed from the Whig leadership in Holland, as it was from everyone else, because William's aims were not the same as theirs. When the Whig leadership with the invasion armada, at Hellevoetsluis, did eventually see the text, many of them were angered by its moderate tone and obvious intention of appealing to Tory, as well as Whig, sentiment.[36]

During the first crucial three months of the Glorious Revolution, down to the beginning of February 1689, William was not yet concerned with how he might evade, or water down, the parliamentary Declaration of Rights which, in the appendix to his

*Declaration*, he had promised. During the decisive phase of the Revolution, that is in the period preceding Parliament's intervention, the Prince's main concerns were still to undermine James by winning extensive English support for the invasion; secondly, to justify his own seizure of power in England as regent with the acquiescence of the peerage – or a selection of it – and the city of London, and lastly, to persuade Parliament to make him king. Hence, even when Williams and his army were approaching London, and James was clearly beaten, William and Bentinck, far from distancing themselves from the *Declaration*, went out of their way to remind everyone of it at every opportunity.[37] When, on his approach, the officers of the London militia sent an address to his camp, assuring him that they would not only support him but that 'it was their firm resolution to venture all that was dear to them to attain the glorious ends of His *Declaration*',[38] they were not trying to box him in but conveying their submission to his constantly reiterated assurances.

Once he had London effectively in his grasp, the Prince continued to deploy his *Declaration* systematically as his chief means of explaining and legitimating every step in his political programme. At the meeting of former members of Parliament which the Prince convened in London a week after his arrival, he asked them to 'advise the best manner how to pursue the ends of my *Declaration*'.[39] In the letters which William, as regent, sent out to the constituencies directing that members of Parliament be elected to attend the Convention which he was summoning, he explained that 'we' were doing so, 'heartily desiring the performance of what we have in our *Declaration* expressed'.[40] On opening the Convention Parliament, on 22 January, the Prince urged members to act with all haste so that the 'ends of my *Declaration* will be attained'.[41]

As Parliament deliberated what to do about the throne and the succession, William was not yet concerned to preserve his future monarchical power as far as possible from constitutional limits because it was very much an open matter whether Parliament would make him king at all. We know that initially there was a great deal of reluctance in both houses to contemplate William as sole, or joint, monarch and that in the Lords there was a large majority against elevating him to the throne.[42] We also know that through his Dutch favourites, Bentinck and Dijkveld, the Prince brought every kind of pressure to bear, threats as well as carrots, to sway members to vote as he wanted. But the most important instrument of pressure was the *Declaration* which was continually kept ringing in members' ears. In other words, in so far as the *Declaration* set limits on royal authority, the manifesto was an asset rather than a handicap to William at the most vital moment of the Revolution and of his political career.[43] The Prince's supporters bombarded wavering MPs with the proposition that 'his unchangeable adherence to what he promised in his *Declaration* shews with what sacredness he will observe his oath as king'.[44]

The paradox of the Convention debate on the future of the throne, however, is that William's *Declaration* also emerged, at this point, as the chief weapon of the Tory loyalist opposition to the dethroning of James.[45] So successful had William's propaganda coup been that his *Declaration* was now conceded by everyone, on all sides of the political equation, as the only basis on which possible courses of action could be taken. For the Whigs it opened up the prospect of setting limits on the crown. For loyalists it was an instrument by which they could hope to exploit the ceaseless assurances of

William and Bentinck that the Prince sought only the aims set out in the *Declaration* and was not after the throne for himself. Clarendon saw at once that the Prince's *Declaration* offered the Tories the best hope of saving James, by following a policy of urging Parliament to concede only what was in the *Declaration*.[46] This then became the strategy of the loyalist grouping as a whole, the bishop of Ely recalling afterwards that 'we saw no other hopeful way to save [the King] and serve him but by treating with the Prince on the foot of his *Declaration*'.[47]

Consequently, when the Convention met everyone was willing to adopt the *Declaration* as a basis of action, Tory MPs such as Sir Robert Seymour, representing the University of Cambridge, and Sir Thomas Clarges, MP for Oxford University, being at the forefront of the clamour. It was Clarges who pronounced: 'I think wee sit here to pursue the ends of the Prince of Orange's *Declaration* and therefore I move that the *Declaration* may be read'.[48] The entire text of the *Declaration* was later reprinted in the opening pages of the Commons journal recording the Convention debate complete with William's promise that 'it is plain that there can be no redres nor remedy offered but in Parliament by a Declaration of the Rights of the Subjects that have been invited'.[49] Parliament on drawing up the Declaration of Rights duly concluded with the words 'to which demand of [the King's subjects'] rights, they are particularly invited by the *Declaration* of His Highness the Prince of Orange'.[50]

Modern historians, Whig and non-Whig in tendency, have alike been intent on focusing attention on the role of the Convention in the making of the Glorious Revolution and have virtually all tended to de-emphasise the role of William III and the Dutch intervention. Along with the Prince and the Dutch state, historians have down-played the Prince's *Declaration*. Whole books of documents on British constitutional history in the late 17th century have been published without including so much as an extract from the Prince's *Declaration*. Yet, it is arguable that this manifesto was by far the most important single document of the Glorious Revolution not excepting even the Declaration of Rights which, to a considerable extent, repeated its stipulations and assertions. Certainly, contemporaries regarded it as *the* document of the Revolution, a text of overriding significance. Furthermore, its contents were much more widely and vigorously debated than those of the Declaration of Rights and this continued to be the case through the 1690s. William III's *Declaration* to the English people, of 10 October 1688, is without doubt an exceptional, even perhaps extreme, instance of the power of the press. With its vast impact, it proved one of the most decisive publications of modern history.

### Notes

1. The historian who has hitherto most emphasised the importance of the *Declaration* of William III is L. G. Schwoerer: see Lois G. Schwoerer, 'Propaganda in the Revolution of 1688-89', *The American Historical Review* 82 (1977), 852-5; Lois G. Schwoerer, 'The Bill of Rights: Epitome of the Revolution of 1688-89' in J. G. A. Pocock (ed.), *Three British Revolutions, 1641, 1688, 1776* (Princeton, 1980),

pp.235-6; L. G. Schwoerer, *The Declaration of Rights, 1689* (Baltimore, 1981), pp.17-18, 115-16.

2. Mark Goldie, 'The Revolution of 1689 and the Structure of Political Argument', *Bulletin of Research in the Humanities*, vol.83 (1980), 479-80.

3. BL MS Add.41823, f.76v. Middleton to D'Albeville, London 28 September 1688 (old style).

4. BL MS Add.41816, f.232v. D'Albeville to Middleton, The Hague, 2/12 October 1688.

5. Ibid, f.238v. D'Albeville to Middleton, The Hague, 5/15 October 1688.

6. Ibid, f.237. Petit to Middleton, Amsterdam, 15 October 1688.

7. Ibid, f.251. D'Albeville to Middleton, The Hague, 21 October 1688.

8. BL MS Add.41816, f.249. D'Albeville to Middleton, The Hague, 20 October 1688.

9. Ibid, f.263. D'Albeville to Middleton, The Hague, 28 October 1688.

10. Ibid

11. Abel Boyer, *The History of King William the Third* 3 vols (London, 1702), I, 229.

12. *The Correspondence of Henry Hyde, Earl of Clarendon... with the Diary*, edited by S. W. Singer, 2 vols, (London, 1828), II, 494.

13. *Correspondence of Henry Hyde* II, 494.

14. Ibid, II, 199-200.

15. Boyer, *History of King William the Third* I, 231; [Edmund Bohun], *History of the Desertion*, (London, 1689), 34; Schwoerer, 'Propaganda in the Revolution of 1688-89', 870.

16. BL G5302. Proclamation of James II, Whitehall, 2 November 1688.

17. [Bohun], *History of the Desertion*, 35-6.

18. J. MacPherson, *Original Papers; containing the Secret History of Great Britain*, 2 vols (London, 1776) I, 286.

19. *The London Gazette*, no.2397 (5-8 November 1688), p.1.

20. Boyer, *History* I, 231.

21. *Some reflections upon the Prince of Orange's Declaration* in *A Collection of Scarce and Valuable Tracts... from the Collection of Lord Somers*, 4 vols (London, 1748), I, 292.

22. Ibid

23. *The Prince of Orange His Declaration: shewing the Reasons why he Invades England. With a shortPreface and some modest remarks on it* (Edinburgh, 1688), p.2.

24. *Seasonable and Honest Advice to the Nobility, Clergy, Gentry, Souldiery, and other the King's Subjects, upon the Invasion of His Highness the Prince of Orange* (London, 1688), p.2.

25. See, for instance, Antoine Arnauld, *Le véritable portrait de Guillaume-Henri de Nassau, Nouvel Absalom, Nouvel Herode, Nouveau Cromwell, Nouveau Néron* (gives Brussels [but Paris?], 1689), pp.34-5, 40, 50, and the *Esprit politique ou l'histoire en abregé de la vie et des actions de Guillaume III de Nassau, Roi de la Grande Bretagne* (gives Amsterdam [but Paris?]), 1695), p.137.

26. [Bohun], *History of the Desertion*, 72.

27. *Engeland Beroerd onder de Regering van Iacobus de II en hersteldt door Willem en Maria, Prins en Princesse van Orangie* (Amsterdam, 1689), pp.246-55; Abraham van Poot, *Engelands Gods-dienst en vryheid hersteld door sijn Hoogheid den Heere Prince van Oranjen* 2 vols (Amsterdam, 1689), II, 167, 205, 213, 231; see also J. I. Israel, 'Introduction' to *The Anglo-Dutch Moment: Essays on the Glorious Revolution and its World Impact*, edited by J. I. Israel (Cambridge, 1991), pp.15-16.

28. Schwoerer, *Declaration of Rights*, 116.

29. W. A. Speck, 'The Revolution of 1688 in the North of England', *Northern History*, XXV (1989), p.194.

30. *The London Courant*, no.4 (18/22 December 1688) p.1.

31. G. G. Arconati Lamberti, *Mémoires de la dernière révolution d'Angleterre*, 2 vols (The Hague, 1702), I, 596.

32. *The Life and Times of Anthony Wood, Antiquary of Oxford, 1632-1695*, edited by A. Clark, 5 vols (Oxford, 1891-1900), III, 286-7.

33. Schwoerer, 'Propaganda in the Revolution of 1688-9', 872.

34. Schwoerer, 'The Bill of Rights', 235.

35. G. Burnet, *History of His Own Time*, 6 vols (Oxford, 1833), III, 300; N. Japikse, *Prins Willem III, de stadhouder-koning*, 2 vols (Amsterdam, 1933), II, 251.

36. Burnet, *History*, III, 308-10.

37. *Correspondence of Henry Hyde* II, 215.

**38.** *A Collection of State Tracts Publish'd on Occasion of the Late Revolution in 1688*, 3 vols (London, 1705), III, 71.

**39.** Israel, 'Introduction', p.16.

**40.** *The Journals of the House of Commons*, X (1688-93) pp. 5, 8.

**41.** Israel, 'Introduction' p.16.

**42.** E. Cruickshanks, D. Hayton, and C. Jones, 'Divisions in the House of Lords on the Transfer of the Crown and other Issues, 1689-94: Ten New Lists', *Bulletin of the Institute of Historical Research* LIII (1980), 61-5.

**43.** Arnauld, *Le véritable portrait de Guillaume-Henri*, 71.

**44.** [R. Ferguson], *A Brief Justification of the Prince of Orange's Descent into England and of the Kingdoms Late Recourse to Arms* (London, 1689), p.36.

**45.** Lois G. Schwoerer, 'A Jornall of the convention at Westminster begun the 22 of January 1688/9', *Bulletin of the Institute of Historical Research* XLIX (1976), 253, 256.

**46.** *Correspondence of Henry Hyde* II, 244, 246; Nicholas Witsen, 'Uitreksels' in J. Scheltema, *Geschied- en Letterkundig Mengelwerk*, 6 vols. (Amsterdam, Utrecht, 1817-36), III, 150-1.

**47.** Robert Beddard, 'The Loyalist Opposition in the Interregnum: a Letter of Dr Francis Turner, Bishop of Ely, on the Revolution of 1688', *Bulletin of the Institute of Historical research*, XL (1967), p.106.

**48.** Schwoerer, 'A Jornall of the Convention', 256.

**49.** *The Journals of the House of Commons*, X (1688-93), p.5.

**50.** Ibid, p.23.

Fig.1 Johannes Luchtmans at an advanced age.
Crayon, c.1791/2, by the German artist Johann Anspach.
Leiden, Stedelijk Museum 'De Lakenhal'.

P. G. Hoftijzer

# Business and Pleasure: a Leiden bookseller in England in 1772

During the early-modern period 'tourism' – travel that is, undertaken for the purpose of both education and entertainment – was generally orientated towards the great centres of European civilization. To educate their minds, but certainly also to have them enjoy themselves, the aristocracy and wealthy bourgeoisie sent their sons to Italy, treasure house of classical history and art, or to France, Europe's leading nation during the 17th and 18th centuries. Other countries attracted less 'tourists', with the exception perhaps of the Dutch Republic, the singular appeal of which can be explained by the abundance of sights within a very small space and surely also by the excellent transport facilities, thus enabling travellers to make a short digression into Holland as part of their more extended grand tour.[1] The British Isles, on the other hand, were not very popular with visitors from abroad, mainly as a result of their unfavourable situation on the north-western fringe of Europe, but also because of a long lasting stigma of backwardness and xenophobia.[2]

Yet during the 17th and 18th centuries it became fashionable among travellers to Britain to combine their commercial, academic or diplomatic visit with a tour of the country, although for various reasons these excursions usually remained restricted to what one Dutch visitor called a 'tourkien' of England, a short tour of southern England based on the triangle London – Oxford – Cambridge.[3] Unfortunately only a small number of the travel journals, notebooks and diaries kept by Dutch travellers to England has survived. Some have later been published, for example the journal of Lodewijck Huygens, son of the well-known Sir Constantijn Huygens, who came to England as a diplomatic attendant in 1651-52,[4] or the account of Allard de la Court, member of a wealthy Leiden family of cloth merchants, who visited England in 1710, among other things to invest his family's capital. De la Court's description of his wanderings through London and south-western England is all the more interesting because of the meticulous list of his purchases added at the end, which includes such varied items as silk stockings, gloves, a yellow bonnet, oranges at the theatre, a gold watch and prints by Van Dyck and Salvator Rosa.[5]

Some 60 years after De la Court another notable inhabitant of Leiden crossed the North Sea. His name was Johannes Luchtmans (1726-1809), who together with his brother Samuel ran Leiden's most renowned publishing and bookselling firm of the 18th century (fig.1). He, too, kept a journal of his English voyage which is preserved among the Luchtmans papers in the Library of the Vereeniging ter Bevordering van de Belangen des Boekhandels at Amsterdam.[6] Although the 19th-century Dutch book historian A. C. Kruseman peevishly remarked that the journal contains hardly anything of interest,[7] this contribution will follow Johannes Luchtmans's perambulations in England during the spring of 1772.

The house of Luchtmans was established at Leiden by Jordaan Luchtmans in 1683.[8] The firm, which from the start was closely associated with Leiden's academic milieu, was continued by Jordaan's son Samuel, who in 1730 was appointed printer both to the university and the city of Leiden. In the latter part of his career he operated in partnership with his two sons, Johannes and Samuel Jr., until in 1755 they took over. While carrying on the publishing activities the two brothers particularly expanded into the international book trade, setting up an extensive network of trade relations with booksellers all over Europe. Proof of the enormous scope of their 'Latin trade' is the *Catalogus librorum compactorum*, a 365-page stock catalogue of bound books published at the beginning of the 19th century, which lists some 20,000 titles from the Luchtmans stores, including numerous incunables and other extremely rare books. Samuel Jr. died in 1780, but Johannes remained in charge of the firm for many more years: when he finally died in 1809, he had been engaged in the family business for over 60 years.

Johannes's trip to England in 1772 was by no means the first time he travelled abroad. According to various memorandum books in the Luchtmans archive, from 1747 onwards he had made regular voyages to the book fairs of Frankfurt and Leipzig.[9] Although such commercial travels were a normal feature of the life of many Dutch booksellers during the old regime, few ever went to Britain. England and Scotland traditionally were recipients, not suppliers of the international book trade, and consequently it was more obvious for British booksellers dealing in foreign books to come to the continent themselves or to use middlemen in order to acquire new selections.[10] However, as the Luchtmans firm had long-established contacts in England, the purpose of Johannes Luchtmans's journey in 1772 clearly was to strengthen existing ties as well as to establish new connections with booksellers in London, Oxford and Cambridge. Johannes even seems to have spoken the English language, a rare phenomenon among continental booksellers, not to mention readers.

Disappointingly, the travel account provides little information on this commercial aspect of Johannes's visit to England, although other documents in the Luchtmans archive can supply important additional details. Nevertheless the journal, which may have been intended by the author to read from to his family at home, is of considerable interest as a personal document, conveying the impressions that England and the English made on this, in spite of all his international connections, still somewhat provincial Leiden burgher.

Johannes Luchtmans left Holland on Saturday 25 April 1772 on the packetboat 'Earl of Bedborough', in the company of his acquaintance Johan Andreas Cunaeus, a jurist and member of the Leiden city council. They had a calm crossing and the following day at five o'clock in the afternoon disembarked at Harwich, where they had tea, scones and 'dunne boterhammetjes' – sandwiches – in the well-known 'Three Cups' inn.[11] On Monday they arrived by coach in London, where Cunaeus took up residence with a

Mr Paris in Great Suffolk Street on the South Bank, while Johannes went straight to the house of Henrik Putman, minister of the Dutch Church in Austin Friars who apparently had invited him to stay.[12]

The following day, Tuesday the 28th, was spent entirely on sight-seeing. In the morning Putman and Johannes visited Drapers' Hall in nearby Throgmorton Street – its garden was a popular promenade among Londoners – and the Bank of England, where Johannes stood amazed by the grandeur of the interior and by the multitude of people, ladies and gentlemen, 'bringing in their money and receiving interest'. Alas there was no time for a visit to Bedlam Hospital in Moorfields, but this was made good by Johannes's spotting John 'Liberty' Wilkes in his coach, whose fame had apparently also spread to Leiden as he was able to recognise him 'from his portrait'. After lunch a short visit was made to Austin Friars, which housed the rather shrunken Dutch congregation,[13] and subsequently they walked to Covent Garden, where, presumably in Drury Lane Theatre, they saw a performance of 'MacBedt' by 'Schakespear'; the theatre was so crowded that they could not get a seat and had to stand all evening.'[14]

Having got somewhat accustomed to the bustle of London life, Johannes began to make his first calls on the booksellers he knew, Samuel Paterson in Essex House in the Strand, Thomas Payne in Cheapside near Mew's Gate, John Nourse at Temple Bar, Benjamin White in Fleet Street and various others. He would continue this practice for the duration of his stay in London and later also in Oxford and Cambridge. Johannes certainly was on good terms with his London colleagues, as he was often invited by them for dinner, and sometimes spent long hours in their company. From the account books in the Luchtmans archives it appears that he made substantial dealings, selling his own books, in particular editions of the classics and scientific works, and buying a great variety of English books. The following list of books, for example, he purchased at the end of his stay from John Rivington, a bookseller in St Paul's Churchyard:

| | £ | | | |
|---|---|---|---|---|
| 4 Tillotson's Works 4 vol.8° | | 2. | 8. | — |
| 6 Joseph Andrews 12° 2 vol. | | 1. | 2. | — |
| 12 Tom Jones 12° 4 vol. | | 4. | 8. | — |
| 6 Grandison 12° 7 vol. | | 3. | 17. | — |
| 1 — dito 6 vol. 8° | | 1. | —. | 6 |
| 2 Robinson Crusoe 12° 2 vol. | | —. | 6. | — |
| 2 Schwerius Mathem. tables 8° | | —. | 18. | — |
| 2 Doddridge Lectures 4° | | 1. | —. | — |
| 2 Herveys Meditations 12° 2 vol. | | —. | 7. | 4 |
| 2 — Theron 12° 3 vol. | | —. | 15. | — |
| 4 Guardian 12° 2 vol. | | —. | 11. | — |
| 1 Martin Philosophy 8° 3 vol. | | —. | 12. | 6 |
| 2 Butler Analogy 8° | | —. | 8. | 4 |
| 4 Hunter on the Teeth 4° | | 2. | 16. | — |
| 4 Longinus ed. Pierce 8° | | —. | 13. | 8 |
| 2 Simpsons Aenoph. mem. 8° | | —. | 8. | 4 |
| 6 Telemachus 12° | | —. | 11. | —[15] |

In addition Johannes bought numerous English literary works from Thomas Cadell, a bookseller in the Strand; among them are four sets of the *Tatler* (4 vols. in-12), Hume's *Essays* (2 vols. in-8), Young *On Opium* (in-8), as wells as the *Works* of Pope (6 vols. in-12), Congreve (3 vols. printed by Baskerville), Dryden (4 vols. in-12), and, last but not least, Shakespeare (8 vols.).[16]

Business, however, was mixed with pleasure. For one thing, Johannes was very fond of walking and much of his sight-seeing was done on foot, often in the company of Putman or one of his English colleagues. He greatly admired the opportunities that London offered for promenading, along streets such as Holborn, 'a nice, wide and long street with beautiful and rich shops', in the splendid garden squares of newly developed Bloomsbury and the West End, in Lincoln's Inn and Gray's Inn, and in the London parks. 'It is very pleasant', he remarked, 'that there are so many walks in town, especially for old people, who do not have to go out of town to divert themselves with walking'. Outings on foot were also made to the villages surrounding London – Islington and Hoxton north of the City, Lambeth and Southwark on the South Bank; twice, moreover, Johannes made a trip by boat from Tower Hill to Greenwich.

On one of their walks Putman and Johannes called at the British Museum at Montagu House to get admission tickets. The actual visit took place on Friday 8 May at six o'clock in the afternoon, when they were shown round by Andrew Planta, one of the curators:

First we went upstairs, where we saw 4 rooms with the Mss. of the Bibliotheca Cottoniana, Regia, Harleiana and Sloana; the last one also has 200 thick volumes of a valuable Herbarius vivus. Then we came into the rooms of Naturalia, fossils, conches and shells, butterflies, insects, birds, etc. which all have been part of the cabinet of Hans Sloane. Downstairs we saw a great many rooms filled with many valuable books belonging to the Museum, which in fact were bought by the Government from the profits of a lottery, and from which also £20,000 had been taken to acquire the cabinet of Hans Sloane, as also a good sum to purchase the house in which all is accommodated. It is a fine building, consisting of a beautiful hall with various rooms on both sides; from the back it commands a pretty garden and the fields up to Hampstead and Highgate. In front there is a large square, at the sides of which live the directors: the upper-librarian, Dr Knight, inventor of the artificial magnet, 3 under-librarians, Dr Maty, Dr Morton and [blank], as also three assistants of whom the eldest is Mr Planta. Afterwards he invited us to his house where we drank a glass of wine before going home.[17]

Guided by his friends Johannes was also taken to the many other sights of London and Westminster: Bartholomew's and Christ's Hospital, Westminster Abbey, where he particularly admired the monument erected for Isaac Newton, the Banqueting House, St Paul's Cathedral, where he climbed the cupola for the panorama, the building of the Royal Society in Crane Court, the Tower, in short all the places any visitor should see. Johannes's mention of these touristic excursions is rather perfunctory and enumerative, not much different from what one finds in contemporary guide books of London.[18] Yet sometimes his descriptions are more detailed, even exalted, as in the case of his visit to the great Rotunda in Ranelagh Gardens:

This building is round in circumference, at least as large as our Mare Kerk [a church in Leiden], though not as high nor having the same sort of dome. The roof rests in the middle upon eight pillars, which are decorated by as many arches. In the centre there is a square fire place which provides sufficient warmth. All round these pillars stand two double rows of benches and tables, and against the wall are built many well-made boxes, equally fitted with benches and tables... On the upper floor there is a gallery with similar boxes and in the middle a fine orchestra with musicians and an organ; from here fair solos are sung by a man and a woman and good concerts are given by the musicians... The entire room is wonderfully illuminated by thousands of lamps in bell glasses as well as candles in numerous beautiful chandeliers. The entries to this room, moreover, are very commodious, so that, when you enter the room when it is fully lit, and you see the multitude of ladies and gentlemen, which this particular evening may have amounted to some 2,000, you are so elated and thrilled by sensation, that you nearly are beside yourself with joy and do not know where you are...

Ample space, too, Johannes devoted to a description of his visit to an exhibition room in the former French Church in Spring Gardens near St James's Park. At the time a display was mounted of the 'Musaeum' of the jeweller Cox, showing all sorts of the most costly mechanical objects, 'elephants moving their trunk, tails and eyes, having turrets on their back with cascades of water, coaches driving round continuously, drawn by horses or flying dragons, a Chinese playing very naturally on a *flute à bec*, and flowers opening and closing automatically'. It was all too much to remember, but luckily Johannes had been able to get a printed catalogue of the collection, which was estimated to be worth some £200,000.

Perhaps most regrettably absent in the journal is an account of the Johnsonian London that Johannes must have witnessed on the streets, in the coffee-houses and restaurants and, above all, in the bookshops, although one wonders whether this down-to-earth Dutchman would have been much at home among the wits of Georgian London. Being an earnest churchgoer, he does, however, comment on religious life in London. Apart from the Sunday services in Dutch at Austin Friars Johannes went to worship in several other churches. Thus he heard a sermon by the eloquent Presbyterian minister Dr James Fordyce in his meeting house at Monkwell Street. Johannes describes him as 'a very able man, whose talents were incomparably fine and whose zeal was apparent throughout the entire sermon', although he confesses that he could not understand a word of what Fordyce had said.[9] On 14 May he attended a special service in St Paul's Cathedral, at which the Archbishop of Canterbury, the Bishop of London and the Lord Mayor and Aldermen of the City were present in full regalia. Johannes was greatly impressed by the music: 'Above on a gallery sat the singers and the boys of the choir of Westminster Abbey and next to the organ a gallery was made for the musicians; there was a kettledrum, a French horn, a double bass and violins, and amongst the singers we heard in between a soloist, who sang admirably'.

But his stay in London was not without other excitement. On the evening after their visit to the British Museum, when Johannes and his host were having a late chat, they were suddenly startled by a loud banging on the door. It appeared that a number of nearby houses in Austin Friars had caught fire and that people in great panic were throwing beds and other furniture out of their windows into the garden surrounding Austin Friars:

Putman immediately took care that the pump leading up to the garden could be used and not long after a fire engine came, which helped much to preserve these houses. It was especially fortunate that the wind was north-east, so the flames and sparks spread to the other side, thus saving Putman's house and the church. Even so I took my trunk into the church, as did the maid and Putman with a box with sermons and papers. The fire then spread to Throgmorton Street, burning down as many as 20 houses as well as Drapers' Hall, looking like an Etna both from Putman's house as from the other side of the church. Meanwhile the church was crammed with furniture of the neighbours. At four in the morning the fire seemed to be lessening and at five it was nearly extinguished. You could hear the sound of collapsing walls and chimneys in those houses that had burned down.

The following day it turned out that a man had perished in the fire; the crowd that found his body among the rubble at first wanted to bring it into the church, but with the help of his sexton and a constable Putman prevented this, as the building was already full with furniture and very wet because of the extinguishing water. The dead man was subsequently moved to a garden shed where people thronged in great numbers to see if they knew him.

During the last two weeks of his stay in England Johannes visited Oxford and Cambridge. Again the main objective was to call upon local booksellers, Daniel Prince and James Fletcher in Oxford and Thomas Merrill and John Woodyer in Cambridge, but again no particulars are given about his dealing with them.[20] In both cities Johannes also visited several colleges, displaying a specific interest in their libraries: in Oxford the library of Christ Church was 'very properly conditioned and with the best books and editions imaginable, all in fine cases', while Queen's College had 'books on chains, placed with the spines turned backwards'. In Cambridge he was particularly impressed by Christopher Wren's library at Trinity College. But why did he have to be so sparing with his words! After a visit to the Clarendon Printing House in Oxford he merely writes that it was a 'costly building; down below we saw the printing presses and upstairs are the type setters', while of the Bodleian Library he dryly remarks: 'surely the largest library I have ever seen, which, apart from printed books contains a considerable multitude of manuscripts'. Only Cambridge's old university library received some more extensive appraisal:

I nearly had forgotten to write that I also saw in a fine square building the wonderfully splendid and rich library of Cambridge, which is unusually large and very orderly and conveniently placed; especially there is a section full with manuscripts, including a small case with oriental manuscripts, which is priceless. Among other things we were shown an Arabic manuscript more than 700 years old, dealing with astronomy and natural history. It was beautifully illuminated and preserved in such a fine state that it was incredible. There furthermore were various curiosities. In another section there were the very first printed works of the classic authors. I was extremely satisfied to have seen this.

From Oxford Johannes also paid a visit to Blenheim Palace, and on his way back to London, to Eton and Windsor Castle. The journey to Cambridge was made in the company of 'Mr Balmer', a London agent of the Luchtmans firm, who was an officer in the Huntingdon militia regiment under the command of the Duke of Manchester. On their way they therefore visited the Duke at his residence Kimbolton Castle, where they were received in a very friendly fashion:

We took a walk through his park, which is very large and full of deer. There also is a fine menagerie with chicken, ducks, turkeys, pheasants and one peacock. The rain prevented us from making a longer promenade, so we returned through an 'English grove' [een engelsch boschje], planted with all sorts of trees and plants. The house itself is stately; beautiful paintings and fine portraits of the Montagu family are hanging in the hall and all the rooms are exquisitely adorned with costly tapestries, paintings and furniture. There were two tables, inlaid with tiny square pieces of marble from all over the world... In one room there was a library, which was not very large though proper, but it is only a part, for as the Duke is a peer of the realm and sits in the House of Lords, he has another house in London, where he also has a library.[21]

After his return from Cambridge to London on 27 May, Johannes's stay was nearing its end. Among the last outings he made was a visit to the instrument maker Edward Nairne, who on the request of the Leiden professor of physics Johannes Allamand had constructed a working model of the Chelsea water works, 'operated by fire and the boiling of water'.[22] His plan to return to Holland on 5 June, however, was thwarted by a letter from his wife and brother, telling him of the serious illness of his two-year old daughter Magdalena Henrietta, 'myn lieve Jetje'.[23] Johannes decided to pack immediately and try and catch the first packetboat home. He left London early on Saturday morning 30 May, accompanied by his friend Putman, who did not want him to travel alone in his sorrow. He left Harwich on Sunday and on Monday at noon landed at Hellevoetsluis. That same evening he arrived home, greatly relieved to find his 'Jetje' much better, 'as also my entire family, for which I cannot thank Heaven enough'. It was the unexpected, yet happy end of what had been a successful and most enjoyable trip.

## Notes

1. For a recent study of English travellers to Holland during the 17th century, see C. D. van Strien, *British Travellers in Holland during the Stuart Period* (Amsterdam, 1989) (Thesis Vrije Universiteit, Amsterdam).

2. There is no general study on foreign travel to Britain. For Dutch visitors during the 16th and 17th centuries, see A. Frank-van Westrienen, *De Groote Tour: tekening van de educatiereis der Nederlanders in de zeventiende eeuw* (Amsterdam, 1983). German travel to England has received relatively great attention; *cf* W. D. Robson Scott, *German Travellers in England 1400-1800* (Oxford, 1953) and M. C. Spieckermann et al (eds.), '*Der curieuse Passagier': deutsche Englandreise des achtzehnten Jahrhunderts als Vermittler kultureller und technologischer Anregungen. Colloquium der Arbeitstelle 18. Jahrhundert, Gesamthochschule Wuppertal, Universität Münster, 1980* (Heidelberg, 1983). For English 'tourists' in their own country see Esther Moir, *The Discovery of Britain: the English Tourists* (London, 1964).

3. Frank-van Westrienen, *De Groote Tour*, p.243.

4. Lodewijck Huygens, *The English Journal 1651-1652*, edited and translated by A. G. H. Bachrach & R. G. Collmer (Leiden, 1982).

5. Allard de la Court, 'A° 1710 Aanteekening ofte journaal van myn reys naar London, met de Hr. Floris Drabbe & Johannis Buckingam', in *De reizen der De la Courts*, edited by F. Driessen (Leiden, 1928), pp.77-121, esp. pp.110-15. Among the prints were *eg*, twelve 'vrouwtjes' by Van Dyck and fourteen 'mannetjes' by Rosa at a total cost of 14½ guilders. On Allard de la Court and his superb art collection see also Th. H. Lunsingh Scheurleer et al, *Het Rapenburg: geschiedenis van een Leidse gracht*, vol.II (Leiden, 1987), pp.325-

90. The gold watch, made by John May and bought for 253 guilders, in 1749 was valued at 170 guilders; ibid, p.478, no.18.

6. 'Reys met de Heer Veertig Cunaeus na Engeland door J. L. 1772.' The library of the Vereeniging is housed in the Amsterdam University Library. An inventory of the Luchtmans archive is in preparation. For a provisional study of the rich holdings of the Luchtmans archive in Amsterdam, see I. H. van Eeghen, *De Amsterdamse boekhandel 1680-1725*, vol.V-1, *De boekhandel van de Republiek 1572-1795* (Amsterdam, 1978), Appendix I, 'Het archief van de Leidse boekverkopers Luchtmans', pp.131-77.

7. A. C. Kruseman, *Aanteekeningen betreffende den boekhandel van Noord-Nederland in de 17de en 18de eeuw* (Amsterdam, 1893), p.620.

8. For a general survey of the history of the house of Luchtmans, see the catalogue of an exhibition held on the occasion of the firm's tercentenary *Luchtmans & Brill: driehonderd jaar uitgevers en drukkers in Leiden 1683-1983* (Leiden, 1983); see also note 6.

9. Abstracts of the travel journals of Johannes and Samuel, who also travelled abroad frequently, are given by Kruseman, op cit, pp.606-22.

10. During the 17th and 18th centuries this position of intermediary was largely held by Dutch booksellers; cf P. G. Hoftijzer, *Engelse boekverkopers bij de Beurs; de geschiedenis van de Amsterdamse boekhandels Bruyning en Swart, 1637-1724* (Amsterdam/Maarssen, 1987), chap.1, and G. Barber, 'Book Imports and Exports in the Eighteenth Century', in *Sale and Distribution of Books from 1700*, edited by R. Myers and M. Harris (Oxford, 1982), pp.77-106.

11. These and following quotations are translated from the original Dutch.

12. Henrik Putman (1725-97), born in Amsterdam, was appointed minister to the Dutch congregation at Austin Friars in 1751. Occasionally he acted as agent for the Luchtmans firm, which in 1784 in cooperation with the Amsterdam bookseller Johannes Wessing published his *Londens tweemalige Nederduitsche Psalm-verwisseling beschouwd*. Putman also was a Fellow of the Royal

Society. *Cf The Marriage, Baptismal, and Burial Registers, 1571 to 1874, and Monumental Inscriptions of the Dutch Reformed Church, Austin Friars, London*, edited by W. J. C. Moens (Lymington, 1884), pp.175, 208.

13. *Cf* J. Lindeboom, *Austin Friars: geschiedenis van de Nederlandse Hervormde Gemeente te Londen 1550-1950* (The Hague, 1950), chap.6.

14. Drury Lane Theatre was partly owned by David Garrick and as Macbeth was one of his favourite parts, Johannes may well have seen him act. Curiously this is the only time a visit to a London theatre is mentioned in the journal.

15. Luchtmans archive, Account book 13, f.442, list dated 29 May 1772. The total sum of £26 10s 12d (one pound = approximately ten guilders) was paid in two terms by means of post bills. On Johannes's dealings with other booksellers, especially John Nourse, see also Barber, 'Book Imports and Exports in the Eighteenth Century', op cit pp.79-84.

16. Luchtmans archive, Account book 13, f.441. The total sum for these purchases, amounting to £18 19s 9d, was paid through Thomas Payne on 20 November. As yet there is no comprehensive study of the reception of English books in the Netherlands during the 18th century. For various introductory contributions see *The Role of Periodicals in the Eighteenth Century. Transactions of the Third Annual Symposium of the Sir Thomas Browne Institute*, edited by J. A. van Dorsten (Leiden, 1984).

17. Planta, a Swiss by origin, was also minister of the German Reformed Church. For the early history of the British Museum, including plans of the layout of Montagu House, see E. Edwards, *Lives of the Founders of the British Museum, with Notices of its Chief Augmentors and Other Benefactors, 1570-1870* (London, 1870; reprinted New York, 1969).

18. A guide book of London available at the time to Dutch visitors was *De leidsman der vreemdelingen, of nodig en nuttig med'gezel beyde voor den vreemdeling en inboorling in hunne wandeling door de steden Londen en Westmunster* (Amsterdam, 1759). It was a translation of *The Forreigner's Guide / Le Guide des étrangers* published at London in 1752.

19. According to the *DNB* Fordyce's eloquence, presence and 'piercing eye' attracted large crowds to Monkwell Street. Perhaps Johannes could not understand him very well because of his Scottish origin.

20. Judging from the account books his transactions with them appear to have been limited. From Woodyear Luchtmans in May only bought for 16s 6d, which in July was balanced by a similar amount on the debit side; Luchtmans archive, Account book 13, ff.440v-441r.

21. George Montagu, 4th Duke of Manchester (1737-1788) was colonel of the Huntingdon regiment and MP for Huntingdonshire. Kimbolton Castle is now a school.

22. Edward Nairne (1726-1806) was an instrument maker and electrician living at Cornhill. In 1782 he constructed 'Nairne's electrical machine' (*DNB*). According to Johannes the miniature steam machine ordered by Allamand had cost £70.

23. She was baptised on 12 November 1769. In 1794 she married the Amsterdam physician Evert Bodel Nijenhuis; it was their son, Johannes Tiberius Bodel Nijenhuis, author of an important study on censorship and the press in the Netherlands, who in 1821 would continue the family business. In 1848 the firm was finally sold to Evert Jan Brill, under whose name it still flourishes.

.

Ernst Braches

# The first years of the Fagel Collection in Trinity College, Dublin

In 1955 Dr Leendert Brummel (1897-1976),[1] librarian of the Royal Library, The Hague, during a conference in Dublin visited the collection of the Dutch Greffier Hendrik Fagel (1765-1838) in Trinity College Library. In 1957 he published: 'The Fagel Library in Trinity College, Dublin',[2] in which he gives information on Fagel and his collection, the planned auction of the books by '*Mr Christie, at Number 5, in Duke Street, St. James's London, On Monday, March 1, 1802, and the Twenty-nine following Days to begin precisely at 12 o'Clock*,'[3] and the rescue of the library to Trinity College Library, Dublin: 'Early in April the bargain was definitely concluded between the Provost and Fagel for £8000. The transport to Dublin, in 115 big bases, cost another £388'.[4]

In 1962, thanks to Dr Brummel and Dr Wytze Hellinga I received a grant to study the Fagel Library and spent three happy months in Dublin, being received with Maartje, my wife, in a most hospitable way by the Board of TCD and the Staff of the Library. During that stay we tried to reconstruct the history of the library after its arrival in Trinity College; made a collection of rubbings of all tooled bindings;[5] and took note of all ownership-entries we could find in the books.

In 1986 Vincent Kinane's 'The Fagel Collection' appeared,[6] which amplifies Brummel's contribution and deals with the first years of the Fagel Collection in Dublin. I shall try to add some further small remarks to Kinane's contribution and to amplify his history of the Fagel Collection after its arrival in Dublin.

'NB On May 11.12.13. & 14 were brought into the Library one hundred & fifteen Cases, containing the Library of Monsieur le Griffier Fagel, purchased by College for £8000 British.' With these words the safe arrival in 1802 of the famous Dutch library is recorded.[7] The 115 numbered cases were not unpacked, for the room at the eastern end, the Long Room, intended to be the future home of the Fagel books, was still in use as the Manuscript Room. On 2 June 1802 case 115 was opened by order of the Board of Trinity College to take out copies of the sale-catalogue of 1801. Of volume I not more than 378 copies were found; and 629 copies of volume II.[8] By decision of the Board, 26 July 1802,[9] copies were presented to fellows and professors of Trinity College in the next few months.[10] Dublin officials received copies bound by local binders, and so did Hendrik Fagel in 1806.[11]

In the beginning unpacking of the collection was obviously not permitted. Two books that were mistakenly removed from their cases were carefully recorded in the

Fagel bindings: Sale-numbers (9224, 1593/243, 9552/2) written on parchment bindings for 1, 3, 5; on diamond-shaped labels for 4, 6, 7, 8. Pressmarks (H.4.12 etc) written on parchment bindings for 1–6; tooled in gold on leather slip for 7–8. (Photograph: The Green Studio, Dublin 1962.)

Library Minute Book on 2 June 1802.[12] On 10 December 1802, another case, number 70, was opened by order of the Provost; the 32 volumes of sale-number 6300 were taken out.[13] These volumes in manuscript, *Mémoires sur plusieurs provinces, viles, généralités, etc. de la France*, might have been considered of strategic value in those Napoleonic days.

In 1803 the room on the first floor above the former Manuscript Room[14] was made ready for the manuscripts of Trinity College, which were packed on 7 February 1803,[15] and unpacked on 8 September 1803, after being brought there the day before.[16] A week after that removal, on 13 September 1803 'They are very busy in the College Library, putting up the Fagel Collection'.[17] From this one may infer that the unpacking had started. This conjecture is strengthened by the record of January 1804 that 19 copies of the Fagel sale-catalogue were found in 'one of the boxes'.[18] On 15 August 1804 the first series of English pamphlets and leaflets is sent out to the binder.[19] In total some 40 volumes were bound in the next two months. On 25 August 1804 the name Fagel Room is recorded; for the first time?[20]

The unpacking of the books was done with a copy of the sale-catalogue in hand.[21] The surviving copy shows that some books were absent or incomplete; on the other hand books were found that had not been entered in the sale-catalogue. Christie's diamond-shaped labels pasted on the spines with the sale-numbers written on them helped to identify volumes with the entries in the catalogue. In TCL these labels were not removed; when missing they were supplied or replaced. From the fact that the sale-numbers figure in the first catalogues of the collection, and that they even figure in the library-stamps, one may infer that they kept playing an important role in the library.

By the end of July 1803 William Chapman presented a bill for over £1000 for 'Carpenters work done ... in the additional Room to the Library'.[22] Kinane does not prove why this bill should concern the future Fagel Room, with its 'fluted oak pilasters with Corinthian capitals that can be seen in Taylor's Illustration'.[23] and with its settees and presses which imitate the arrangement in the Long Room. I presume that the bill concerns the new Manuscript Room and I take the line that the unpacking of the Fagel books started in the unaltered former Manuscript Room, *ie* with the shelves fixed for their former use. I assume that from September 1803 the volumes were arranged on these shelves in order of the sale-numbers. By that procedure the books were immediately available to the public; the distribution of sale-catalogues to Fellows and Professors of Trinity College and the value attached to the sale-numbers argue for this hypothesis.[24] Now the scholars could ask for books by mentioning the sale-numbers from the catalogues they had received.

Did the Librarian know from the beginning to what extent the presses in the former Manuscript Room could accommodate the Fagel Books? On 25 March 1802 Dr Thomas Elrington had estimated 'the footage of shelving that the collection occupied in the house that Fagel had leased to store it [the collection]. He calculated that ... there were 5300 feet of books; he later revised this upwards to 5528 feet.'[25] In may 1803 the board of TCD had resolved that strict duplicates of the Fagel Collection were to be removed to the Lending Library of TCD.[26] It must have been obvious that there was not enough shelfroom; but only after the presses had been filled definitely could the real extent of the overflow be known.

This second, definite, arrangement started on the same fixed shelves of the old Manuscript Room, and in the old presses indicated with single letters A-Z.[27] It is still to be proved that an arrangement by subject was intended. Geography can roughly be discerned in presses A-B; in presses E-G classics; in H political tracts; in I coins; biology and gardening in M-N; English history in Q; general history in R-V; theology in W-Z. The folio formats were put up on the lowest shelves, the quarto's higher, and smaller formats such as octavo and duodecimo on the highest shelves. But the fixed shelves for the former Manuscript Room were accommodated to the former proportions of formats and were not adapted for the Fagel Collection. Smaller formats were put up on shelves intended for bigger formats, and folios were laid on shelves that were too low. A carpenter had to be ordered to adjust the distance between the shelves to the formats and thereby gain space. After that operation new, empty shelves for smaller formats could be filled with books and the last openings in the rows filled. An overview of top rows and last spaces in shelves makes clear that even volumes belonging to other subjects were placed there, and that the principle of subject-arrangement was over-ruled by the need to close all the gaps. This indicates how difficult it must have been to accommodate the last part of the collection after gradually arranging the books in the presses along the alphabet. Then, at last, it was possible to figure out how much extra room was needed. Two windows in the northern wall had to be sacrificed to make room for presses.

This procedure can be followed in the accounts. The last phase of the definite placing of the Fagel books starts in the beginning of 1806. Carpenter Tim McEvoy (on 12 April 1806) in an account to the Library) includes 'one and a quarter days taking sundry dimensions in Fagel Library to settle books'.[28] On 18 March a Library Account Book notes the first payment for assistance in placing the books.[29] Throughout 1807 the carpenter's work on the Fagel shelving continues. In September 1807 a bill is submitted for 'plastering the backs of 2 windows in the New Library'.[30]

The placing continued through 1808. 'Various students were paid sums for their help.'[31] The placing also involved work by the binder who put leather slips on the spines of leather bindings and stamped the press numbers in gold. About July 1808 the binder, Richard Edward Mercier, received £40 for 'littering' in the Fagel Room.[32] Kinane writes: 'Michael Logan was engaged throughout 1808 and early 1809 lettering and numbering the volumes *in situ* and in preparing the catalogues'.[33]

When the books were taken out of sale-catalogue order and definitely placed on the shelves a concordance between sale numbers and new pressmarks was necessary. Probably another copy of the sale-catalogue (now lost) was used to jot down the pressmarks next to the sale-numbers. There exists one copy of the sale-catalogue with all the pressmarks entered.[34] A similar inscribed copy of the catalogue was probably used for preparing the *Fagel Local Catalogue* (paper dated 1801), in which, next to the pressmarks, plain sale-numbers (no titles) were entered.[35] This local catalogue (press-marks to sale numbers) might have been used in composing its counterpart: a concor-dance of sale-numbers to pressmarks. This concordance has been given the deceptive title *Catalogus Bibliothecae Fagelianiae* (paper dated 1801).[36] The title indicates that the concordance was used as a complement to the *Catalogus Bibliothecae Fagelianae ordine alphabetico* by Dr John Barrett, in which authors and titles have been arranged alphabetically, and in which only sale-numbers have been entered; hardly any pressmarks. The history of this alphabetical catalogue dates back to 4 May 1803, when two copies of the sale-catalogue were given to Dr Elrington to dissect.[37] In this way a rough alphabetical catalogue was constructed, from which the *Catalogus Bibliothecae Fagelianae ordine alphabetico dispositus labore & autographo Johannis Barrett S.T.P.* (paper dated 1796) was copied.[38] On 7 May 1803 Dr Barrett was busy with this project and he finished it eventually in 1807.[39] Dr John Barrett was also involved with the placement. He was paid £100 for this and for his alphabetical catalogue on 7 November 1807.[40]

The catalogues Michael Logan was preparing were probably the *Fagel Local Catalogue* (pressmarks to sale-numbers) and concordance *Catalogus Bibliothecae Fagelianiae* (sale-numbers to pressmarks),[41] which complemented John Barrett's *Catalogus Bibliothecae Fagelianae ordine alphabetico* (authors/titles to sale-numbers).

Both *Catalogi Bibliothecae Fagelianae* (Barrett's alphabetical copy and the concordance) do not show wear and tear. After 1815 alterations in the Fagel Collection are not entered in these catalogues; they never were very popular. A manuscript copy of Barrett's catalogue, with pressmarks, to be dated after 1824-26 fared the same.[42] The sale-catalogue was preferred. During my visit to the Fagel Library, long after the publishing of the impressive printed catalogue of Trinity College Library, I found that browsing in the Fagel Room stacks still is most convenient with a copy of the sale-catalogue in which the pressmarks have been entered.[43].

In the beginning of 1809 matters were drawing to an end. 'In February 1808 and in the first quarter of 1809 [George Stapleton] was paid for "gilding and shading… large letters in New Library".'[44] On 23 February 1809 the last account of carpenters Tim McEvoy & Son for Fagel shelving was settled.[45] On 1 March 1809 finally the Board 'ordered that the Fagel Library be opened forthwith'.[46] That is to say: Fellows, Professors and other scholars were from now on allowed to enter the Fagel Room and find themselves the books they wanted; and to sit down on the settees to study them.

The Fagel Room, crowded as it already was in 1809,[47] had yet to endure an invasion of copyright books,[48] for which preparations were made about 1856:[49] the cases B-Y were raised to the ceiling: 19th-century invaders were put up there from 1857.[50] Probably at the same time the last settees were removed to make room for low presses that got double pressmarks, such as FF.[51]

## Notes

1. C. Reedijk, 'Leendert Brummel', *Jaarboek van de Maatschappij der Nederlandse Letterkunde te Leiden*, 1987-88, (Leiden, 1989), 150-162. See also R. B. McDowell, 'The acquisition of the Fagel Library', *Friends of the Library of TCD. Annual Bulletin*, 2 (1957), 5-6.

2. L. Brummel, 'The Fagel Library in Trinity College, Dublin', in L. Brummel, *Miscellanea Libraria*, (The Hague, 1957), pp.204-33.

3. *Bibliotheca Fageliana. A catalogue of the valuable and extensive Library of the Greffier Fagel, of the* Hague: Comprehending a choice Collection of Books, in various Languages, in Theology and Ecclesiastical History; in Classical and Philological Learning, and in most Branches of Polit Literature; in Philosophy, Physics, and Natural History; in Painting, Architecture, Engraving, and the whole Body of Arts and Sciences: in Chronology, Egyptian, Greek and Roman Antiquities; in Ancient and Modern History and Topography, including many choice Books of Prints: in Geneology and Jurisprudence, and in Geography, Voyages and Travels; Digested by Sam. Paterson. Part I. Which will be sold by auction by Mr Christie, at Number 5, in Duke Street, St. James's, London, on Monday,

*March 1, 1802, and the Twenty-nine following Days, to begin precisely at 12 o'Clock. To be viewed on Monday, February 22 and to the Time of Sale.* Part I of the catalogue contained 5246 numbers. 'When the second volume appeared, which had no title-page and raised the numbering to 9844, cannot be stated with certainty.' (Brummel, p.226).

**4.** Brummel, p.227.

**5.** These rubbings have been used by Dr J. S. Storm van Leeuwen for *De achttiende-eeuwse Haagse boekband in de Koninklijke Bibliotheek en het Rijksmuseum Meermanno-Westreenianum* (The Hague, 1976) and for 'Un groupe remarquable de reliures amstellodamoises ou contribution à l'étude des reliures du xviiie siècle, in *De libris compactis miscellanea* (Brussels, 1984), pp.321-74.

**6.** Vincent Kinane, 'The Fagel Collection', in *Treasures of the Library–Trinity College Dublin*, edited by Peter Fox (Dublin, 1986), pp.158-69.

**7.** In 1962 I made a note that the quoted text is entered without date in the Minute Book TCL 1785-1861 between the entries of 18 March and 2 June 1802. Kinane, p.160, n.7: TCD MUN/LIB/2/1 (Library Minutes).

**8.** Minute Book TCL: 'June 2. By desire of the provost opened Box N⁰.115, and took out all the copies of the 1st part of the Catalogue of the Fagel Library, being 301. Sent to the Provost 25 Copies. Took out also Memoire Pour la suppression du Belasting, which through mistake was not replaced in the Box. With the copies of the catalogue was also put L'Art de former Les Iardins Modernes, which had fallen out of one of the Boxes. N⁰.3900.' Minute Book TCL: 'July 19. Placed in the presses 629 copies of the 2nd part of the Catalogue of the Fagel Library, 38 copies of the 1st part, and 39 of the same in boards.'

**9.** Minute Book Trinity College Dublin, 26 July 1802, p.393: 'Catalogues of the Fagel Lib. ordered to be given to each Fellow + Professor.'

**10.** The first presentation on 27 July 1802, Minute Book TCL: 'It having been ordered by the board that each fellow and professor should be allowed a Copy of the Catalogue of

the Fagel-Library, the 2nd part was given to Dr Brown (July 27) the first part having been proveniently lent to him'.

**11.** Minute Book TCL: 'Aug.16.1802. Gave Mr Mercier (by desire of the Provost) five Copies blue paper [wrappers] of Fagel Cat. both parts: one to be elegantly bound in Morocco for the Lord lietenant: & the other four to be bound for the Provost.' Minute Book TCL: 'July 2.1806... Gave Mr Mercier, by order of the Board 7 Copies of Fagel's Catalogue Parts 1st & 2d to be bound in 7 Vols. & 6 of them to be presented to Mr Fagel late possessor of the Library, & one to Hentry Alexander Esqu: they having requested that favour.' Kinane, p.164: '6 July', n.21: TCD MUN/LIB/2/1 (Library Minutes).

**12.** Minute Book TCL, 2 June 1802.

**13.** Minute Book TCL:'Decr.10.1802. Dr Elrington by desire of Provost, opened Case N⁰.70 of the Fagel Lib. & took thence N⁰.6300, 32 Vols: which I placed in the MS Room in the Press with the Icelandic Mss.'

**14.** Kinane, p.160, no.9: TCD MS 4960 (T. Elrington's Minutes (personal) of Board Meetings 1801-3, 8 May 1802).

**15.** Minute Book TCL: 'Feb.7.1803 Put the MSS into boxes prepared for that purpose & numbered.'

**16.** Minute Book TCL: '1803 Sept.8. Put all the MSS, Books of prints &tc on the Shelves in the Presses in the New MS Room: the Boxes (17) containing them having been conveyed into that room the preceding day.'

**17.** Letter of E. Ledwich on this date, mentioned in McDowell, p.5-6.

**18.** Minute Book TCL: 'Jan.28. Found in one of the Boxes of the Fagel Library 19 copies of the first part of the Catalogue, & lodged them in the Librarian's Press.'

**19.** Minute Book TCL: 'Aug.15.1804. Gave Mr Mercier to bind of the Pamphlets of the Fagel Library.' Minute Book TCL 'Aug.27. the Bookbinder sent in bound all the Books sent him on Aug. 14th.15th & 17th. Those of the Fagel Library were left in that Room.'

**20.** Minute Book TCL: 'Aug.25.1804... He

[Mr Cary the bookbinder] sent in also the six Vols of Pamphlets (being the other six) which were put up in the Fagel Room.'

21 Sale-catalogue 1802, Part I, found on 20 August 1962 in the Quinn-Room by Miss M. Pollard, and moved to the Fagel Collection, where it got pressmark N.12.61a. Entries next to number 3009, 3981 and on p.153 prove that it has been used for checking while unpacking. Most numbers are ticked off.

22. Kinane, p.161, n.13: TCD MUN/P/2/187/3 (Buildings).

23. Kinane, p.161. Kinane takes the line that the bill concerns the reconstruction of the old Manuscript Room. I do not agree with him.

24. That the sale-catalogue was really a tool, is demonstrated by the following. Dr Browne, who received his copy on 27 July 1802, mislaid it. The Minute Book TCL: 'Nov.19 [1803] Sent D$^r$ Browne a Copy of Fagel Cat. 2 parts: on his promise to return it when he should find the former copy given him.'

25. Kinane, p.160, and no.5: TCD MUN/LIB/12/1 (Elrington's Diary).

26. Kinane, p.161, n.20. TCD MS 4960 (Elrington's Minutes): 'On 16 July the Board had taken another step towards their sorting by resolving that strict duplicates in the collection were to be put into the Lending Library.' In 1844 other duplicates were removed; they are probably identical with the books found in 1908 in the Librarian's Room. In 1962 in press P. 14-18 I found some uncatalogued duplicates; and incomplete books in press BB.

27. Shelves A 1-10; B 1-12; C 1-12; D 1-12; E 1-9; F 1-10; G 1-16; H 1-16; I 1-9; K 1-9; L 1-9; M 1-9; N 1-10; O 1-10; P 1-10; Q 1-10; R 1-13; S 1-12; T 1-13; U 1-13; V 1-10; W 1-10; X 1-10; Y 1-10; Z 1-11.

28. Kinane, p.161, n.16: TCD MUN/P/2/191/22 (Buildings).

29. Kinane, p.164. Extra help was needed to keep pace with the carpenters (shelves) and bookbinders (pressmarks).

30. Kinane, p.160, n.19: TCD MUN/P/2/197/78; MUN/P2/199/62 (Buildings).

31. Kinane, p.164.

32. Minute Book TCL.

33. Kinane, p.164, n.23: TCD MUN/LIB/11/9/16a, 21a-b; MUN/LIB/11/10/3,5 (Library Accounts). The lettering and numberings might concern the parchment bindings, on which the pressmarks were written by hand.

34. The pressmarks in the annotated sale-catalogue with the ample title *Fagel Library Classed Catalogue* (Fag.N.12.61) were entered after September 1836, but go back to pressmarks in a older copy.

35. Folio. The title *Fagel Local Catalogue* is on the spine. Between the leaves of the original catalogue (paper 1801; red-ink pagination) lightblue paper (dates 1832, 1853, 1854, 1872) is added. A note on the removal of a manuscript on 22 May 1815 makes it clear that the *Fagel Local Catalogue* (1801 paper) must have been composed before that date.

36. The title *Catalogus Bibliothecae Fagelianae* is on the spine. The move of the manuscript on 22 May 1815 makes it clear that this *Fagel Catalogue* (1801 paper) must have been composed before that date. Removals to the Lending Library are entered in this catalogue.

37. Minute Book TCL: 'May 4.1803... Sent D$^r$ Elrington four Parts (*ie* 2 Sets) of Fagel Catalogue to dissect.'

38. Folio. This catalogue probably has been used formerly in loose quires, each paginated separately. The 'Nota libri in Cat. Fageliana' (column 1) and the title (column 2) have been inserted totally; the column 'Nota libri in Bibl.Fagelianae' is only inserted on the first 16 pages. This catalogue is just an extract of the printed sale-catalogue, as can be demonstrated by printing errors as 'Gegagten' (3510)for 'Gedachten', 'Woorboek' for 'Woordboek' (119), 'Rotterdam 1651' for 'Amsterdam 1751' (117). The catalogue is mentioned by Kinane, p.161, n.11: TCD MUN/LIB/1/21 = MS 1707 (Library Catalogue).

39. Kinane, p.164, n.22: TCD MUN/LIB/11/9/3, 5, 17, 19, 20 (Library Accounts). Kinane's statement: 'The Librarian, Dr John ('Jacky')

Barrett, was busy extracting an alphabetical catalogue from the subject arrangement of the sale catalogue' (p.160), based on TCD MS 4960 (Elrington's Minutes), 7 May 1803 (p.169, n.10), needs modification: John Barrett was busy copying the slips.

**40.** Kinane p.161, n.12: TCD MUN/LIB/11/9/5 (Library Accounts): 'This *Catalogus Fagelianna* ordine alphabetico dispositus was eventually delivered to the Library in November 1807.' See also Kinane, p.164, n.22: TCD MUN/LIB/11/9/3, 5, 17, 19, 20 (Library Accounts).

**41.** They were not ready in September 1804. The sentence in Minute Book TCL: 'Received all the above sent in by Mercier, bound: on Sept^r.24^th which were same day put [up] in the Library [& entered in both Catalogues] among the other Books of the Fagel Collection'. The words in square brackets [ ] have been struck through in the original. They are to be considered as slips of the pen made by somebody who followed the general practice in TCL.

**42.** Voluminous manuscript with pressmarks: *Liber impressorum qui in Bibliotheca Fageliana adservantur Catalogus* (volume I on paper 1824 and 1825; volume II on paper 1825 and 1826).

**43.** For the Dutch political tracts in the Fagel Collection the readers could use the manuscript catalogue that may be attributed to François Fagel the Elder (1649-1746): *Inventaris van politique en andere tractaten* (spine: Catalogue of the Fagel Tracts No.7593). Kinane (p.165, n.25: TCD MUN/LIB/1/23: MS 3726 – Library Catalogues) owes the attribution of the manuscript catalogue of pamphlets in the Collection to François Fagel (1659-1746) and the estimated percentage of pamphlets covered by this catalogue (80%) to my report.

**44.** Kinane, p.161, n.19: TCD MUN/P/2/197/78; TCD MUN/P/2/199/62.

**45.** Kinane, p.161, n.17: TCD MUN/P/2/193, 194, 197, 199 (Buildings).

**46.** Kinane, p.164, n.24: TCD MUN/V/5/5 (Board Register).

**47.** Kinane (p.160, p.164) estimates that the Fagel Collection contains at least 20,000 volumes. The Number Books of Trinity College Library give 17,539 (1835-9); 17,539 (1840); 17,605 (1841); 17,618 (1842); 17,617 (1843); 17,602 (1844); 17,604 (1845); 17,599 (1846); 17,598 (1847); 17,537 (1848). I found an entry that 104 volumes of duplicates were 'removed out of the library'; these volumes were obviously not placed; they play no part in the Number Books. The varying numbers in 1844 and 1848 are caused by removal of volumes to the MS Room. In 1845-6 three volumes and a duplicate were removed.

**48.** Along the southern wall there were two cupboards with glass doors, GG and HH, in which precious folio-volumes and some manuscripts were placed, complemented with other, more common volumes. These cupboards might have been part of the former Manuscript Room. In or after 1853 manuscripts were removed from GG and HH to the Manuscript Room. The open places were filled with 19th-century books as time went on. FF and TT were built and filled before 1853.

**49** According to E. H. Alton, 'Some notes on the library and the cost of its building', *Friends of the Library of Trinity College Dublin* (1948), 10-12, big changes took place in the period 1856-62.

**50.** Raised presses since 1857: B 13-17; C 13-17; D 13-17; E 10-14; F 11-14; G 17; I 10-16; K 10-17; L 10-16; M 10-15; N 11-15; O 11-16; P 11-16; V 11-13; W 11-17; X 11-12; Y 11-20. Lower presses since 1854: QQ, RR, TT, VV. Raised presses since 1872: K 18-19; L 17-18; M 16-18; N 16-18. The Number Books show the filling of the new shelves to begin with 1858.

**51.** Press II was filled with Fagel leftovers.

# T. A. Birrell

# *'A Sentimental Journey' through Holland and Flanders by John Gage*

John Gage (1786-1842)[1] was the fourth son of Sir Thomas Gage, 6th Bart, of Hengrave Hall, Suffolk. He studied law in the chambers of Charles Butler (1750-1832) and was called to the Bar at Lincoln's Inn in 1818, but never practised. He became an FSA in 1818 and was Director of the Society of Antiquaries from 1829 till his death in 1842. Gage was a serious scholar and by no means a dilettante, and he took his duties as Director of the Antiquaries very seriously. Besides a number of important archaeological papers and two books of local history, he produced the first published account of the Benedictional of St Aethelwold (1832) – a landmark in the study of late Anglo-Saxon art – and an edition of the Chronicle of Jocelin of Brakelond (1840), which was the inspiration for Thomas Carlyle's *Past and Present* (1842). The Gages were a very old and much ramified recusant family, and through his family connections John Gage moved easily in the political and social circles of his time. He was renowned for his courtesy and affability, and he even got on well with that rabid anti-Papist, Sir Thomas Phillipps, Bart.[2]

The hitherto unpublished account of what he calls his 'Sentimental Journey' in Holland and Flanders in 1815 was written up from notes on his return to England, and was intended to be read by his family and friends: it is now on deposit in the University Library, Cambridge.[3] Besides affording some insight into Gage's temperament and interests, it also provides an eyewitness account of the battlefield of Waterloo only nine days after the battle.

Gage had certainly read Sir Joshua Reynolds's *A Journey to Flanders and Holland in the Year 1781*, but unlike Reynolds, he was not concerned solely with looking at paintings. As might be expected, he was interested in ecclesiastical art and architecture, and he also had a general interest in social customs, dress – especially of females – and landscape. Nevertheless, his tour of Holland certainly seems somewhat hasty and superficial – he 'did' Leiden in half a day. He had probably intended to spend more time in Belgium, but his tour was cut short by the aftermath of Waterloo. But despite these drawbacks, his narrative has considerably more intrinsic interest than the conventional travel diary of the period.[4]

With characteristic English *insouciance*, Gage set out on his travels in the early days of June 1815, just as Napoleon began to assemble the Grande Armée on the Franco-Belgian frontier. On Tuesday 6 June he left London for Hengrave Hall and on 9 June he left Hengrave, picked up the coach from Bury St Edmunds to Ipswich, and went from thence by chaise via the Shotley Gate ferry to Harwich, to avoid the long way round by Manningtree:

On entering the boat at Shotley Gate, the stillness of the evening, the brightness of the tranquil waters, the shipping and other objects in the distance, raised poetical sensations. Charon's boat and the Stream of Oblivion were before me, and perhaps I should have continued musing, until I found myself in New Worlds, if the stench of the fish on the beach as I approached the shore had not recalled *one* certainly, if not more, of my senses, and announced to me I was at Harwich.

The gentle self-mockery is typical of much of the rest of the narrative.

Gage embarked on the *Prince of Orange* packet boat at 4 pm on 10 June, but the ship was delayed by adverse winds, and he did not arrive at Hellevoetsluis till 5 pm on the 12th. After much haggling with porters over tips, he reached Maassluis to await a carriage for The Hague:

The fair was beginning at Maaslandsluys, and in the gingerbread stalls I observed women whose dresses I have as yet seen nowhere else, though I am told I shall find them in North Holland: a pink jacket turned up with white cuffs, a white frill and handkerchief, with a muslin cap close to the head covering the hair entirely, and hanging down the neck in the form of lappets, [and] a black and yellow petticoat.

He left Maassluis at 10 pm, passed through Delft in the dark, and arrived at The Hague, at the Marshall de Turenne Inn, at 1 am on 13 June. After a few hours' sleep, he made for the Maison du Bois, the residence of the Orange family after their return to Holland in 1814:[5]

The Queen of the Netherlands being at the palace, it was conjectured there would be no admittance for strangers… I made the attempt, and in vain did I make love to the housekeeper: she did not understand me. It is singular, not a soul in the palace could either speak French or English, except the nurse of the Princess Mary Anne; and after waiting a considerable time she came down and offered to conduct me round the house. The nurse was an Englishwoman, and to this circumstance I was indebted for my *entrée*. Going down the principal stairs of the palace, the Queen and her daughter, the Princess Mary Anne, passed us, [and] her Majesty did me the honour to make me an inclination of her august head! The Queen appears to be about 35 years of age, thin, and rather tall, of a pale complexion. She wore a French muslin morning dress, and a straw hat…

The saloon is the only princely apartment in the palace: it is formed by the Rotunda in the centre of the building… in this room the royal family always take their coffee and hold their converzatione: for a large state room, it has more real comfort than any I ever saw… My fair conductress told me she came from Bedfordshire; her attachment to her charge the princess Mary Anne appeared great. I was pleased with her telling me just after the Queen had passed, that her mistress was *en déshabillé*, and looked very different when dressed. At parting, the woman would not receive any money and expressed the pleasure she always felt in showing any attention to English families. *Mem*. I believe she is the only person in Holland who would refuse money!

Gage then went on to Scheveningen and returned to The Hague for dinner. He did not visit the Mauritshuis, so warmly recommended by Sir Joshua Reynolds, but left The Hague for Leiden at 6.30 pm on a *trekschuit*:

The canal through which we passed is lined with trees, and on each side, particularly in the environs of The Hague, are numberless villas. The Dutch style of laying out grounds needs no comment, particularly when it is explained that the people themselves now pretend to show you pleasure grounds à l'anglaise. The statuary, pagodas, summerhouses, boathouses, bowers, painted scenery etc. crowded the banks. In the summerhouses looking immediately on the water the Dutch were all smoking, drinking tea etc. The women are remarkably clean in their persons, and I observed some who looked very pretty in their strait caps... I confess I think the English have a very erroneous idea of Dutch beauty: the complexion of the Dutch women is remarkably fine, and I did not see that grossness of person given to a *Vrouw* by our countrymen. The Dutch as far exceed in beauty the Flemish, as they do a Hottentot Venus: the neatness of their persons and the manner of adjusting their caps, prepossesses.

On arriving at Leiden at 9 pm he immediately called on Jacobus Murray,[6] the publisher and bookseller in the Breestraat, to arrange for a hasty tour of the town on the following day. At 1 pm on 14 June he left Leiden by boat for Haarlem, visited the church and heard the famous organ, and went on to Amsterdam. He arrived there at 10 pm at the Hotel Doelen, where he met up with Mr and Mrs Fitzherbert of Swynnerton, Staffordshire, to whom he was related.[7] On the morning of 15 June he toured the dockyards at Amsterdam and admired the floating docks and dredgers, and in the afternoon he visited the Oude Kerk and the Botanical Garden. In the evening he went to the police for his passport:

and refusing to pay money which I had done nowhere else for my pass, I was most grossly insulted and Mr Fitzherbert's Swiss servant who accompanied me was nearly locked up for the night... I felt so much disgust and my temper was so much ruffled, I hardly recovered myself until I got out of Amsterdam. What blessings does England possess in her happy Constitution!

Despite this rather Pooterish episode, he spent the following day visiting 'Felix Meritis'[8] and the Palace on the Dam. His admiration of the paintings in the Palace was rather subdued, but at least he disagreed with Reynolds's adverse judgement of the 'Nightwatch':

The Wouvermans, Wenixs, Vander Helsts and Gerard Dous all please me much, but my mind was not carried from the earth. I was surprised not to find any very considerable paintings by the masters of the Flemish School. Has the national jealousy prevailed on this occasion? of Rubens there are few relics! The celebrated Nightwatch by Rembrandt is censured by Sir Joshua Reynolds – it is however worth attention. The extraordinary yellow tint in this picture is to be found on a painting by the same master of the Marshal de Turenne on horseback in the collection of Lord Cowper.

He left Amsterdam at 6 pm by carriage with the Fitzherberts and arrived at Utrecht. On the 17th it rained, and they did not go out till the evening. On Sunday 18 June (the day of the Battle of Waterloo) he went to church in the Catholic chapel in the Meesterstraat and later saw a 'train de bois' sailing down the Vecht:

Immense poles of timber, the riches of Germany, are joined together in the form of rafts, each raft being connected by a cross rope which at the turn of the river has the appearance of so many joints. On these rafts many hundreds of people come down the Rhine with their families, a whole colony, having wooden houses on the rafts and provided with food and every comfort for a journey of several weeks. In their progress they sell their wood and return home on foot. The wood cottages I saw on the train de bois were remarkably neat.

On 19 June he called on the police at Utrecht, only to discover that in the course of the *fracas* at Amsterdam he had been given the passport of somebody else. His servant was therefore despatched to Amsterdam to rectify the mistake. After an early dinner he went with the Fitzherberts in an open carriage to visit the Moravian Brethren at Zeist:[9]

The beauties of the environs of Utrecht soon dissipated the gloom of the morning, and the delightful appearance of the village of Zeist brought back all my *gaieté du coeur.* We stopped at an auberge belonging to the *frères Moraves.* The institution forms a very fine square divided by the road and an avenue of trees. The society is composed of the followers of John Huss; they live together in community under certain regulations. There are *soeurs* as well as *frères.* The women wear close caps of muslin with folds very like ears on each side of the head, which looked more like the cranium of an ape than anything else. These caps are tied with a ribband, the colour of which varies according to the class of humanity to which each belongs. Virgins wore red, widows white, married women blue ribbands. All communications between the *frères* and unmarried *soeurs* is forbidden, and if a *frère* wants a wife she is sent for from some other society, and the *soeurs* at Zeist are in the same manner proffered in marriage among other societies…
      We amused ourselves in the repository which contains a suite of rooms, each occupied by productions from the hands of the society. The members of the society are paid for their labour and the profits go to the general benefit. In some respects they affect to imitate the primitive Christians! The variety and the excellency of the different articles displayed in the repository were temptations not be resisted, and we purchased a cargo of toys etc. We were summoned from our merchandise by the ringing of a bell to attend the chapel. At the doors a *frère* and a *soeur* were in waiting: Mr Fitzherbert and his excellency [*ie* Gage himself] accompanied the *frère,* and Mrs Fitzherbert to our amusement was reluctantly conducted to the other side of the chapel by a *soeur*… After the discourse the *soeurs* sang a psalm. Mr Fitzherbert and myself planted ourselves at the door where the *soeurs* made their exit, and we thought one or two of the monkies very pretty.

As his passport had not yet arrived from Amsterdam, Gage also spent 20 June in Utrecht. He went over the silk mills and visited the celebrated bookshop of Johannes Althier (1758-1840),[10] at the corner of the Domsteeg:

There is an excellent bookseller's shop at Utrecht opposite the old church. Mons. Althier the proprietor I found extremely obliging. Books are very scarce on the continent and it may seem extraordinary but I could not procure here the *Histoire de l'Eglise Metropolitaine d'Utrecht,*[11] which was printed at this place and is not considered a scarce work in England.

His passport arrived in the evening, and he heard rumours of the fighting on 16 June and of the death of the Duke of Brunswick at Quatre Bras. On the morning of 21 June he heard news of the French defeat on the 18th:

The evening before it was doubtful whether the English were not in retreat, and the French at Brussels. An Englishman will imagine that Utrecht must have been in ferment in the midst of such events. No such thing: the apathy of the Dutch character was gloriously preeminent! Victory or defeat seemed to me to have no effect upon those people of Utrecht. I fancied last night the government was not popular, and I have reason to think the Dutch are jealous of the English and dislike their interference.

Gage parted company with the Fitzherberts, who were going on towards Hanover, and he himself left Utrecht at noon by boat for Rotterdam, via Bodegraven and Gouda, where he visited the church. He arrived at Rotterdam about 11 pm. On the morning of 22 June he visited Mr Ferrier, the consul at Rotterdam, who confirmed the report of the victory at Waterloo. At 5 am on 23 June he set out for Antwerp in a diligence as far as Dort, crossed the Hollands Diep, continued by diligence to Breda, and arrived at Antwerp at 9 pm:

On entering Brabant I exclaimed with Voltaire, 'Adieu canals, canots, canaille!' Holland is certainly the *chef d'oeuvre* of art, and a person who travels there will acknowledge all the merit due to the Dutch for their industry: his curiosity will be gratified continually but he will not fancy a long sejour in Holland. I doubt whether you would, for pleasure, twice make the tour of Holland.

On 24 June he visited the docks and the cathedral at Antwerp, both of which he admired. His opinion of the Dominican church was much more critical:

It is crowded with statuary, and I observed they were putting a fine cope upon one of the figures. I also remarked the same in the Cathedral of Notre Dame, where a large figure of the B. Virgin was decked out most outrageously. I think such childish ornaments are much better dispensed with: they take from the nobleness of the temple, and frequently in strangers produce impressions of much more consequence than the mere feelings of pity and contempt! As you enter the Dominicans there is a most ludicrous promenade made to resemble the Garden of Olives, terminating with the tomb of Christ. A crowd of statues line the walls up to the tomb, on the top of which is a large figure of Christ triumphant, from whose side an immense stream of blood is represented to flow into a small cup held by a figure representing the B. Virgin. How people can degrade the mysteries in such a manner is to me surprising. I forbear saying further on the exhibition of this place.

Gage also visited some of the hospitals and convents at Antwerp which were already nursing over 10,000 wounded from the Waterloo campaign.

On Sunday 26 June he set off in a cabriolet for Brussels, pausing at 8 am at a small village 'to hear prayers'(the old recusant idiom for hearing Mass). He also stopped briefly to look at Malines Cathedral just as High Mass was beginning:

In this church are a profusion of statues and paintings, one or two of which pleased me, but as our carriage was waiting at the door of the cathedral, I had only time to distract half the congregation by a hasty exhibition of my person!

On his entry into Brussels he began to see the signs of war, a week after the battle:

It was Sunday, all the shops were shut, it rained, and nothing was to be seen but sick and wounded in carts, on litters, or at the windows, whilst here and there the military passed backwards and forwards, or a few sorrowful countenances met the eye. A secret horror crept upon me, and I almost wished myself away.

He put up at the Hotel de Bellevue, the largest hotel in Brussels, where he met Sir James Craufurd, a relative by marriage, who had lost his eldest son in the battle. Craufurd was a singularly unpleasant man, quarrelsome, vain and overbearing – which makes all the more praiseworthy Gage's subsequent kindness to him in his time of sorrow.[12] The old Prince of Condé was also staying at the same hotel. Gage attended his levée that evening, in the course of which an aide-de-camp brought Condé the news of Napoleon's abdication.

On Monday 26 June Gage visited various wounded friends, including Lieutenant Michael Browne, son of the 5th Viscount Kenmare, and brother of Lady Mary Anne Gage. Browne's regiment, the 1st Battalion of the 40th Foot, had arrived in Belgium at the end of May, direct from the disastrous expedition to New Orleans. They had marched from Ghent to Waterloo on the morning of 18 June, and were stationed in reserve in the centre of Wellington's line, where they passively endured heavy artillery fire from the flank during the entire afternoon, before joining the final charge of the day at 8 pm. Browne's thigh was completely shattered by artillery fire, and his leg was amputated above the knee: he retired on half pay in 1816 and died in 1825 at the age of 32.[13]

The horrors of war did not inhibit Gage from visiting some of the art collections recommended by Reynolds:[14]

At Danoots the banker's I found a Hanoverian General occupying his best apartment in which was his fine collection of pictures. The Hanoverian was fast asleep on a handsome couch and Danoot obligingly showed me his pictures, and I passed round, without waking the poor fellow, who I understood had a fractured thigh. There are some beautiful paintings in this small collection, which is noticed by Sir Joshua Reynolds in his tour through Flanders. Here are two fine sketches by Rubens, the Rape of the Sabines, and the women preventing the Romans and Sabines from fighting... I was delighted with a Teniers, the subject is Boors shooting at a target, the countenances and action are admirable. As I was fearful of disturbing the slumbers of the Hanoverian, I took only a hasty look at the collection and I have since regretted I did not visit the pictures again – they struck me much.

The most remarkable English figure in Brussels society was Thomas Creevey (1768-1838) the Whig MP for Thetford.[15] It was a shrewd public relations exercise on Wellington's part to choose Creevey as the first civilian to whom he gave an account of the battle of Waterloo: no one could spread a story more quickly than Creevey. Gage knew Creevey through his contacts with Catholic Whig circles: he had called on him on the evening of his arrival in Brussels and was invited to dinner on the Monday afternoon:

I dined with the Creeveys and found the society of Mr Creevey rather enviable, as he was acquainted with the Duke of Wellington and all the leading characters, and had personal knowledge of the most interesting circumstances which have passed in Brussels. In the evening I made the round of my sick friends; tomorrow I intend to visit the field of Battle which I am most anxious to tread.

The following day, 27 June, Gage went with Sir James Craufurd to recover the remains of his son, Captain Thomas Craufurd of the Scots Guards.[16] They passed through the stench and chaos of the Forest of Soignies, arrived at the village of Waterloo, and made their way to the château at Hougomont, on the right flank of Wellington's line, where Captain Craufurd had been killed. Gage's account of the scene, nine days after the battle, is worth quoting at some length:

In front of the right of Lord Wellington's centre was the Hougomont farm which stood on a declivity, composed of large buildings, having a garden of some acres with very thick walls above it, a small hop ground below and a deep lane with a very strong hedge and double ditch running round a croft or orchard at the head of the garden: here were placed the Guards... The Hougomont farm was the very key of Lord Wellington's position, the Nivelles road ran very near it, and the deep lane before noticed came from that road under the house covering the troops... The garden was well laid out, two *allées vertes* crossed it in different parts, and you came upon a terrace as you entered the garden. The French getting possession of a small wood above the farm, repeatedly charged down a lane leading by the farm, into the deep lane below. The buildings looking on the wood alluded to, were battered to pieces; the farmhouse was entirely unroofed, a great part of it having taken fire from a shell: many French prisoners were burnt to death in this farm. The garden wall opposed to the French lines was very thick, and was a great point of defence. Against this spot, the very key as I have said before of Lord Wellington's position, the French directed all their efforts from ten o'clock in the morning till night... In the field at the head of the garden leading from the little wood I observed all the marks of the most obstinate contention. A whole line of fine young trees were taken off by the range of cannon precisely at the same height. Hats, caps, and the remains of every species of army accoutrement, still remained on the field, and heaps of slain lay buried beneath a slight covering of earth; the fires were still smoking where the dead were burning. The ground looked as if every inch had been contested for and, if I may use a strong expression, seemed as if it had sweated with blood and filth. Near a gate at the head of the garden fell poor Craufurd; we found his stock on the spot. I observed a tree standing by this gate, and so many bullets had struck the tree, you could hardly have put two fingers in any direction without touching them... I did not see any perfect human bodies on the field, though several were taken out of the corn the day I was there. Parts of humanity were still visible and the barrows made here and there over the field were many of the very slight coverings... I observed some mutilated remains.

In the Hougomont garden Sir James Craufurd's son had been buried the morning after the battle in part of his clothes, and in a blanket, with every decency the moment would allow. We had one of the Guards with us for our guide and he directed us to the spot, and we had no difficulty in finding the body. Raphael, to paint the horrors of civil war, in his battle of Constantine and Maxentius,[17] has represented a father taking up his son, who had fought on opposite sides. None but a father can feel the sentiments which are there expressed, none but a Raphael paint them! This picture loses its force when I look upon the scene in the Hougomont garden: a father opening the winding sheet of a beloved son who had fallen in battle eight [*vere* nine] days before! I retired down the garden and indulged feelings I could not repress. As I returned to Sir James through the garden, I could not help remarking that while devastation reigned round the garden in every horror, the garden itself remained unchanged. The enemy never penetrated this spot, which was so well protected by its walls and the thick hedges round it, and excepting where some of our troops were stationed behind the wall fronting the enemy, all the walks, beds of flowers, and fruit trees, were in the same state as before the battle... The pigeons were the only tenants I observed in this sorrowful farm. I understand these pigeons during the battle flew over the head of our troops in distraction, and our troops were at a loss to conceive where they came from.

I remained on the field of battle nearly four hours, and confess I left the ground with horror. The scene I had witnessed in taking up poor Craufurd, and the general appearance of the whole field, were sufficient to awake every feeling. It was dusk before we reached Mont St Jean, where we had left our carriage… It was nine in the evening before we got to Waterloo… It was very late before we reached Brussels, and I retired to rest with my head full of battles and every misery attendant on human nature which war can bring.

At Sir James Craufurd's request, Gage agreed to take the body of Captain Craufurd back to England for burial in the village church at Hengrave. Gage spent most of 28 June visiting his wounded friends in Brussels; in the evening he walked on the ramparts and in the park, and was amused to see the Prussian soldiers waltzing to the music of their regimental band. On 29 June he set out for Ghent, intending to meet Sir James there, and proceed with the corpse to Ostend. However, Sir James did not arrive at Ghent till the evening of 30 June. On 1 July the body was put on a boat for Bruges, accompanied by Sir James's servant, and Gage himself went from Ghent to Bruges in a cabriolet:

As I passed along the road, I observed for the first time a brace of partridges, and I had the impudence to attempt to slay one of them with my pistols. I was much amused at the hurried manner of a countryman who passed me at the moment I got out of the carriage with a pistol in my hand: I believe he thought I was going to shoot him! I should not forget to notice that when I left the field of battle on the evening of the 27th, as I approached Mont St Jean, I heard a partridge call several times in a cornfield bordering on the Nivelles road: I should have thought so much firing would have driven all the birds away.

On arriving at Bruges he had no time to look at the town, or even to visit the convent of his friends, the English Augustinian Canonesses, who had stayed at Hengrave Hall from 1794 till 1802, to avoid the troubles of the French Revolution.[18] Gage hastened to meet the boat and spent the night with the corpse outside Ostend; at 4 am on 2 July he went down to the harbour and hired a small packet boat. At 8 am on 3 July he landed at Wivenhoe and sent his servant to Colchester to fetch a hearse for the body. He himself reached Hengrave Hall in the evening.

In *The History and Antiquities of Hengrave in Suffolk* (London, 1822), Gage describes the monuments in Hengrave church, including that of young Craufurd, and gives the following extract from the parish register:

Thomas Gregan Craufurd, late lieutenant in the 3rd Regiment of Foot Guards, eldest son of Sir James Craufurd, Bart, who fell bravely fighting in the battle of La Belle Alliance, at Waterloo in Flanders, on the 18th June 1815, was buried in Hengrave church, being brought over from Brussels on the 5th of July 1815. Aged 22 years and 4 months.

With characteristic modesty, Gage makes no mention of how the body reached its last resting place.

## Notes

1. In later life he took the name of John Gage Rokewode.

2. See Bodley MSS Phillipps-Robinson *passim*.

3. ULC Hengrave Hall MS 42. The entire journal consists of about 20,000 words. In the following extracts, spelling and orthography have been slightly modernised where necessary.

4. James Simpson's *A visit to Flanders in July 1815, being chiefly an account of the field of Waterloo*, (Edinburgh, 1815), is extremely dull and pompous, yet it ran to four editions. Robert Southey's *Journal of a Tour in the Netherlands in the autumn of 1815* (London, 1902), is of course well known, but lacks Gage's spontaneity.

5. In 1800 it had been used as a brothel. See R. Fell, *A Tour through the Batavian Republic during the latter part of the year 1800* (London, 1801), p.74.

6. Murray's father, according to Gage, was a Scotsman from Perth. See also A. M. Ledeboer. *Alfabetische Lijst der Boekdrukkers en Uitgevers in Noord Nederland* (Utrecht, 1876), p.122: he records the brothers Murray, Jacobus and Jan Anthony, in business from 1780 to 1808; C. C. van der Hoek took over the business in 1822. The surviving Murray brother must therefore have carried on the business alone from 1808-1822.

7. He was also related to the family of Fitzherbert Brockholes, of Claughton Hall, Lancs.

8. An institution for the furtherance of the arts and sciences, founded in 1777; it still exists today.

9. The real founder of the Herrnhuter 'Brüdergemeine' was Graf Nikolaus von Zinzendorf (1700- 60). At the invitation of the Princess of Orange a colony of the Brethren from Holstein settled at Ysselstein in 1737, and in 1746 they moved to Zeist. See A. Bost, *History of the Moravians* (London, 1862), pp.310-11, and *Fortsetzung von David Cranzens Brüder Historie*, dritter Abschnitt (Barby, 1804), pp.7, 159-61; vierter Abschnitt (Gnadau, 1816), pp.273, 339-47.

10. Johannes Althier, a Swiss emigré from St Gallen, in business at Utrecht 1787-1840, one of the leading antiquarian booksellers of his time. See A. M. Ledeboer, *De Boekdrukkers, Boekverkoopers en Uitgevers in Noord-Nederland* (Deventer, 1872), p.357.

11. [G. Dupac de Bellegarde], *Histoire Abrégée de l'Eglise Metropolitaine d'Utrecht* (Utrecht, 1765). Dupac de Bellegarde was a fervent French admirer of the schismatical, Jansenist, 'Old' Catholic Church in Holland.

12. Sir James Craufurd had married Gage's cousin, Maria Teresa Gage, sister of Henry Viscount Gage of Firle, Sussex. Craufurd had been British resident at Hamburg and later plenipotentiary at Copenhagen. There was a strong streak of insanity in the Craufurd family. Sir James's mother and sister had both died insane. His brother, General Robert Craufurd (1764-1812), of Peninsular War fame, was a manic-depressive, and his other brother, General Sir Charles Gregan Craufurd (1761-1821) was declared by the Duke of Newcastle to be 'not quite right' (*sc.* in the head). Sir James's own *Mémoires* (Paris, 1820) and his correspondence printed by Sir Patrick Blake (Bury St Edmunds, 1811) give a sufficiently repulsive picture of the man. See also E. Dard. *Un Rival de Fersen*, (Paris, 1947), pp.110-11 and *History of Parliament, s.v.* Charles and Robert Craufurd.

13. For the Hon Michael Browne, see C. Dalton, *The Waterloo Roll Call* (London, 1890), p.136 and R. H. R. Smythies. *Historical Records of the 40th. (2nd. Somersetshire) Regiment*, (Devonport, 1894), pp.178, 187 and 569.

14. Sir Joshua Reynolds, *Works*, edited by E. Malone (London, 1801), II, 264-67.

15. There is no entry for Creevey in *DNB*; the fullest account is by R. G. Thorne in the *History of Parliament*. Creevey held the constituency of Thetford in the interest, indirectly, of Gage's friend Bernard Howard, Duke of Norfolk. In his reminiscences of Waterloo, Creevey recalled that Wellington 'praised greatly the Guards who kept the farm (meaning Hougomont) against the repeated attacks of the French'; see *The Creevey Papers* (London, 1970), p.151.

16. Thomas Craufurd had served with the Scots Guards as an ensign in the Peninsular War (*ie* from the age of 17), and was acting captain at Waterloo. The Scots Guards held the orchard and the sunken road at Hougomont, and the Coldstream Guards held the garden. Gage was under the mistaken impression that Thomas Craufurd was in the Coldstreams. See F. Maurice. *The History of the Scots Guards* (London, 1934), I. 407; II, 302.

17. A fresco in the Sistine Chapel.

18. P. Guilday, *English Catholic Refugees on the Continent* (London, 1914), pp.385-6, and J. Gage, *History and Antiquities of Hengrave* (London, 1822), p.76.

Frits Knuf

# *For Anna*

*Anna has many loves: Bill, The British Library, books – many books and on many subjects.*
*One of her bibliographical loves is the Amsterdam bookseller and publisher Theodorus*
*Crajenschot who was active from 1745-18_ _.*

*With this short description and illustration of an exceptionally fine edition by Crajenschot I*
*would like to pay tribute to Anna and thank her for many years of good and faithful friendship.*

*Over the years Anna has systematically collected data about Crajenschot, a Roman Catholic*
*bookseller in a not very Catholic age, publisher of prayer-books, devotional works and*
*occasional publications. One of these occasional works is:* Huwelijkszangen ter
Echtvereeniging van den Heere Ernst Friederich Binquebanc, en Jonkvrouwe
Anna Catharina Wegener. Echtelijk vereenigd binnen Amsterdam, den llden van
Slagtmaand, MDCCLXX. *Te Amsterdam, bij Theodorus Crajenschot, Boek- en*
*papierverkooper op den hoek van de Herengracht en Heisteeg In den berg Sinai, 1770. [16]pp.4°.*
*With large symbolic title-vignette by C. F. Fritzsch; T. Crajenschot excud. (fig.1). There is a*
*detailed 'explanation of the title-plate' signed 'in respect' followed by six marriage-poems by*
*various members of the family.*

*It is interesting that there are several enclosures in the book. One is a splendid symbolic*
*cut-out print of two doves and two hearts forged together with the caption: 'Mejuffrouw*
*A. C. Wegener Als Bruid' (Miss A. C. Wegener as a bride). There is also a much later*
Huwelijkszang aan den Heer Mr F. Binquebanc en Mejufvrouw A$^a$. C$^a$. Wiethoff;
ter gelegenheid van derzelver Echt- Ver- ééniging, gevierd binnen Amsteldam, den
30sten Sept$^b$, 1815.

*There are twelve pages of little handwritten poems by family and friends. One of these*
*poems, entitled 'Van 's Mans Vader', ends strangely enough with the lines '... Now that old*
*age's attire adorns your skull, your years strive swiftly grave-wards...' – not a very cheerful*
*contribution to a wedding-feast.*

*Clearly this beautiful Crajenschot edition (fig.2) remained of sentimental value for the*
*family, in view of the more modern addition to the old book.*

*I wrote this little piece partly in order to hear from Anna Simoni why she is interested in*
*Crajenschot and when she will write her bibliography of his works, but above all as thanks for,*
*and a token of, friendship.*

Fig.1   Title-page of the *Huwelijkszangen.*

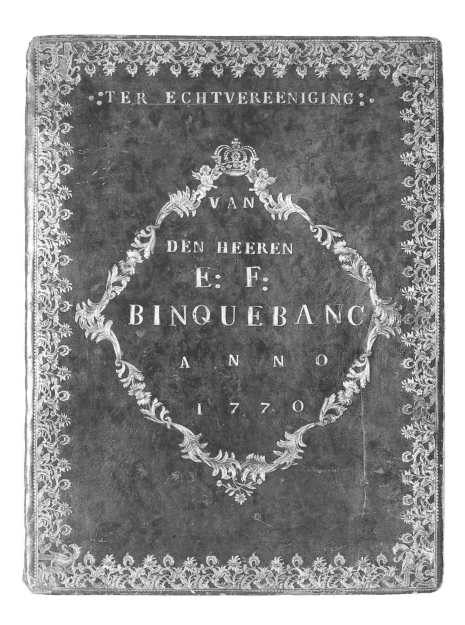

Fig.2 Binding of the volume for E. F. Binquebanc.

# Bibliography of the published works of Anna Simoni to the end of 1990

## Dennis E. Rhodes

**1953**

'Guillaume Haudent and the first translation of Poliziano's *Rusticus*', *The Library*, 5th series, vol. 8 (1953), 111-17.

**1955**

Review of: Benjamin Christie Nangle, 'The Monthly Review. Second series, 1790-1815. Indexes of Contributors and Articles' (Oxford, 1955), *The Library*, 5th series, vol.10 (1955), 224-25.

**1956**

*Dictionary of Anonymous and Pseudonymous English Literature (Samuel Halkett and John Laing)*. Volume eight, 1900-1950, by Dennis E. Rhodes and Anna E. C. Simoni (Edinburgh, London: Oliver and Boyd, 1956), pp.viii, 397.

**1959**

Review of: 'Börsenblatt für den deutschen Buchhandel', Jahrg.15, 1959, *Book Collector*, vol.8 (1959), 443-44.

**1962**

Review of: I. H. van Eeghen, 'De Amsterdamse boekhandel 1680-1725. Vol.1, Jean Louis de Lorme en zijn copieboek' (Amsterdam, 1960), *Book Collector*, vol.11 (1962), 363-64.

— Review of: Irvin B. Horst, 'A Bibliography of Menno Simons, *c.*1496-1561, Dutch reformer' (Nieuwkoop, 1962), *Book Collector*, vol.11 (1962), 502, 505.
—*Dictionary of Anonymous and Pseudonymous English Literature (Samuel Halkett and John Laing)*. Volume nine by Dennis E. Rhodes and Anna E. C. Simoni (Edinburgh, London: Oliver and Boyd, 1962), pp.viii, 479.

**1963**

Review of: J. A. van Dorsten, 'Thomas Basson, 1555-1613, English Printer at Leiden' (Leiden, London, 1962), *The Library*, 5th series, vol.18 (1963), 71-72.

**1964**

Review of: I. H. van Eeghen, 'De Amsterdamse boekhandel 1680-1725. Vol.2, Uitgaven van Jean Louis de Lorme en familieleden' (Amsterdam, 1963), *Book Collector*, vol.13 (1964), 88, 91.

**1965**

Review of: Jean Peeters-Fontainas, 'Bibliographie des impressions espagnoles des Pays-Bas Méridionaux', 2 vols. (Nieuwkoop, 1965), *Book Collector*, vol.14 (1965), 576, 579.

**1966**
Review of: John Landwehr, 'Dutch emblem books' (Utrecht, 1962) and 'Fable-books printed in the Low Countries' (Nieuwkoop, 1963), *The Library*, 5th series, vol.21 (1966), 257-58.

**1969**
Review of: I. H. van Eeghen, 'De Amsterdamse Boekhandel 1680-1725. Vol.3' (Amsterdam, 1965) and 'Idem. Vol.4' (Amsterdam, 1967) *Book Collector*, vol.18 (1969), 109-10.
— Review of: 'Studia bibliographica in honorem Herman de la Fontaine Verwey' (Amsterdam, 1968), *The Library*, 5th series, vol.24 (1969), 252-53.

**1970**
'The Printing of Portraits and Privileges: the *Handvesten ende privilegien* published by Johannes Tongerloo, The Hague, 1663, and related works', in *Essays in honour of Victor Scholderer*, edited by D. E. Rhodes (Mainz: Karl Pressler, 1970), pp.369-401.
— 'Where Museum and Library meet: two specialized Museums in The Netherlands', *Museums Journal*, vol.69, no.4 (March 1970), 164-66.

**1971**
' "Not in Van Doorninck": the authorship of *Yerlant verlost en hersteld*', *Quaerendo*, 1/4 (1971), 302.
— 'The Shape of Things to Come?', *Book Collector*, vol.20 (1971), 197-201.
— 'Visit to the Elgin Marbles', *British Museum Society Bulletin*, no.7 (June 1971), 14-15.

**1972**
'Dutch Clandestine Printing, 1940-1945', *The Library*, 5th series, vol.27 (1972), 1-22; 8 plates.
— Review of: John Morris, 'Correspondence of John Morris with Johannes de Laet, 1634-1649', edited by J. A. F. Bekkers, Van Gorcum's litteraire bibliotheek, 17 [Assen, 1970], *The Library*, 5th series, vol.27 (1972), 151-53.
— Translation of the words of Bach's Cantata no.82 'Ich habe genug' (It is enough) in: Thames Chamber Orchestra concert programme, Friday, 24 November [1972], Queen Elizabeth Hall, London.

**1973**
'The Gauger gauged, or a Bibliographical Coelacanth', *Archives et bibliothèques de Belgique*, 44 (1973), no.3-4, pp.593-98.

**1974**
'A Present for a Prince', in *Ten Studies in Anglo-Dutch Relations*, edited by Jan van Dorsten, Publications of the Sir Thomas Browne Institute, Leiden. General Series, no.5 (Leiden: Leiden University Press; London: Oxford University Press, 1974), pp.51-71.
— Review of: 'Catalogus van de historische bibliotheek van het Nederlands Legermuseum in het voormalige Magazijn van Holland thans Armamentarium te Delft. Dl. 1' (Leiden, Delft, 1969, 1971), *The Library*, 5th series, vol.29 (1974), 344-45.

— *Publish and be Free: a Catalogue of Clandestine Books printed in The Netherlands 1940-1945 in the British Library* (The Hague: Martinus Nijhoff, in association with British Museum Publications Ltd for the British Library, London, 1975), pp.[6], 289; plates.
— 'Newton in the Timberyard: the device of Frans Houttuyn, Amsterdam', *British Library Journal*, vol.1 (1975), 84-89.
— Review of: F. F. Blok, 'Contributions to the history of Isaac Vossius's library' (Amsterdam, London, 1974), *The Library*, 5th series, vol.30 (1975), 254-55.
— Review of: 'Contributions à l'histoire des bibliothèques et de la lecture aux Pays-Bas avant 1600' (Brussels, 1974), *The Library*, 5th series, vol.30 (1975), 347.
— 'Van Helderen/Heldoren/Hoorn', *Quaerendo*, 5/4 (1975), 344.

**1976**
'The Mockers mocked: the Brussels play of Saint Ignatius, 1610, and its Dutch counter attack', *Archives et bibliothèques de Belgique*, 47 (1976), no.3-4, 644-49.
— 'A Ghost no more: a contribution to the bibliography of Joannes David, S.J.', *De Gulden Passer*, jaarg, 54 (1976), 64-71; 3 plates.
— 'Hendrik Nicolaas Werkman and Werkmaniana in the British Library', *British Library Journal*, vol.2 (1976), 70-88.
— Review of: J. G. C. A. Briels, 'Zuidnederlandse boekdrukkers en boekverkopers in de Republiek der Verenigde Nederlanden omstreeks 1570-1630' (Nieuwkoop, 1974), *The Library*, 5th series, vol.31 (1976), 262-64.
— 'New light on a Grotius attribution', *Quaerendo*, 6/4 (1976), 374.

**1977**
'A Catalogue of Seventeenth-century Books from the Low Countries in the British Library. [A note]', *British Library Journal*, vol.3 (1977), 189.
— 'Haarlem's Modest Muse: anagrams, their solution, and the truth about a Haarlem worthy', *Quaerendo*, 7/2 (1977), 153-72.
— 'Hiel's Dutch Crossing: slow but sure', *Dutch Crossing*, no.2 (July 1977), 22-24.
— 'Catalogus van zeventiende-eeuwse Nederlandse boeken in de British Library', *Dokumentaal*, 6 (1977), 54-55.
— Review of: H. de la Fontaine Verwey, 'Uit de Wereld van het Boek. II: Drukkers, liefhebbers en piraten in de zeventiende eeuw' (Amsterdam, 1976), *TLS*, 9 December 1977, p.1455.
— Review of: Marja Keyser, 'Dirk Philips 1504-1568: a catalogue of his printed works in the University Library of Amsterdam' (Nieuwkoop, 1975), *The Library*, 5th series, vol.32 (1977), 384-86.

**1978**
'Bilingual Poet: William Fennor, alias Wilhelmus Vener, Enghelsman', *Neophilologus*, vol.62 (1978), 151-60.
— 'An early Makeblyde edition from Louvain at the British Library', *Ons Geestelijk Erf*, dl.52 (1978), 33-38.

**1979**
Review of: I. H. van Eeghen, 'De Amsterdamse Boekhandel 1680-1725. Vol.5, De

boekhandel van de Republiek 1572-1795' (Amsterdam, 1978), *Book Collector*, vol.28 (1979), 293, 294 and 297.

— 'Lulofs to the rescue: a Contribution to the History of Vondel Studies', *Dutch Crossing*, no.8 (July 1979), 55-65.

— 'Balthasar Bekker and the Beckington Witch', *Quaerendo*, 9/2 (1979), 135-42.

— 'Van Helderen/Heldoren/Hoorn: the case decided', *Quaerendo*, 9/1 (1979, 261.

### 1980

'Bearwood, Tree, Flatfish & Co.: some punning Dutch devices', in *Hellinga Festschrift* (Amsterdam: Nico Israel, 1980), pp.447-66.

— 'Balthasar Bekker: some recent additions', *British Library Journal*, vol.6 (1980), 108-22.

— 'Jus Belli sabaudici: evidence found, evidence wanted', *Quaerendo*, 10/3 (1980), 250-53.

— Review of: J. A. Gruys and C. de Wolf, 'A Short-title Catalogue of Books printed at Hoorn before 1701' (Nieuwkoop, 1979) and 'De Computer als hulpmiddel bij bibliografische ontsluiting: catalogus van Hoornse drukken 1591-1718 in de Universiteitsbibliotheek van Amsterdam' (Amsterdam, 1979), *The Library*, 6th series, vol.2 (1980), 378-81.

### 1981

'A Clusius variant', *Quaerendo*, 11/1 (1981), 67-69.

— Review of: H. de la Fontaine Verwey, 'Uit de Wereld van het Boek. III: In en om de "Vergulde Sonnewyser" ' (Amsterdam, 1979), *TLS*, 13 February 1981, p.179.

### 1982

'A Postscript to the Bilingual Poet', *Neophilologus*, vol.66 (1982), 638-39.

— Review of: J. A. Gruys and C. de Wolf, 'Typographi & bibliopolae Neerlandici usque ad annum MDCC thesaurus' (Nieuwkoop, 1980), *Book Collector*, vol.31 (1982), 383-85.

—'Paulus Sismus, forgotten physician', *Quaerendo*, 11/4 (1981), 325-27.

### 1983

'Rhetorical conundrum: *Der Reden-rijcken Springh-Ader* (Haarlem 1614) re-examined', *Quaerendo*, 13/1 (1983), 38-49.

— 'The Books at Dyrham Park', Pt.1, *Book Collector*, Vol.32 (1983), 171-88; pt.2, *ibid*, 283-95.

— 'A Pageant + Emblesmes = Dutch X', *Dokumentaal*, 12 (1983), 74-79.

### 1984

Review of: Otto S. Lankhorst, 'Reinier Leers (1654-1714), uitgever en boekverkoper te Rotterdam' (Amsterdam & Maarssen, 1983), *The Library*, 6th series, vol.6 (1984), 189-91.

— 'The Book of Franciscan Saints by Cornelius Thielmans, 1610: a question of title', *British Library Journal*, vol.10 (1984), 158-72.

— 'John Wodroephe's *Spared Houres*', in *Studies in seventeenth-century English literature, history and bibliography: Festschrift for Professor T. A. Birrell* (Amsterdam, 1984), pp.211-32.

## 1985

'Laurels for the Bishop: a school celebration in words and images, Antwerp, 1711', *Jaarboek* 1985 – Koninklijk Museum voor Schone Kunsten, Antwerpen, 289-308.
— 'Poems, Pictures and the Press: observations on some Abraham Verhoeven newsletters (1620-1621)', *De Gulden Passer*, jaarg, 61-63 (1983-85), 353-74.
— 'Terra Incognita: the Beudeker Collection in the Map Library of the British Library', *British Library Journal*, vol.11 (1985), 143-75.
— 'Henrick van Haestens, from Leiden to Louvain via "Cologne"', *Quaerendo*, 15/3 (1985), 187-94.

## 1986

— Review of: Marie Mauquoy-Hendrickx, 'Les estampes des Wierix conservées au Cabinet des Estampes de la Bibliothèque Royale Albert I$^{er}$: catalogue raisonné enrichi de notes prises dans diverses collections' (Brussels, 1978-83), *The Library*, 6th series, vol.8 (1986), 83-85.

## 1987

Review of: 'Erasmiana Lovaniensia. Catalogus van de Erasmus-tentoonstelling in de Centrale Bibliotheek te Leuven november-december 1986' (Louvain, 1986) and 'Memorabilia Erasmiana: Die *Adagia*. Führer durch die Ausstellung im Globenraum der Bibliotheca Augusta' (Wolfenbüttel, 1986), *The Library*, 6th series, vol.9 (1987), 393-96.
— Georges Dogaer, *Flemish miniature painting in the 15th and 16th centuries.* [Translated by Anna E. C. Simoni and others.] (Amsterdam: B. M. Israel, 1987), pp.192; illus.

## 1990

*Printing as resistance.* [Published as the fourth chapter of the *Ambachtelijk Groeiboek*, also as a separate issue of the same edition, in 150 copies.] (Leiden: De Ammoniet, 1990), pp.[20].
— *Catalogue of Books from the Low Countries 1601-1621 in the British Library* (London: The British Library, 1990), pp.xviii, 842; illus.
— Review of: F. W. van Heertum, 'A critical edition of Joseph Swetnam's *The Araignment of Lewd, Idle, Froward and Unconstant Women (1615)*' (Nijmegen, 1989), *English Studies*, vol.71, no.3 (June 1990), 283-85.
— 'The Hidden Trade-Mark of Laurence Kellam, Printer at Douai', *Ons Geestelijk Erf*, dl.64 (1990), 130-43.
— Review of: 'Bibliographie de l'humanisme des anciens Pays-Bas... Supplément 1970-1985', *etc* edited by Marcus de Schepper and Chris L. Heesakkers (Brussels, 1988), *The Library*, 6th series, vol.12 (1990), 246-48.

# Index